NETWORK CONTROL AND ENGINEERING FOR QoS, SECURITY AND MOBILITY, V

IFIP – The International Federation for Information Processing

IFIP was founded in 1960 under the auspices of UNESCO, following the First World Computer Congress held in Paris the previous year. An umbrella organization for societies working in information processing, IFIP's aim is two-fold: to support information processing within its member countries and to encourage technology transfer to developing nations. As its mission statement clearly states,

> IFIP's mission is to be the leading, truly international, apolitical organization which encourages and assists in the development, exploitation and application of information technology for the benefit of all people.

IFIP is a non-profitmaking organization, run almost solely by 2500 volunteers. It operates through a number of technical committees, which organize events and publications. IFIP's events range from an international congress to local seminars, but the most important are:

• The IFIP World Computer Congress, held every second year;
• Open conferences;
• Working conferences.

The flagship event is the IFIP World Computer Congress, at which both invited and contributed papers are presented. Contributed papers are rigorously refereed and the rejection rate is high.

As with the Congress, participation in the open conferences is open to all and papers may be invited or submitted. Again, submitted papers are stringently refereed.

The working conferences are structured differently. They are usually run by a working group and attendance is small and by invitation only. Their purpose is to create an atmosphere conducive to innovation and development. Refereeing is less rigorous and papers are subjected to extensive group discussion.

Publications arising from IFIP events vary. The papers presented at the IFIP World Computer Congress and at open conferences are published as conference proceedings, while the results of the working conferences are often published as collections of selected and edited papers.

Any national society whose primary activity is in information may apply to become a full member of IFIP, although full membership is restricted to one society per country. Full members are entitled to vote at the annual General Assembly, National societies preferring a less committed involvement may apply for associate or corresponding membership. Associate members enjoy the same benefits as full members, but without voting rights. Corresponding members are not represented in IFIP bodies. Affiliated membership is open to non-national societies, and individual and honorary membership schemes are also offered.

NETWORK CONTROL AND ENGINEERING FOR QoS, SECURITY AND MOBILITY, V

IFIP 19th World Computer Congress, TC-6, 5th IFIP International Conference on Network Control and Engineering for QoS, Security and Mobility, August 20-25, 2006, Santiago, Chile

Edited by

Dominique Gaïti
Université de Technologie de Troyes, France

 Springer

Network Control and Engineering for QoS, Security and Mobility, V

Edited by D. Gaïti

p.   cm. (IFIP International Federation for Information Processing, a Springer Series in Computer Science)

ISSN: 1571-5736 / 1861-2288 (Internet)

eISBN: 10: 0-387-34827-1

ISBN: 13 978-1-4419-4193-0
Printed on acid-free paper

eISBN: 13 978-0-387-34827-8

9 8 7 6 5 4 3 2 1
springer.com

NETCON 06

vi

A Zero Burst Loss Architecture for star OBS Networks

Xenia Mountrouidou*, Vishwas Puttasubbappa**, Harry Perros*

*Computer Science Department,
North Carolina State University,
Raleigh, NC 27695, USA
{pmountr, hp}@csc.ncsu.edu
**Ericsson IP Infrastructure,
920 Main Campus Drive, Suite 500
Raleigh, NC 27606, USA
vishwas.puttasubbappa@ericsson.com

Abstract. Performance studies point to the fact that in an OBS network, the link utilization has to be kept very low in order for the burst loss probability to be within an acceptable level. Various congestion control schemes have been proposed, such as the use of converters, fiber delay lines, and deflection routing. However, these schemes do not alleviate this problem. It is our position that in order for OBS to become commercially viable, new schemes have to be devised that will either guarantee zero burst loss, or very low burst loss at high utilization. In a previous paper [1], we described effective zero burst loss schemes for OBS rings. In this paper, we present a zero burst loss scheme for star OBS topologies. Further research into the topic is required.

1   Introduction

Optical Burst Switching provides a good solution for transporting bursty traffic in an all optical network. The fundamental unit in an OBS network is a burst: a collection of packets grouped into a size that may vary according to the characteristics of the specific network. The most attractive feature of OBS is that it is all-optical; meaning, there is no OEO conversion of data within the OBS network. This characteristic reduces the overall system cost, but more importantly, offers a high speed and transparent network, independent of technology or data rate.

An OBS network consists of end-devices that we refer to as edge nodes. Edge nodes can operate both as transmitters and receivers of bursts. These devices are connected to various electronic packet-switched networks, such as IP, ATM and frame relay, and they also have one or more OBS interfaces. Each edge node is connected to one or more core OBS node which are interconnected through a mesh network. Each core node is an all bufferless optical cross connect (OXC). This means that the burst data are transmitted optically all the way

Please use the following format when citing this chapter:

Mountrouidou, X., Puttasubbappa, V., Perros, H., 2006, in IFIP International Federation for Information Processing, Volume 213, Network Control and Engineering for QoS, Security, and Mobility, V, ed. Gaïti, D., (Boston: Springer), pp. 1–18.

to their destination. Multiple bursts can be transmitted onto the same fiber simultaneously, since each fiber carries W wavelengths.

The main characteristic of an OBS network is the separation between data and control planes. Payload data is received and assembled into data bursts at each source edge node in the electronic domain, transported through one or more optical core nodes in the optical domain, and delivered to sink edge nodes where they are converted back to the electronic domain and disassembled into their constituent data packets for delivery to respective data sinks. In order to transmit a burst, a connection has to be established through the bufferless optical network. This is done by sending a control packet (also referred to as the setup packet in this paper) that includes information such as: source address, destination address, and duration of the burst. The control packet is transmitted optically in-band or out-of-band or it is transmitted electronically out-of-band, and it is processed by each core node electronically.

Another feature that distinguishes an OBS network from any other optical network is that the transmission of data is performed in bursts. The burst aggregation algorithm that is used to formulate the burst shapes the traffic in the OBS network. There are several algorithms for burst aggregation in the current literature. These algorithms consider a combination of the following parameters: a pre-set timer, a maximum burst size and a minimum burst size. When the timer expires, an edge may form a burst. Burst aggregation algorithms may offer QoS by adjusting their characteristics, such as timeout and/or minimum/maximum burst sizes corresponding to the traffic demand [2], [3].

Various resource reservation schemes have been proposed for the transmission of a burst (see Perros [4]). One of these schemes is *on-the-fly connection setup* with *delayed setup* and *timed release*. In the on-the-fly connection setup a control packet is first sent and then after a predetermined offset the corresponding data burst is sent. An OXC allocates the necessary resources within its switch fabric so that as to switch the incoming burst at the time the burst is due to arrive (delayed setup) for a period of time equal to the burst duration (timed release).

The on-the-fly connection setup scheme, which is the prevalent scheme, leads to burst loss. This is because, the setup request may be refused by an OXC due to contention at the required output port. However, this may not be known to the edge node at the moment of transmission of the burst. Burst loss is a negative characteristic in a high speed OBS network that promises to deliver QoS.

Several solutions to alleviate the problem of burst loss have been proposed such as fiber delay lines (FDL), wavelength conversion and deflection routing. A small number of FDLs ([5], [6], [7]) could be used in order to reduce burst loss. Fiber delay lines require lengthy pieces of fiber, and therefore they cannot be commercialized. Wavelength conversion is a viable solution to the burst loss problem. In this case, an incoming burst on a wavelength that is currently in use at the destination output fiber, can be converted to another free wavelength. Finally deflection routing ([8], [9]) may offer an alternative path to the destination device and divert a burst that would be lost otherwise. This path may include more hops making deflection routing an ineffective method. Also, bandwidth has to be reserved especially for the overflow traffic over the path that the deflected burst will take.

Obviously in order for OBS to become commercially viable, new schemes have to be devised which will either guarantee a zero burst loss or a very low burst loss at high utilizations. In [10] we described zero burst loss access protocols for OBS rings that are efficient and they can also provide QoS for different classes of customers, such as HDTV streaming, non-real time high priority variable bit data, and best effort data. In this paper, we describe a zero burst loss scheme for star OBS networks. Obviously, more research along these lines is required.

The paper is organized as follows. In Section 2, we review various congestion control schemes that have been proposed for OBS networks. These schemes do not alleviate the problem of burst loss. Our zero burst loss scheme is described in Section 3. Results related to the performance of this scheme are given in Section 4. Finally the conclusions are given in Section 5.

2   Congestion Control Schemes

Congestion control in Optical Burst Switching (OBS) networks is an important research area. It is well known that OBS networks are prone to high burst losses and congestion can push these burst losses to alarming proportions. Although congestion control and congestion avoidance is an over-studied topic when it comes to IP and ATM networks, it poses several new and unresolved questions for OBS networks. Since an OBS network functions largely independent of any electrical or optical buffers at its core, congestion control schemes that are applied to buffered networks like ATM differ considerably in their architecture to that of OBS networks.

It is a well recognized fact that acceptable blocking rates in OBS mesh networks can be achieved only when the links are under-utilized. For example, in Figure 1 we give a plot of the blocking probability against utilization. This plot was obtained using both analytical and simulation models (see [10] for details) under the following assumptions. The graph is for a single outgoing wavelength in a core OBS node with 20 input and output fibers, 100 wavelengths per single fiber, 20 converters (i.e. 20% conversion rate), and with the ability for partial wavelength conversion with degree of conversion 20. Such an under utilized wavelength does not carry a high appealing factor for service providers who would always want to run their links heavily loaded.

In an OBS network, congestion and contention are closely related aspects. The boundaries that distinguish these two ideas are quite ambiguous. It is our conviction that contention and congestion drive each other, but the former is more transient in nature than the latter. Contention leads to burst loses due to lack of wavelengths at a core OXC. But the bursts arriving immediately after the losses might just pass through fine. Congestion occurs over a longer time frame and leads to increased contention problems over a longer time period.

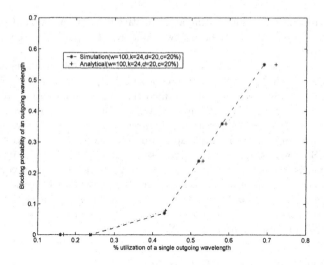

Fig. 1. Blocking vs Utilization

Research in OBS hitherto has mainly focused on contention resolution and there have been few contributions that have focused on congestion control. Several different approaches have been investigated in the literature including TCP -based approaches [11] [12], load balancing [13], alternate routing and deflection routing [14], [15], [8]. Below, we review some congestion avoidance schemes. For a more detailed discussion, please refer to Puttasubbappa [16].

2.1 Deflection routing

Deflection routing at a core OXC involves the selection of a different output fiber than the intended one, if the burst cannot be switched through the original output fiber. Deflection routing has its advantages and disadvantages.

1. The offset needs to be recalculated since the deflected burst takes a different path.
2. Offset recalculation will require intermediate nodes to be equipped with FDLs to delay the deflected bursts if necessary.
3. Deflected bursts may arrive out of order at the destination. End nodes may thus have to store large amounts of data.
4. Deflected bursts may end up in a loop and never reach their destination
5. There have been studies [17] [18] which indicate that deflection routing is ineffective at high traffic loads.

Deflection routing in OBS networks requires that the core nodes are equipped with FDLs. Using FDLs, a burst can be delayed for an extra amount of offset time and then sent over the deflected path. It has to be noted that the process of deflection and offset recalculation can happen several times along the journey of a burst. A core node on receiving a setup message looks at its routing table to determine the next hop based on the destination information the setup message carries. Since the node has knowledge about the current usage of the wavelengths on each outgoing link, it can determine whether this particular outgoing link is congested. The core OXC may maintain not just the primary next hop routing entry but also secondary and tertiary next hops. Thus, each node based on its local information can choose any of the other next hops in case the primary is congested. It then has to calculate the additional offset value in case the route now chosen is longer (i.e. more hops) than the one the burst was traversing in. (This of course assumes that it knows how many hops the new route consists of). This additional delay is made up using FDLs. In case there is an absence of sufficient FDLs available to delay the burst, the burst will have to be dropped.

Some of the issues arising out of this mechanism are:

1. The amount of FDLs may be limited.
2. There are publications [17] [18] that deal with several aspects of this method. Key points arising out of these studies are:
   (a) Excessive deflection may lead to a congestion collapse
   (b) Excessive deflection may lead to longer end-to-end delays
   (c) Deflection routing may lead to re-ordering of bursts since bursts may take different routes, and thus higher layer protocols like TCP might find it difficult to operate optimally.

Absence of any optical buffering in the network complicates things in the sense that a burst once released with an offset value cannot be slowed down. Intermediate core nodes have no way of manipulating the offset and thus little can be done to prevent a burst loss in the presence of congestion. An alternative solution to the use of FDLs is to set all offsets to a value that is an upper bound of all offsets and it is such that the burst can be deflected any number of times (assuming no cycles), but still stays behind the setup message. This method may lead to possible under-utilization of the network.

Deflection routing itself can be implemented using several strategies found in protection and restoration of networks, such as:one hop deflection, path deflection, and N:1 deflection. In one hop deflection, each core node maintains next-hop primary, secondary and tertiary routes for a packet heading towards a particular destination. In the presence of congestion on an outgoing link, an alternative next hop is chosen by the core node. In path deflection, each core node calculates primary, secondary and tertiary paths to each destination. When the outgoing link of the primary (secondary) path gets congested, the core node chooses the outgoing link of the secondary (tertiary) path and this path has to be followed to the destination. Path deflection can either be implemented through source routing or using pre-establish GMPLS paths (LSPs). In bypass $N : 1$ deflection, a congested link of a group of N links can be bypassed by using an alternate link, similarly to the $N : 1$ technique in protection and restoration of networks.

It was shown by simulation that deflection routing is not an effective means to lowering the burst loss which can be greatly reduced with a few converters with restricted converter capabilities. (see Jonandula [19])

2.2 Feedback based schemes

This is a subject that has been studied quite extensively, e.g. the ABR scheme in ATM networks. Feedback messages relay the bandwidth usage and utilization of links back to the ingress OBS nodes thus enabling them to harness the dynamic state of the network. The feedback messages can either be sent as separate control messages or can be piggybacked to control messages traversing in the opposite direction resulting in minimization of control messages.

Feedback messages can be used to assist deflection routing. Specifically if OXCs know the utilization levels of links ahead of them, they can deflect bursts away from a congested link. Feedback mechanisms can also be used to determine the rate of burst transmission by the sources based on the congestion levels in the links the bursts are supposed to traverse. A feedback based setup has been studied for congestion-based routing techniques in [14]. Such a feedback based based routing technique has been shown to reduce loss probabilities.

2.3 Path recalculation

The congestion control techniques described in the previous sections can be seen as short-term schemes since they operate at smaller time scales. Path recalculation can be seen as a long-term congestion control scheme since it operates at a much larger time scale than the above schemes.

The motivation for path recalculation is that the state of the network in terms of congestion might reach a stage when short-term schemes can no longer be effective. In such a scenario, a radical change in routing paths needs to be made at a larger topological area.

The path calculation can either be distributed or centralized with a master node. Irrespective of the routing architecture, this mechanism facilitates a new routing pattern and thus a chance for the stagnant network to solve its congestion problems. Different source-destination flows between all pairs of nodes that satisfy quality of service criterion of the optical signal can be calculated.

3   A zero burst loss scheme for star networks

As shown in Figure 1, presented in the previous section, the utilization per wavelength has to be kept extremely low in order for the burst loss to be within an acceptable level. Congestion control schemes, such as deflection with FDLs, do not lower significantly the burst loss (see Jonandula [19]). As mentioned above, in order for OBS to become commercially viable, we will need schemes which either eliminate burst loss all together, or provide a very low burst loss but high utilizations.

In this section, we discuss a zero burst loss solution for star OBS networks. Current technological developments permit the transmission of an optical signal over a long fiber without intermediate amplification or signal restoration. This trend, obviously, is only going to continue in the future. In view of this, it is not hard to imagine that a single OBS core node can serve edge nodes over a large geographical area, whereby an edge node may be as many as 1,000 kilometers away from the core node. If the density of edge nodes is high, then multiple OBS core nodes can be used, as shown in Figure 2. In this case, each edge node has one OBS interface for each core node it is connected to. In the remaining of this paper, we will assume a single OBS core node, since the additional OBS nodes are independent of each other.

In a star configuration, it is possible to provide zero burst loss, if we let the core node do the scheduling. That is, the offsets are determined by the core node. Each edge node sends a control packet to the core node requesting a transmission of a certain duration to a particular destination edge node directly connected to the core node. Using a simple horizon scheduler, for each outgoing fiber the core node can manage all the burst transmissions without any loss. However, the propagation delays for far away edge nodes may take this toll on the network throughput. Below we describe the bimodal burst switching architecture that provides a solution to the issue of long propagations.

3.1 Bimodal Burst Switching Architecture

This architecture referred to as Bimodal Burst Switching (BBS) uses the delayed setup timed-release scheme compound with two modes of operation. The first mode (Mode 0) applies to an edge node that is close to core node, and the second mode (Mode 1) applies to a distant edge node. BBS can cover a large geographical area (1,000 km radius) and it is implementable in hardware as described in [20]. Also, it assumes that the OBS core node is a bufferless switch equipped with full conversion on each outgoing fiber.

Each edge node is linked to the core node via an upstream and a downstream fiber, each carrying W wavelengths. Furthermore, each edge node may use both operation modes to send data, depending on its proximity to the core node. Therefore, in a network that has N edge nodes, each edge node may include $2N - 2$ destination queues, where packets are classified based on the destination and the mode of operation. The core node has a number of parallel switching planes equal to W, the number of wavelengths in a WDM link. The number of edge nodes that the core node can support is equal to the number of dual ports per switch plane.

This architecture introduces an innovative scheduler that performs the flow regulation of the traffic that arrives at each edge node. The scheduler is embedded in the controller of the core node. The core node does not use buffers on either inputs or outputs. The main structures that are used by the

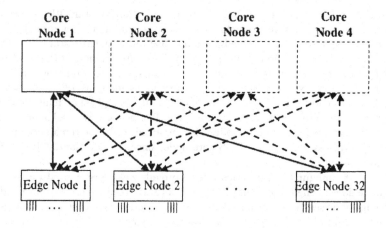

Fig. 2. Star OBS Network topology

controller in order to make a scheduling decision is the *Calendar* and the *M-element array*. The Calendar keeps track of the time when the uplink wavelengths to each edge node are going to be free. It consists of K elements. Preferably K is equal to $N * W$, where W is the number of wavelengths per fiber and N the number of edge nodes. We may also use a two-dimensional array with N rows and W columns to store the Calendar structure. If an element that belongs to the ith row and wth column of the Calendar is equal to j, then this means that the wth wavelength of the edge node i is free at time slot j. The time slot of the Calendar structure is long enough to allow a contiguous period of time to schedule bursts and short enough to have small delays between bursts. It is usually between $1msec$ and $1\mu sec$. The M-element array keeps track of the availability of the output edge nodes. It consists of M elements, where M is $N * W$. We use a two-dimensional array with N rows and W columns for the M-element array elements, that are stored in the same way as the Calendar elements.

The scheduling algorithm, implemented by the controller, consists of two modes, Mode 0 and Mode 1. This differentiation is based on the proximity of the edge node to the core node. The proximity is determined by measuring the round-trip propagation delay between the edge node and the core node. Mode 0 is used for edge nodes that are at a small distance d from the core node ($d \leq 100\ km$) and consequently have a small round trip propagation delay. On the other hand, Mode 1 is more suitable for distant edge nodes ($d > 100\ km$) that have a large propagation delay. As will be explained below the main difference between these two modes is that in the first mode the flow rate regulation is provided to waiting bursts whereas in the second mode it is provided to anticipated bursts.

Mode 0 scheduling. In this case, an edge node sends requests to transmit bursts to its ingress OXC. These requests are sent by the edge node at fixed intervals. The operation of Mode 0 is as follows:

- **Transmission:** Edge node i receives packets which it then buffers to the appropriate destination queues. In an OBS network with N edge nodes, there exist $N-1$ Mode 0 destination queues at each edge node. Every T μsec, the edge node checks the input queues and forms bursts subject to a minimum and a maximum burst size. For each burst it issues a burst request that is stored at the burst request queue. Each edge node has one request queue where it stores all the burst requests for any destination, until they are sent to the core node. Each request consists of a number of fields such as: source, destination, size and an ID number.

- **Scheduling:** Every T μsec edge node i sends all the burst requests it has stored until that moment in a single control packet to the core node. This procedure needs time equal to one-way propagation delay to be completed. Once the control packets reach the core node, the controller that implements the scheduler decides when the burst will be transmitted using the *shortest horizon* scheduling policy. This decision is formed using the Calendar and the M-element array. The scheduler scans the Calendar to find the first uplink wavelength of any edge node that is free, then calculates the horizon for the specific edge node's requests. The horizon for each burst request is computed as the difference of the time slot at which any downlink wavelength of destination is free, to the time slot that the uplink wavelength of the source is free. (Full wavelength conversion is assumed). The burst that is destined to the edge node which has the minimum horizon value is served first. According to the proposed scheduling policy it is preferred to schedule the minimum negative value, because this means that the destination is available earlier than the source, so the source may start transmitting immediately. For example, if source edge node i has a free uplink wavelength at time slot 10 and requests to transmit to destination edge nodes j and k that have free downlink wavelengths at times 5 and 15, the horizons are -5 and 5. It is preferable to schedule the request destined to j since the source can start transmitting to it immediately.

After a request is served the Calendar and the M-element array are updated. Then the Calendar is scanned in order to find the next available wavelength and the above scheduling procedure is repeated, until all the requests that the edge nodes sent at this time are scheduled. When all the requests are scheduled, the core node sends permits to the edge nodes containing information as to when they can transmit their bursts. An edge node may receive permits on its downlink wavelengths while at the same time it is sending new requests on its uplink wavelengths. Interleaving burst requests and permits reduces the waiting time of a request.

It is clear that this mode depends highly on the round trip time. The delay of a burst request is equal to one round trip time plus the queueing delay.

The queueing delays of a particular burst request depend on the number of requests that are scheduled prior to this.
- **Reception:** Each destination edge node receives bursts from the core node which are buffered electronically, disassembled to packets and then delivered to its users through other interfaces.

Mode 1 scheduling. In Mode 1 burst switching, data is still transmitted in bursts, but the initial phase in OBS where an edge node sends a request to its ingress OXC has been eliminated. Mode 1 scheduling is preferable when the propagation delay is large. Unlike Mode 0, a Mode 1 edge node does not issue burst requests. Rather, the edge node requests and is allocated a fixed bandwidth for each destination during the initialization phase. This bandwidth is calculated based on the traffic between the edge node and each destination edge node, and it is made available to the edge node in the form of burst sizes. These burst sizes are fixed in time and they repeat periodically.

Let t_{ij} μsec be the transmission time allocated to the traffic from i to j, and let this be repeated every T μsec. Then the bandwidth allocated to edge node i for transmitting traffic to edge node j is $(t_{ij}/T)*V$ $Gbits/sec$, where V $Gbits/sec$ is the transmission speed. The edge node communicates the values t_{ij}, $j = 1, ..., N$, $j \neq i$ and T to the controller. The controller issues automatically a burst request of duration t_{ij} every T μsec for each destination, where $t_{ij} \leq T$ for every $i, j = 1, 2, ...N$. These burst requests are then scheduled following the same procedure as in Mode 0 operation. Next the scheduler issues permits which are sent to the edge node. It is clear that the core node defines a different bandwidth allocation for every stream ij. This offers a flexibility to satisfy the different traffic requirements of each stream. We note that the bandwidth allocated to each Mode 1 edge node by the controller can be renegotiated using specially designed messages. Such renegotiation will take place when the traffic arriving at an edge node changes significantly. Adapting the bandwidth allocation to the traffic demand is considered as a congestion avoidance scheme. Therefore, the BBS architecture prevents burst loss due to congestion.

The Mode 1 operation is summarized as follows:

- **Transmission:** The edge node may transmit the data it has gathered up to this moment based on the permit information. In this case there is no minimum or maximum burst size used to define the size of a burst. This means that the burst aggregation algorithm used at the edge nodes does not have an effect in the burst characteristics when using Mode 1. The burst size B is defined by the transmission time t_{ij} as: $B <= t_{ij} * V$ $Bytes$. When a Mode 1 edge node i receives a permit it will transmit data for the duration t_{ij}. Assume, for instance, that the data it has requires 112 μsec to be transmitted. Assume also that $t_{ij} = 100$ μsec. Then in this case, it will not be able to transmit all the data, and 12 μsec worth of data will remain in its buffer. On the other hand, if it has 80 μsec worth of data, then it will transmit all its data and the remaining 20 μsec of the t_{ij} period will be unused.

- **Scheduling:** The controller creates a burst request of duration t_{ij} for every destination $j \neq i$, and for every Mode 1 edge node i, every T units of time. These requests are then placed at the scheduler's queue, and they are scheduled in the same manner as Mode 0 burst requests. Notice that the burst requests are generated by the controller and not by the edge nodes. Transmission permits are then sent to the Mode 1 edge nodes.
- **Reception:** The destination edge node j receives bursts which are buffered electronically, disassembled to packets and then delivered to its users.

The main difference between the two scheduling modes is that in Mode 0 already existing bursts are scheduled whereas in Mode 1 permits for anticipated bursts are issued. Generating fixed size requests for every edge node requires no knowledge whether they have bursts to transmit. Also it does not require knowledge of the size of their packet queues. This may lead to bandwidth loss if the edge nodes do not have data to transmit to every destination, or if they have smaller queues than the fixed size that is set. Also it may lead to larger delays if they have larger bursts than the bandwidth allocated. This is why we may need to adjust the bandwidth allocation when the arrival traffic pattern at the edge nodes changes.

The operation of the bimodal scheduler is depicted in Figure 3. In the case of a nearby edge node (Mode 0), the edge node sends all the burst requests it has accumulated up to this moment every fixed period of time, say every 256 μsec. The core receives the requests, schedules them according to the shortest horizon scheme and then sends permits to the edge nodes. Finally, the edge nodes transmit their bursts according to the permits they received from the core. The fixed period used to send requests is short, and as a result it provides a continuous supply of permits to the edge nodes.

In the case of a distant node (Mode 1) the core node creates burst requests periodically which are then scheduled according to shortest horizon. When a Mode 1 edge node receives a permit, it transmits data for a fixed period of time. The main difference in this scheme is that there are no requests from the edge nodes to the core node. This provides a more efficient scheme since the one-way propagation is large.

4 Simulation results

In this section we evaluate the performance of the BBS architecture using simulation. N edge nodes and one core node were simulated. We assume that edge nodes 1 to $N/2$ are within a small distance d from the core node, where 10 km $< d <$ 100 km, which means that they are served using Mode 0 scheduling. The remaining edge nodes $N/2 + 1$ to N are more than 100 km away, which means that the core node serves them using the Mode 1 scheduling mechanism. Burst aggregation is performed using timeout and minimum/maximum burst sizes. The minimum burst size and maximum burst size were fixed to 16 kB and 112 kB respectively.

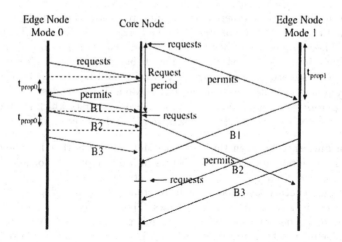

Fig. 3. The operation of the bimodal scheduler

Furthermore, the burst aggregation period T was set to 256 μsec. The same period T is used for convenience as a request period for Mode 0 edge nodes and as a permit period for Mode 1. The one way propagation delay between an edge node and the core node for Mode 0 edge nodes was set to 500 μsec, which means they are at a 100 km distance from the core node, and for Mode 1 edge nodes to 5,000 μsec, which means they are at 1,000 km from the core node. In this study we have assumed out-of-band signaling. The signaling messages can also be implemented in-band, but this was not considered here. Finally, renegotiation of the bandwidth allocation in Mode 1 scheduling is expected to take place less frequently compared to the time scales of the burst transmission operation, and it was not considered in our simulation study.

Each edge node has a 10 MB electronic buffer to store the packets that arrive from external sources. The arrival process is an Interrupted Poisson Process (IPP) as described in [21]. This IPP arrival process is an ON/OFF process, where both the ON and OFF periods are exponentially distributed. Packets arrive back-to-back using Poisson distribution with rate λ during the ON period. The transmission speed is 10 Gbps. Packets do not arrive during the OFF period. The packet length is assumed to be exponentially distributed with an average of 500 bytes. The last packet of the ON period may be truncated so that its last bit arrives at the end of the ON period. The squared coefficient of variation c^2 of the packet interarrival time was used to characterize the burstiness of the packet arrival process. This coefficient is defined as the variance of the packet inter-arrival time divided by the squared mean packet inter-arrival time. Assuming that the distribution of the ON period is exponential with average $1/\mu_1$ and the distribution of the OFF period is exponential with average $1/\mu_2$ we have:

$$c_{IPP}^2 = 1 + \frac{2\lambda\mu_1}{(\mu_1 + \mu_2)^2}$$

where λ is the arrival rate of a packet during the ON period and $\frac{1}{\lambda} = \frac{(500 Bytes)}{(10 Gbps)} = 0.4\mu$sec. Finally to characterize completely the arrival process the *average arrival rate* is used, given by:

$$average\ arrival\ rate = \frac{(10 Gbps)\mu_2}{\mu_1 + \mu_2}$$

Given the c^2 and the average arrival rate we calculate the quantities μ_1 and μ_2. In our simulation experiments c^2 was set to 5 and 20, and the arrival rate was varied from 6 Gbps to 100 Gbps. Packets arriving at an edge node were assigned to a destination using the uniform distribution. This arrival process captures the burstiness of the Internet traffic, especially when voice and video are transferred. It is also confirmed experimentally that it models accurately the traffic in a network [22], [23].

The simulation outputs consist of the mean overall delay per packet for all nodes and the percentage of utilization of an uplink or a downlink wavelength. In all the figures provided, the results are plotted with 95% confidence intervals estimated by the method of the batch means [24]. The number of batches is set to 30 and each batch consists of at least 10,000 bursts/edge node. The confidence intervals are very narrow and as a result are barely visible in the figures.

The Bimodal Burst Switching (BBS) scheme is compared against the case where all N edge nodes operate under the Mode 0 scheme, indicated in the graphs as "Mode 0". BBS is also compared against the case where all N edge nodes operate under the Mode 1 scheme, that is the bandwidth allocation scheme, indicated in the graphs as "Mode 1". We recall that in the BBS scheme edge node 1 to $N/2$ operate under Mode 0 and edge nodes $(N/2 + 1)$ to N under Mode 1. The calculation of the intervals t_{ij} for Mode 1 was based on the average arrival rate. Full wavelength conversion was assumed.

An overall picture of the delay per packet when all edge nodes are scheduled using the three scheduling schemes under study for c^2=5, is shown in Figure 4 (a). The average arrival rate at every edge node is 6 Gbps. The delay of a packet is the time elapsed from the moment it fully arrives at an edge node to the moment it is delivered to a destination edge node. That is, it consists of the queueing delay at edge node plus the propagation delay from the transmitting edge node to the destination edge node. Edges nodes 1 to 5 are at short distance from the core node (i.e. they have 500 μsec one-way propagation delay) and edge nodes 6 to 10 are far away (i.e. they have a 5,000 μsec one-way propagation delay). Packets arriving at each edge node were assigned to a destination node using the uniform distribution. The increased delays of the traditional OBS scheme can be easily seen in this figure. As the number of wavelengths increases, we observe an almost linear decrease in the packet delay for the BBS and Mode 1 schemes. The difference between Mode 0 and BBS evident: Mode 0 overall average delay per packet is much higher. An interesting observation is that the average delay per

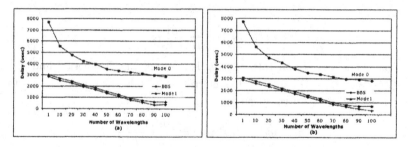

Fig. 4. (a) Mean packet delay for all 10 edge nodes vs. number of wavelengths for c^2=5, (b) Mean packet delay for all 10 edge nodes vs. number of wavelengths for c^2=20

packet for the BBS and the Mode 1 are very close. This leads us to the conclusion that differentiating our scheduling technique between distant and closeby edge nodes does not offer a large improvement on the average delay per packet. Figure 4(b) gives the average delay per packet when the input traffic is burstier, i.e. $c^2 = 20$. This burstiness corresponds to traffic that may have long intervals of silence (OFF period), like VoIP or video. It can be observed that there is no significant difference for the BBS and Mode 0 schemes when the burstiness increases.

Figure 5 shows the percentage of utilization of an uplink/downlink wavelength. The uplink and downlink wavelength utilization is the same. That is because the same arrival process to each edge device was assumed and destination nodes are uniformly chosen. When we use only one wavelength in our model, wavelength utilization approaches 60%. All three schemes have the same utilization. As mentioned above Mode 1 scheduling scheme is used to schedule bursts that are not yet formed at the edge node. If the wavelength utilization is high, this means that there is always a burst formed for each destination in every edge node that is scheduled using this scheme. Then the bandwidth that is allocated periodically is not wasted. On the other hand, the utilization per wavelength decreases since the number of wavelengths increases and there are more alternative paths for a data burst. This means that lower per wavelength utilization does not affect Mode 1 and BBS schemes if the input traffic and the overall utilization remains the same (60% for all wavelengths in one fiber link).

Figure 6 shows how the average delay per packet is affected when the average arrival rate of the input traffic is varied and the rate of packet arrivals is set to 100 Gbps for all three scheduling schemes, with all other parameters remaining the same as above. There is one uplink and one downlink wavelength for every fiber link. When the average arrival rate is >80 Gbps we get very high delays for Mode 0 and BBS, whereas Mode 1 gives very high delay when it is >90 Gbps. These delays are not drawn in this Figure. The BBS and Mode 1 schemes scale well when the average arrival rate increases. Mode 0 on the other hand has a high increase in the mean delay when the average arrival rate is >60 Gbps. This proves that BBS and Mode 1 are suitable for the high bandwidth demands.

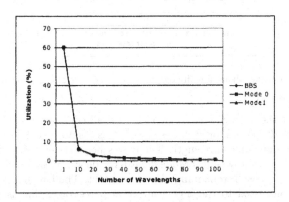

Fig. 5. Mean utilization for all 10 edge nodes vs. number of wavelengths

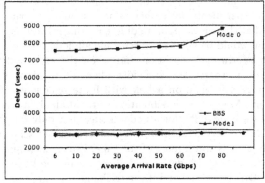

Fig. 6. Mean packet delay for all 10 edge nodes vs. average arrival rate

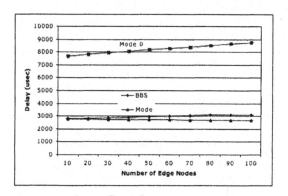

Fig. 7. Mean packet delay for all edge nodes vs. number of edge nodes for $c^2=5$

In Figure 7 the average delay per packet for all edge nodes is plotted when the number of edge nodes for $c^2 = 5$ is varied. It is assumed that W = 1, i.e. one uplink and one downlink wavelength. The BBS scheme scales well as the number of edge nodes increases, whereas Mode 0 has large delays. It is also observed that Mode 1 scales very well, remaining almost constant. The low delays of Mode 1 and BBS is contrasted to the high utilization percentage, that is about 60% when only one wavelength is used.

At this point the limitation of Mode 1 compared to BBS is exposed. Based on our simulation experiments both schemes have similar performance, therefore one would think that there is no point in differentiating scheduling in two modes. Mode 1 scheduling would be efficient to schedule all nodes. This is not the case. Mode 1 requires bandwidth allocation and when the edge nodes increase in number we have to increase the bandwidth allocated to each one of them as well. This may not be feasible on a link with finite bandwidth. On the other hand BBS is using Mode 0 in combination with Mode 1. Therefore, it does not need to allocate bandwidth for all edge nodes, but only for those that are scheduled using Mode 1. Furthermore Mode 1 scheduling scheme may waste useful bandwidth, as it is static most of the time. When the input traffic is low, the bandwidth allocated by Mode 1 scheduling may be too large, and therefore it will be wasted. On the other hand if the traffic is too high, there will be large delays as the packets will have a longer queueing time. Therefore, if the traffic pattern changes oftenly, Mode 1 scheduling is not efficient. Further work on the evaluation of the BBS scheme, can be found in [25].

5   Conclusions

In order for OBS to be commercially viable, schemes have to be devised that provide very low burst loss at high utilizations or are burst loss free. In this paper, we presented a burst loss free scheme for star OBS networks. More than one star OBS network can be used in order to provide large geographic coverage. How these separate start networks can be linked together so that the entire resulting network is burst loss free, is a problem currently under investigation.

References

1. Puttasubbappa, V., Perros, H.: Access protocols to support different service classes in an optical burst switching ring. (In: Networking 2004)
2. Choi, J., Choi, J., Kang, M.: Dimensioning burst assembly process in optical burst switching networks. In: IEICE Transactions on Communications. Volume E88-B. (2005) 3855–3863
3. Vokkarane, V., Jue, J., Sitaraman, S.: Burst segmentation: an approach for reducing packet loss in optical burst switched networks. In: IEEE International Conference on Communications. Number 5, IEEE (2002) 2673–2677
4. Perros, H.G.: Connection-oriented networks: SONET/SDH, ATM, MPLS, Optical Networks. Wiley (2005)
5. Yoo, M., Qiao, C., Dixit, S.: Qos performance of optical burst switching in IPover-WDM networks selected areas in communications. IEEE Journal on Areas in Communications 18(10) (October 2000) 2062–2071
6. Gauger, C., Dolzer, K., Scharf, M.: Reservation strategies for FDL buffers in OBS networks. In: Proceedings of the IEEE International Conference on Communications, IEEE (2002)
7. Yoo, M., Qiao, C., Dixit, S.: The effect of limited fiber delay lines on qos performance of optical burst switched WDM networks. In: Proceedings of the IEEE International Conference on Communications. Number 2, IEEE (2000) 974–979
8. Hsu, C.F., Liu, T.L., , Huang, N.F.: On the deflection routing in QoS supported optical burst-switched networks. In: IEEE International Conference on Communications. Number 5, IEEE (2002) 2786–2790
9. Kim, S., Kim, N., , Kang, M.: Contention resolution for optical burst switching networks using alternative routing. In: IEEE International Conference on Communications. Number 5, IEEE (2002) 2678–2681
10. Puttasubbappa, V., Perros, H.: An approximate queueing model for limited-range wavelength conversion in an OBS switch. (In: Networking 2005)
11. Wang, S.: Using TCP congestion control to improve the performances of optical burst switched networks. IEEE ICC'03 (International Conference on Communication) (2004)
12. Wang, S.: Decoupling Control from Data for TCP Congestion Control. PhD thesis, Harvard University (1999)
13. Battiti, R., Salvadori, E.: A load balancing scheme for congestion control in MPLS networks. Technical report, Universita di Trento (2002)
14. Vokkarane,, G.T.V., Jue, J.P.: Dynamic congestion-based load balanced routing in optical burst-switched networks. IEEE Globecom (2003)
15. Kim,, S.K.N., Kang, M.: Contention resolution for optical burst switching networks using alternative routing. In Proceedings of IEEE ICC (2002)
16. Puttasubbappa, V.: Optical Burst Switching: Problems, Solutions and Performance Evaluation. PhD thesis, North Carolina State University (2006)
17. Morikawa, X.W.H., Aoyama, T.: Deflection routing protocol for burst switching WDM mesh networks. In proceeding of Opticomm (2000) 257–266
18. Wong, A.Z.H.V.Z.R.E., Zukerman, M.: Reduced load Erlang fixed point analysis of optical burst switched networks with deflection routing and wavelength reservation. The First International Workshop on Optical Burst Switching (WOBS) (2003)

19. Jonandula, V.: Performance analysis of congestion control schemes in OBS mesh networks. MS thesis (2004)
20. Beshai, M.: Burst switching in a high capacity network. US Patent (2001)
21. Fischer, W., Meier-Hellstern, K.:   The Markov-Modulated Poisson Process (MMPP) cookbook. Performance Evaluation 18 (1992) 149–171
22. Karagiannis, T., Molle, M., Faloutsos, M., A.Broido: A nonstationary poisson view of the internet. IEEE INFOCOM (2004)
23. Heffes, H., Lucantoni, D.M.: A Markov modulated characterization of packetized voice and data traffic and related statistical multiplexer performance. Journal on Selected Areas in Communications SAC-4(6) (1986) 856–868
24. Perros, H.G.: Computer simulation techniques: the definitive introduction. Available at: http://www.csc.ncsu.edu/faculty/perros/books.html (2003)
25. Mountrouidou, X., Perros, H., Beshai, M.: Performance evaluation of optical burst switching schemes for grid networks. In: GridNets 2005, IEEE (2005)

Safeguarding the Transmission of Biometric Measurements Used for Authenticating Individuals

Ernst L. Leiss

Ernst L. Leiss, Dept. of Computer Science, University of Houston,
coscel@cs.uh.edu

Abstract: Various biometric measurements can be used to establish the identity of individuals. Common to many of them is the fact that a significant amount of information is collected and transmitted; this information is then used to compare the captured biometric data with the previously recorded information identifying a particular individual. If the two pieces of information are similar, it is assumed that the identification is carried out correctly.

An important problem in this process is the safeguarding of the transmission of the captured information. In many cases, it cannot be assumed that the channel over which this information is transmitted is secure. Therefore it is crucial that the process be viable even if the channel is insecure. We outline an approach that ensures the security and integrity of this process. We demonstrate that this approach is highly effective in that it requires only minimal additional storage capacity and virtually no additional processing capacity to be functional.

Support of this research under NSF grants DUE 0313880, SCI 0453498, and OISE 0519316 is acknowledged.

1. Introduction

The authentication of users in shared systems is an important problem; it has numerous solutions [2, 3, 5, 10]. Historically, computer systems have used passwords to establish the bona fides of a would-be user. Passwords have a number of advantages and disadvantages. Among the advantages are the following:

Please use the following format when citing this chapter:

Leiss, E.L., 2006, in IFIP International Federation for Information Processing, Volume 213, Network Control and Engineering for QoS, Security, and Mobility, V, ed. Gaïti, D., (Boston: Springer), pp. 19–26.

Compactness: Extremely little information must be stored to carry out the identification process.

Universality: It is easy for anyone to invent a password.

There is an unlimited number of passwords.

Passwords can be retired and replaced at will.

The use of passwords is extremely efficient: Both providing new passwords and using passwords to verify identity is very fast.

Among the disadvantages are the following:

The connection between user and password is tenuous at best: There is no inherent connection between user and password, other than that the user invented the password.

Passwords are typically not unique: Many users tend to invent the same passwords.

While the compactness of passwords was an attractive feature for earlier computer systems, with their limited space, the disadvantages of passwords have provided the impetus for the study of alternative means for authenticating users. The most important of these are biometric measurements [8, 11].

Biometric measurements extract information that is tied directly to the physical properties or aspects of a user. They may be either entirely descriptive or capture abilities as well. Among the descriptive ones are fingerprints, retina scans, iris scans, hand geometry, face authentication, and DNA. Among those that capture abilities are signature-based verification, voice authentication, and methods based on keystroke dynamics. Common to all are the following features:

The biometric measurements are intimately tied to a specific individual.

They are more or less unique: Within reason, they uniquely identify a specific individual (see more specific discussion below).

The amount of data captured is significantly larger than that for passwords. Also, the amount of storage to accommodate the data against the captured data are compared is much larger.

Biometric measurement data must be similar to the stored data to generate a much. This is in marked contrast to the situation for passwords, where an exact match is required. In other words, biometric data require a **similarity** condition to be satisfied, while password schemes require a test for **equality**.

It is important to understand the implications of the similarity test, especially when contrasted with the equality test. While passwords are very definite, biometric measurements are inherently approximate; in most cases, there is a good deal of variability (of the objective aspects that are measured [most biometrics] or of the actual measurements [DNA]). Therefore, it is entirely inappropriate to apply a test for equality, which is of course precisely called for with passwords. Indeed, if one were to apply a test for equality in the context of biometric measurements to determine whether a match is present, virtually all tests would result in rejecting the authentication attempt.

Fingerprints [6] have been used for about a century to identify persons, primarily perpetrators of crimes. Fingerprints are generally assumed to be entirely unique.

However, not all individuals have suitable fingerprints, either because of missing fingers, medical conditions, or work-related abrasion. Typically, a great deal of fingerprint information is captured, but only certain aspects (called indicia) of the captured data are extracted and used in the similarity test. The amount of information used to establish valid matches (the number and type of indicia) varies.

Retina scans [7, 8] are based on the pattern of blood vessels in an individual's eye retina. The information contained in the measurements is generally considered to identify uniquely a given individual. The method is fairly intrusive and therefore not commonly employed.

Iris scans [8] are similar to retina scans and use the iris of the eye instead of the retina's blood vessel pattern; however, they are significantly less intrusive. They are considered to identify uniquely a given individual; even identical twins are said to have different iris scans. A substantial amount of data is captured which is then used to compute a similarity relation as basis for determining whether a match is present.

Hand geometry [4] uses geometric aspects of the hand and specific physical characteristics of hand and fingers. The data captured are either several 2D images or a 3D image. Again, a good deal of information is captured (approximately one hundred different measurements). However, it is not entirely clear how unique the resulting measurements are; typically, hand geometry is used to identify individuals drawn from a relatively small set (e. g., access control to a specific facility).

Face authentication [9] is easily the oldest technology for identifying individuals – of course not by computer, but by humans in their daily interactions. In the context of computer-based authentication, it is in fact one of the newest technologies. It measures geometric facial structure (distance between eyes, nose, mouth, jaw, etc.), either in 2D (not very reliable) or 3D. Measurements use either visible or infrared light (the latter being known as thermal imaging). The method is supremely non-intrusive; it is in fact the only biometric authentication approach that can be administered without knowledge and cooperation of the subject and also at a distance. A large amount of data is captured in this process. The similarity test is correspondingly complex.

DNA [1] is of course the ultimate identifier (except that it cannot differentiate between identical twins). While it has major drawbacks within the context of computer-based authentication, it shares with the other biometric approaches the aspect that a great deal of data must be captured in order to obtain enough of a basis to carry out a similarity test.

Signature verification [8] extends the classical signature approach (which only considers the final result, the signature) and includes information captured in the process of supplying the signature, such as pressure exerted on the surface during portions of the signature, variation of the angle of pen to surface for portions of the signature, speed of producing segments of the signature, and so on. Again, a good deal of information is captured which provides the basis for the similarity test against the stored template of information associated with a specific individual.

Voice authentication [7] employs specific characteristics of an individual's speech to identify that person. Because of the variability of a person's speech depending on factors such as medical conditions (cold, asthma, etc.) and fatigue, the similarity condition is especially crucial. Again, both the stored template (voice sample) and the captured voice record imply significant data requirements.

Finally, the (mechanical) way a user types text at a keyboard can be used to authenticate that user. While the discriminative power of keystroke dynamics [7] is limited (it is unlikely that millions of typists can be reliably differentiated from each other by this approach) and the failure rate is larger than with other biometric methods, it shares with them the fact that a substantial amount of data must be captured and transmitted in order to apply this approach.

A major disadvantage of all biometric approaches over password schemes is that it is (virtually) impossible to change biometric aspects of a person. In particular, this imposes dramatically more stringent security and integrity requirements on the operation of such methods, since it is not possible to "assign" to a human a new biometric measurement in case the original one was compromised. This is in marked contrast to passwords where the consequence of discovering the theft of a password is the issuance of a new one. This is possible because there is no tight link between the password and the individual. In the case of biometric information, this link is very tight and for all practical purposes indissolvable.

2. The Problem of Intercepts

We will assume in the following that sufficient security and integrity conditions are satisfied at the two endpoints of the process. In other words, we assume that the capturing device is reasonably secure and that the system involving the storage of the template and the processing of the similarity condition satisfies the requisite security and integrity constraints. This assumption is generally realistic because the two endpoints tend to be under the control of the agent interested in the proper functioning of the authentication process. Our specific concern for the purpose of this paper is with the transmission of the captured data.

The problem of intercepts can be stated as follows: Assume that biometric measurements of an individual requesting access are captured at an access point; these data are then transmitted to a central facility where it is determined whether a match between the captured measurements and the stored template exists. This involves carrying out the similarity test. If a match does exist, the individual is granted access; otherwise additional attempts may be permitted before access is definitively denied. The problem we address here is the following: How can we avoid that a third party intercepts the captured measurements for the purpose of reusing them at some other time and in an illicit way? While the inclusion of timing information may impede this replay attack, this is fraught with difficulties; in particular, this assumes that the measurement capturing access point is impervious to any attacks, in particular to schemes that cause it to change its local time. Since synchronization in this approach is crucial, the ability of the central processing facility to synchronize the times of the local measurement stations may be compromised and result in resetting the time, which in turn would defeat the approach using timing information to safeguard against replay attacks. This synchronization is needed more within the context of biometric measurements than for passwords because of the significantly larger amount of data transmitted. This is true even if the data to be transmitted are first encrypted (in this case the timing information would be part of the encrypted data).

3. The Proposed Solution

The problem of intercepts can be avoided by using the scheme described below. Here we assume that no reliable timing information is available. We require that the biometric measurements be encrypted before transmitting them, using some reasonably strong encryption method. An important implication of this assumption is the following [5,10]: Changing a single bit in the ciphertext (here the transmitted, encrypted measurement data) implies that the decryption of this modified ciphertext results in a plaintext that differs from the original plaintext in about half of all bits. In other words, a small change in the ciphertext will result in a huge change in the resulting plaintext.

We now exploit the fact that biometric measurements, in contrast to passwords, contain a great deal of redundancy: changing portions of a password most likely will result in another, valid password, while changing portions of biometric measurements will result in data that do not correspond to any real person. To put it differently, if we require passwords to consist of between 6 and 12 characters, using letters and digits, then there are more than four quintillion different passwords, even though there are fewer than ten billion persons; thus, each person would have almost half a billion passwords. On the other hand, biometric measurements may have a size of several hundreds to many thousands of bytes (that is, orders of magnitude more than passwords). Therefore, enormous redundancies are present in them.

It follows that because of the redundancy involved, because of the way measurements are taken, and because of the variability of human physical characteristics, no two different measurements are identical. This implies in particular that encountering identical measurements are an incontrovertible proof of a replay attack!

The leaves us with two issues to resolve: How to detect identical measurements, and how to ensure that attackers cannot produce artificially small variations in the measurements. The second question is easily addressed: Since the measurements are encrypted before transmission, the attacker has no access to the plaintext, but only to the ciphertext. Since a change in the ciphertext dramatically affects the resulting plaintext, such changes will result in (decrypted) measurements that are totally unrelated to the stored template. Therefore the match is guaranteed to fail.

Finally we come to the detection of identical measurements. Here, we assume that at the central storage facility, every successful measurement (i. e., every measurement that resulted in a successful match) is stored; then every subsequent access request consists of two parts, the test whether the measurement that was transmitted is identical to any previously transmitted measurement, and the similarity test as before. While the similarity test is most likely carried out on the basis of plaintext data (that is the transmitted encrypted data must be first decrypted), the test for equality can be applied either to cipherdata or decrypted data. (Recall that all modern password schemes operate exclusively on cipherdata!)

It is important to understand that the similarity tests involved in biometric data are quite complicated; in fact, some of the schemes mentioned above do not operate in real time, for this reason. An inherent problem is the fact that there is neither an order relation nor a proximity relation between the biometric measurements. (For example, there is no natural order of fingerprints in which "similar" fingerprints would be close to each other while dissimilar ones would be far apart.) However, the test for equality is extremely efficient: it is essentially binary search which runs in time proportional to the logarithm of the number of items to be compared against!

One problem with the above scheme is the amount of data that would have to be stored. Assuming that each measurement is 1kB, we would have to provide 1kB for each successful match. This may be considered excessive. However, it can be drastically reduced: Instead of storing the entire measurement data, we can apply a hash, such as MD5 or SHA [3,10], and reduce the amount of data to a significantly smaller amount. Given the random distribution of the hashes, it is reasonable to limit the size to fifteen bytes; this yields a space of potential hashes of size 2^{60}, or well over 100 sextillions (10^{20}), which is more than sufficient to differentiate between the fewer than ten billion humans alive. Yet, even if there are a million successful accesses in a year, the system requires additional storage capacity of no more than 150MB during a ten-year operation, a rather small amount in view of today's capacities of storage media.

It should be clear that the length of the hashes can be considered a parameter – if more space is available (or fewer access requests are anticipated), longer hashes can be used. Note that using a hash that is too short will (on average) result in more accesses being rejected as supposed replay attacks (a false negative, from the user's perspective). To illustrate this, assume the hash length were only one byte; thus, there are only 16 different hashes. Consequently, the likelihood that an access request is rejected as a supposed replay attack is 1 in 16. Note that in practice and given the characteristics of typical biometric measurement systems, once an access request is rejected as a replay attack, the individual requesting access is most likely asked to repeat the access request, generating a new set of biometric measurement data. Given the general nature of the processes, it is virtually inconceivable that this new set is identical to the previous one; in other words, the new data set is different if this is a legitimate measurement, and not a replay attack. Therefore, the likelihood of the second request being rejected again is greatly reduced, if it is legitimate! How many such repeat attempts are permitted is a policy issue. Important for us is that observation that repeated legitimate measurements necessarily result in different data sets being transmitted and compared against the stored template. This clearly enhances the usability of the approach without sacrificing any aspect of security of the overall system.

4. Conclusion

We have outlined an approach that safeguards against a replay attack within the context of using biometric data for authentication purposes. This scheme works in the absence of reliable timing information. It exploits intrinsic aspects of biometric measurements, namely their redundancy and their variability. The resulting method is highly efficient (it requires virtually no additional time to process the information, compared with the generic approach that does not safeguard against replay attacks); it also functions well with a relatively small amount of additional space.

Bibliography

[1] C. T. Clelland, V. Risca, and C. Bancroft. Hiding Messages in DNA Microdots. Nature 399:533-534, 1999.

[2] A. Conklin, G. Dietrich, and D. Walz: Password-Based Authentication: A System Perspective, Proc. 37th Hawaii Int'l Conf. System Sciences, 2004.

[3] S. Garfinkel: *Web Security, Privacy, and Commerce*, Second Edition, O'Reilly and Associates, Sebastopol, CA, 2002.

[4] Ingersoll-Rand Corp., IR Recognition Systems, last web site access 10 Aug. 2005, http://www.recogsys.com/company/index.htm.

[5] E. L. Leiss: *Principles of Data Security*, Plenum, New York, NY, 1982.

[6] D. Maltoni, D. Maio, A. K. Jain, and S. Prabhakar: *Handbook of Fingerprint Recognition*, Springer, New York, NY, 2003.

[7] Microsoft informit.com, Access Control Systems, last web site access 10 Aug. 2005, http://www.informit.com/guides/content.asp?g=security&seqNum=149&rl=1.

[8] Z. Riha and V. Matyas: Biometric Authentication Systems, Tech. Report FIMU-RS-2000-08, Faculty of Informatics, Masaryk Univ., Hungary, Nov. 2000.

[9] T. D. Russ, M. W. Koch, and C. Q. Little: 3D Facial Recognition: A Quantitative Analysis, 38th Ann. IEEE Int'l Carnahan Conf. Security Technology, Albuquerque, NM, 2004.

[10] B. Schneier: *Applied Cryptography*, Second Edition, John Wiley and Sons, New York, NY, 1996.

[11] J. Woodward: *Biometrics and Strong Authentication*, Osborne/McGraw-Hill, Emeryville, CA, 2003.

The risks analysis like a practice of secure software development. A revision of models and methodologies

José Carrillo Verdún[1], Gloria Gasca Hurtado[1], Edmundo Tovar Caro[1] and Vianca Vega Zepeda[2]

1   Universidad Politécnica de Madrid, Departamento de Lenguajes y Sistemas Informáticos e Ingeniería de Software, Madrid, España, {jcarrillo,etovar}@fi.upm.es; glogasca5@yahoo.com WWW home page: http://www.upm.fi.es

2   Universidad Católica del Norte, Departamento de Ingeniería de Sistemas y Computación, Antofagasta, Chile, vvega@ucn.cl WWW home page: http://www.ucn.cl

Abstract. The following document, presents and analyzes the Risks Analysis in the whole software development life cycle, framed like one of the recommended practices for secure software development. It present and compare a set of Risk Analysis methodologies and strategies, considering like criteria some classifications propose by different authors and the objectives that they persecute to orient them towards of evaluation criterion for the secure software development.

1   Introduction

When a new software product is developed, assuring the incorporation of all functionalities required by the users to the new system is not enough, a set of quality characteristics exists which must consider it at software designing and implementing time. On these quality characteristics, exist diverse models and standards developed, under which different quality attributes are considered, they can vary of model in model. Between these attributes, they are possible to be mentioned for example, software mantenibility, reusability, correction, integrity, efficiency and security, among others and vary according to the model.

In relation to the security, the increasing technology incorporation in all organizational processes, has caused that this attribute acquires real relevance, that at present, multiple researches are made, like one carried out in the United States in 2003 [1], where representatives of the industry, academy and the Government, met them for analyze the consequences of the vulnerabilities of the developed software products under the traditional development models, that models do not incorporate

Please use the following format when citing this chapter:

Verdún, J.C., Hurtado, G.G., Caro, E.T., Zepeda, V.V., 2006, in IFIP International Federation for Information Processing, Volume 213, Network Control and Engineering for QoS, Security, and Mobility, V, ed. Gaïti, D., (Boston: Springer), pp. 27–39.

adecuately the security like a necessary characteristic throughout the software development life cycle. This forum, in addition, has made a series of recommendations to follow with the purpose of improving the development processes in the software developer organizations.

At the present time, several works and proposals about software development, indicate the importance of studying and investigating the products security. For example, the process proposed by Software Engineering Institute of the University of Carnegie Mellon, Team Software Process, which has evolved to the TSP-Secure, or the CMM model, developed by the same Institution, that it has served as base for the development of CMM System Security Engineering.

In general, the software security is limited by the work that develops the operators of the implemented systems to protect the vulnerabilities identified in the organization, having a great infrastructure mounted and handled by people who determine and raise the security policies; but software that they protect, has been designed with the security that deserves?, From the beginning of their construction, has been considered the different properties from security and they have been developed throughout its implementation?

This article deals with the Security focused on development process, being centered in a revision of the practice of the Risks Analysis from different aspects. In the first place techniques and approaches are described taking like main reference the McGraw proposal for secure software development (section 2). The McGraw's proposal shown in fig 1, introduces best practices of security and involves a interdisciplinary atmosphere to apply them and to develop them, with the purpose of fighting against the problems which it is exposed software, specifically about connectivity, extensibilidad and complexity [2].

Later (section 3), appear different risks management methodologies. And finally, a comparative of risks analysis tools is made, which raises certain practices like security tests application, threats models use, attacks patterns and risks analysis (section 4).

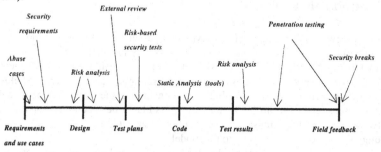

Fig. 1. Software development life cycle - McGraw's proposal

2 Risk Analysis

Throughout this document the concepts software security have been treated from the quality perspective, locating the security like an attribute of the same one.

Between the diverse concepts that exist of quality, it has been taken like reference that is mentioned in [3]. That one reference to that the quality is given by the client requirements, it is to say that "the quality exists in a product when it is apt for the use that the clients that buy it give him." Considering this definition of quality, it is important to focus the Risks Analysis like a support element to identify those problems that affect a software development project.

In the software development processes models Spiral, considered like a realistic approach for great scale systems, the Risks Analysis is also proposed throughout the software development life cycle [4]. This Paradigm uses an evolutionary approach, allowing to the developer and the client to understand and to react to the risks in each level. It uses the creation of prototypes like a risk reduction gear[1]. The Spiral Model recommends the iterative Risks Analysis within the phases of the software development life cycle, defining explicitly the stages in which it must be made, which agree with the McGraw's model [2]; where it recommends the accomplishment of the Risks Analysis of high level in the early phases and its iterative application throughout the service software development life cycle, specially in the Testing stage [5].

McGraw in [6], raises the security is due to incorporate throughout the software development cycle whole, with the purpose of include characteristic emergent like: to specify what must be protected, who must to be in charge and by how long must become that protection.

The security is always related to the information and the services that must be protected, therefore it has relation with the intruders skill, who attack the system. The risk analysis, specially in the design level, allows to identify the main security problems and their impact [7], once identified and classified allows to establish the guide of software security tests.

The attack models are a very useful tool for the identification of the risks that can affect a new software product. The classification and identification of the attacks models that Whittaker proposes [8] and the risks taxonomy propose by Wang and Wang in [9] gives facilities to do the risks identification task by means of possible attacks to the system.

Some studies made[2] sustain the importance that it has to specially do an risks analysis in early stages of the software development. In addition, Microsoft informs that more than 50% of the software security problems they are in design defects, nevertheless, the work for measure the software security and the risks are important throughout the software development life cycle [6].

As it is observed in fig 1, and like it has considered in the preceding paragraphs, it recommended to do the Risk Analysis in the Requirements, Design and Tests stages. In the following sections, some approaches for each one of these stages are described.

---

[1] http://www.itlp.edu.mx/publica/tutoriales/analisis/index.html
[2] www.cio.com/archive/021502/security.html

2.1 Risk Análisis in Requirement level

Next three strategies considered in [5] are enunciated , they describe the risks analysis process in the Requirements phase:

1. **SecureUML**: It is a methodology for access control policies modeled and for the handling of the integration model in the software development. SecureUML is located in the access control and the security requirements models for applications in predictable atmospheres.
2. **UMLsec**: It is an extension of UML that allows the security characteristics modeled related to confidentiality and access control[3].
3. **Abuse Cases Model**: Proposed by Sindre and Opdahl as a way to understand the form in which it would be possible to be responded to the applications threats in less controlable surroundings; they describe the functions that the system does not have to admit.

2.2 Risk Análisis in Design level

In the Design level, the risk analysis must fulfill characteristics like the indicated in [6]: a consequent system vision, the high level of system knowledge and the consideration of the typical vision of analysts and developer when they belive in the sufficiency to describe and to discover the design problems in the code level. In adition, it is also necessary to consider the business risk analysis and the architectonic risk analysis:

1. **Business Risk Analysis**: The companies wants answers as opposed to the investment and to the cost. Therefore, to appraise the impact is a primary target at the moment for do the risk analysis, considering that a good strategy considers questions of cost of the project, so that the direction of the organization can decide the investment in software in relation to the direct cost (responsibility, wasted productivity and reelaboration) as indirect cost (reputation and damage of mark) [10].
2. **Architectonic Risk Analysis**: Similar to the previous one, this analysis measures the technical security exposition in the proposed design of an application and it connects them with the impact of the company. Beginning with a representation of high level of the design, the analysis team considers each one of the modules, interface, interaction, etc. against the well-known attack methodologies and their success probability. In order to provide a general visualization of the security state of a software system, the analysts apply the analysis against the individual design subcomponents [10].

2.3. Risk Analysis in the Testing level.

The risks evaluation in the Testing phase, it allows to evaluate the system against the different risks that affect the product quality. The Risk Analysis in this stage

---

[3] www4.in.tum.de/~umlsec/

allows the project team to arrange and to compare the quality risks with the other categories risks. Categories as like they are defined in [3]:

a) **Financial risks**: It affects the project budget.
b) **Schedule Risks**: They affect the time assigned to project
c) **Feature Risks**: They affect the product characteristics, generally their development obtained a mistaken result.
d) **Quality Risks**: They affect the relation client - satisfaction.

This analysis assures the evaluation of product quality risks and the failures identification in different attributes from quality, not only in the software functionality. The Risk Analysis also will have to be do having in account other characteristics, like the Rex Black's recommendation in [3]. The same author proposes the accomplishment of Risk Analysis under three techniques:

1. **Informal technique**: It works well without considering the development process maturity. The author proposes the use of a table with three columns where the Risks, the error mode associated to the risk will be enunciated and finally a column of Priority, determining evaluation ranks. For the risks idenficación, the errors and specially the priority; the author raises a meeting with a team of project key people.

2. **Standard ISO 9126 Approach**: This standard proposes that the software system quality can be measured throughout six very important characteristics:

Functionality: System Capacity requeridad

Reliability: The system works when it is needed and how it is needed.

Usability: The System can be to use like instinctive, comprehensible and useful for the users.

Efficiency: Resources use.

Mantenibility: System update facility.

Performance: System answer capacity.

Like in the Informal Technique, the Risk Analysis process, is developed defining quality sub-characteristics also identified in the standard - within which is the security – and the priority levels related to the test of each area are determined for the project stakeholders.

3. **Failure Mode and Effect Analysis (FMEA)**: It is a tool that reviews the potential product or the process failures, it values the risk priorities[4]. This tool appears in spreadsheet format and it admits a easy analysis evaluation. The use of this method is advisable specially on development projects very structured, with the purpose of formalizing the of quality risk analysis process. An example of application of this tool is described in [3].

The key of an Risk analysis that supports the software development process in iterative form, from early stages like design, to final stages like Testing; it is the accomplishment of a good analysis, using tools and methodologies able to bring to light software problems that with the tests or a delayed Risk analysis would not be identified or would be correct easily and consequently it obtain a unsecure software development.

---

[4] http://web2.concordia.ca/Quality/tools/11failuremodeanalisys.pdf

José Carrillo Verdún1, Gloria Gasca Hurtado1, Edmundo Tovar Caro1 and Vianca Vega Zepeda2

3 Risks Management Methodologies

In order to be able to develop a secure software product, able to proactively resitir the attacks which is exposed, it is essential to consider the risks throughout the development cycle. With this objective, different strategies and frameworks have been proposed, they harnesses the risks identification, allowing managing them, that is to say, to plan, to implement and to control the measures against the risks and vulnerabilities founded.

3.1. Risks Management Proposals

Next, some strategies propose appear to develop the risks management. They have been selected by the endorsement and recognition that have the organizations who have developed them.

Risk Management Framework (RMF): This proposal has been elaborated by Cigital, where the business goals determine the risks, the risks lead the methods, the methods measure the yield, the measures handle the decisions support and the decisions support handles the reajuste/reelaboration and the aplicationn quality [6]. The RMF intention is to assume a capable, consequent and repetible approach for the risks prevention. The Cigital's proposal describes in [11] like a iterative process, it trim in five basic activity stages, concentrated in following the trajectory, visualizing and to understand the process with respect to the software risk. This structure has been applied in the software field during almost 10 years [11] and the design that presents allows to discover the company risks, including those of software. RMF consists of five fundamental stages:

1. **Understand the Business Context:** The business objectives and risks are identified. The analyst will have to extract and to describe the objectives of the company, the priorities and circumstances to understand the software risks perfectly [11].
2. **Identify and link the Business and Technical Risks:** It must identify business risks. Aid to define and to direct the use of technical methods to extract, to measure and to mitigate the software risk. On the other hand, the technical risks, involve impacts like unexpected system faults, failures in the software controls, data modification. This stage is understood like one of the best practices of Fig 1.
3. **Synthesize and Rank the Risks:** Within the two previous stages, it will find many evident risks, nevertheless the sintetización and priorización of these will have to serve to give value to the analysis process that is tried to make.
4. **Define the Risks Mitigation Strategy:** This strategy will be defined under the business context. It must identify the validation techniques that are going to be used to mitigate appropriately the risks.
5. **Carry out Fixes and Validate:** When a strategy is defined (step 4) it must be executed. When identifying a problem it must be rectified, following the defined strategy. This process must be measured in relation to the risk mitigación strategy.

Finally the Cigital's proposal raises an additional activity but not less important, to inform and to report.

Framework for Managing Information Security Risk: Software Engineering Institute (SEI) of the University of Carnegie Melon, has developed the evaluation strategy OCTAVE (Operationally Critical Threat, Asset and Vulnerability Evaluation), whose objective is to measure the organizacional risk and it focuses in strategic and practical aspects. Aid to an organization to take decisions on the basis of the risks from confidentiality, integrity and availability of the critical assets associated to the information that has its [12]. In this context, the SEI also proposes a Risks Managing Framework [13] it is a risks identification process and its address. Next, they briefly describe each one of the stages that conforms the cyclical process:
1. **Identify:** The objective of this stage is to anticipate the risks, before problems appear. As result it obtains a set of documented risks, including critical assets, threats and vulnerabilities.
2. **Analyze:** This point is the of specific risk analysis. The obtained result is the impact and probability of occurrence of each identified risk and a mitigación approach of such risks.
3. **Plan:** The actions are determined to develop to improve the organization security and the critical assets protection. As result is obtained: protection strategy; risks mitigation plan; action plans, budget, success criteria, indicators for to monitor the fulfillment of the action plans and the allocations of responsibility for the implementation of these plans.
4. **Implement:** Its objective is to execute the defined action plans.
5. **Monitor:** It is the track process of the action plans to determine its fulfillment. Some results of this stage are: Completed actions, progress reports, indicators risk.
6. **Control:** In this stage it determines if the personnel adjusts to the defined action plans, and if the organizacionales changes have caused new risks. As result new decisions can be obtained on changes in the plans or due to the new risks identification.

Magerit: Information Systems Risks Analysis and Management Methodology. The reason of being of Magerit is directly related to the generalization of the use of the electronic, computer science and telematics means, it supposes evident benefits; but also it gives rise to certain risks that must be diminished with security measures which they generate confidence. Magerit allows to know the risk that the work elements are put under, being considered an essential procedure[5]. This methodology proposes a methodical approach that allows to make decisions with foundation and to rationally explain the taken decisions. The risk determination is made by means of six steps defined methodically in [14], they are:
1. To determine the eminent assets for the organization.
2. To value such assets based on the cost that would suppose for the organization to recover it of a failure of availability, integrity, confidentiality or authenticity.
3. To determine to what threats are exposed those assets.
4. To value the vulnerability of the assets to the potential threats.

---

[5] http://www.csi.map.es/csi/pg5m20.htm

5. To consider the impact, defined as the damage on the assets derived from the materialization of the threat.
6. To consider the risk, defined as the impact weighed with the rate of occurrence of the threat.

Integrated approach for risks mitigation: The Institute of Technology of Californian Jet Laboratory Propulsion along with the University of Californian At Davis, has developed an integrated approach for security risks mitigation [15], it form of the following components:
a) **Vulnerability Matrix (Vmatrix):** It is a data base that contains catalogued vulnerabilities taxonomy and that can be acceded like library.
b) **Security Assessment Tools (SAT):** It is a tools list available, where the intention of each one is included.
c) **Properties-based Testing:** It tries to cover the existing emptiness between the formal verification and the ad-hoc verification.
d) **Model-Based Security Specification and Verification:** It is used to verify if they are fulfilled the wished security properties.

The authors indicate that although, each component can be applied in independent form, when applying them altogether, it obtain benefits like the developing system trustworthiness is increase.

3.2. Proposals Analysis

The strategies presented in the previous section, they are coincident in several points. Perhaps one of most important is the implicit recognition that it is impossible that the 100% of the detected risks they are eliminated, thus is necessary and imprecindible the risks priorización based on the damage that can cause, of such way to invest greater resources in those than can cause greater losses to the organization. Others of the agreement points are given by the iterative approach of the proposals, reaffirming of this form the fact that the risks and threats can be varying through the time, thus, it due to do constants revisions and adjustments to the new organizations reality. The three first proposals are oriented to give processes to follow to manage the risks, however, the last integrated approach proposal, is but well a tools set that facilitates this work.

4 Risk Analysis Tools

Next, it briefly describe a tools set for the risk analysis development, which in the following section will be put under a classification and comparison on the basis of the criteria explained down. The tools selection has been do having in account the prestige and experience of the organizations who have developed them or who suggest them as successful tools for the risk analysis.

Microsoft's STRIDE: *Spoofing, Tampering, Repudiation, Information disclosure, Denial of service and Elevation of privilege[6]*, it is a commercial tool, developed to support the threats identification in the software development. Keith Brown, in their book "The .NET Developer's Guide to Windows Security"[7], enunciates the importance of the threats modeled when software is development and designs and he raises as guideline for his modeled the use of this tool. As well, Kenneth van Wyk[8] raises the accomplishment of risks analysis to prevent threats in the software development and he relates the utility of this tool like support to the work, effort and time that a good risks analysis requires.

Sun's ACSM/SAR: It was created to evaluate of formal way the software development and to determine its security level. Mark G. Graff and Kenneth R. van Wyk[9] study the code maintenance within software development because they consider it vital for the security and they propose methodologies and practices for the security software development from the point of view of evaluations for this analysis. For that reason its proposal enunciates tool ACSM/SAR and ASSET like good elements for the developer.

ASSET: Automated Security Self-Evaluation Tool is the automated version of questionnaire "Security Self-Assessment Guide for Information Technology Systems", created by National Institute of Standards and Technology (NIST). This questionnaire looks for to help in the systems security evaluation that has an organization. ASSET is forms of two tools: ASSET-System, this one is the interface that allows to respond the questionnaire; and ASSET-Manager which orders and summarizes the questionnaire application results.

Siemerns CRAMM: Risks Valuation Tool. It includes in addition, other tools that approach tasks like: to identify the impact of the risk valuation in the company, to measure the threats and the vulnerabilities, to identify risks and justifying the required controls, based in the risk valuation. Within the advantages of this tool, the developers argue[10] that it has an excellent capacity to determine requirements for specific controls like: Authentication Level, Encriptation and Hardware Protection, to identify security functional requirements required by the new application, to develop security requirements, evaluation of a security atmosphere, among others.

Cigital's SQM Solutions: Cigital Software Quality Management, was created under the motto "To identify and to eliminate software security defects during the software development and it test" the product Cigital SQM tries to offer a new series of solutions and services for software quality developed around innovating products. In addition, this tool combines the risks prevention, software measurement and software process improvement to help the companies to lead the cost of the quality software development.[11]

SecureUML: It is done on the UML base (Unified Modeling Language). This tool considers the advantages to integrate security engineering in the software

---

[6] http://books.slashdot.org/article.pl?sid=05/11/21/1442228

[7] http://pluralsight.com/wiki/default.aspx/Keith.GuideBook/What%20Is%20A%20Security%20Principal.html

[8] http://www.esecurityplanet.com/views/article.php/3417561

[9] http://www.cedarlug.org/article.php?story=2004040617250150

[10] http://www.insight.co.uk/files/datasheets/CRAMM%20(Datasheet).pdf

[11] http://www.cigital.com/news/index.php?pg=art&artid=110

development life cycle, with the purpose of facilitating the mature security development beyond avoiding the infraction of the security policies.[12]

UMLSec: Its objective is to raise an approach based on UML (Unified Modeling Language) it allows to express the information related to the security by means of diagrams in the system specification. Therefore UMLsec is defined under the UML profile, in particular when associating the security restrictions of a software design, references to a formal semantics of a simplified UML fragment[13].

Failure Mode and Effect Analysis (FMEA): It is a methodology to analyze and to discover all the potential system error ways, its effects and how to correct or to mitigate these failures. It is the analysis procedure more used in the initial stages of the systems development like Conceptual Design stage[14], nevertheless there are authors like Rex Black that considers the possibility and utility of this tool to eliminate all the potential system failures, therefore they focus it in the Testing stage. It is a specific methodology to value the system, the design, the process, or the service in the different possible ways in that the failures (problems, errors, risks, consequences) can happen [16].

Pilar: The risks analysis and management methodology Magerit (section 3) in its second version[15], is accompanied by the risks analysis and management tool PILAR, elaborated by the National Cryptoanalytic Center and the Spain Public Administrations Ministry; it allows to define the assets and threats of an information and communications system, with object to determine its safeguard that allow to reduce the risk to which is put under the system[16]. PILAR constitutes a tools set that supports to the information system risks analysis and management, following the Magerit 1.0 methodology and that at the present time offers:

a) Pilar-1: qualitative analysis, before entering a detailed quantitative analysis.

b) Pilar-2: detailed quantitative analysis, with the purpose of obtaining results of the investment recovery in its safeguard, in terms of declining risk[17].

5. Risk Analysis Tools Comparative

The following table shows a classification and comparison of the described tools. This classification uses some criteria proposed by McGraw (Column Type) and others defined by the authors of this article (Column Security).

The criterion "Type" indicates the classification given by McGraw in [5]. In the comparative that appears it indicates the objective that looked for to reach at the time of its development:

• Commercial: Those methodologies done with an aim to commercialize it like support to certain task within the software development.

---

[12] http://www.foundstone.com/resources/whitepapers/wp_secureuml.pdf

[13] http://www4.in.tum.de/~juerjens/papers/uml02.pdf

[14] http://www.nepss.org/presentations/dfr9.pdf

[15] http://www.revistasic.com/revista64/propuestas_64.htm

[16] http://www.boe.es/boe/dias/2004/11/23/pdfs/A38750-38750.pdf

[17] http://www.ccn.cni.es/medidas_tecnicas/herramientas.htm

- Standards: They are tools, standards or methodologies done by official institutions and proposals like standards of risk analysis.
- Security: It has been catalogued because they have been thought under the criteria of software security or secure software, is to say that the security aspects are the main objective to support within the development of the risk analysis.

The criterion "Security", determined by the authors of this investigation, looks for to categorizar the methodologies and tools considering the support levels that can offer these methodologies in the security requirements analysis for the software development, from a low level at a high level, of the following form:

** :	Low Level
*** :	Mean level
**** :	High Level
***** :	Very High Level

Table 1. Risks Analysis Methodologies and Tools Classification.

Tool or Metodology	Type	Security
Microsoft's STRIDE	Comercial	****
Sun's ACSM/SAR	Comercial	***
ASSET	Comercial - Standard	***
Siemerns CRAMM	Comercial	***
Cigital's SQM Solutions	Comercial-Security	*****
SecureUML	Comercial- Security	****
UMLSec	Comercial- Security	****
Pilar	Standard	**
Failure Mode and Effect Analysis (FMEA)	Security	****

Of this form, the Low Level indicates that the mentioned methodology or tool allows to make an risk analysis, but that its philosophy has not been thought directly in analysis of software security aspects, whereas the Very High Level, it will occur to a tool that has been constructed or raised under the philosophy of the software security aspects, considering the difference between security software and safe software (critical).

When the table is analyzing, it can be observed that most of the risks analysis tools were not developed for its exclusive application in the software security development, but well, they are of general use. The approaches and strategies of security and risks evaluation in the organizations, have been focused like a necessity by the increasing incorporation of the information technology, although it is certain, the software products are part of this technology, at the time of making the risks analysis, would be due to incorporate particular considerations, as threats and typical attacks that frequently happen, and also the vulnerabilities generated by errors or negligences in the design and implementation of these products.

The objective to describe the security aspects of the methodologies mentioned, is to focus future research works directed to support the Risk analysis like a good practice within the life cycle, framed in the proposal of figure 1.

6 Conclusions

The importance of Risk Analysis in the early stages of the software development life
cycle, like it has been showed previously; it extends from the product quality to the
security and evolve to such an extent that wakes up the interest of the business in
aspects like costs and investment return.

In the security scope, if the requirements and necessities of an organization are
not considered from the early stages of the software development life cycle and these
are not evaluated in the other development stages, hardly it will be obtained a system
robust, able to repulse the attacks so common in the present time.

Every day the organizations take more serious the security problems, and this is
demonstrated with the different initiatives taken to do that the software developers
become aware from the importance of improving their processes, incorporating
practical that they look for to reach the security product implementation, proactive to
the attacks. The necessity to incorporate the study and application of the security
software life cycle under the standards parameters and associated quality models to
good practices, with the purpose of having developments able to respond and to face
the attacks and the systems attackers, it is complemented with the preoccupation of
the industry, the academy and the commerce giving as result variety of efforts in the
search to raise solutions to this problem.

The study and the Risk Analysis Tools comparative made present the beginning
of the investigation that are developing the authors of the present article, leaving laid
the way to investigate thorough the methodologies, tools, standards and principles to
establish development models with practices and evaluations at the right moment to
guarantee the quality, evaluating in first instance the security in the software
development. Mainly the study to the practices raised by McGraw, shown in fig 1,
for the security software development is left open.

References

1.   N. Davis, W. Humphrey, S. Redwine, G. Zibulski, and G.
McGraw, "Processes for producing secure software," *Security
& Privacy Magazine IEEE*, vol. 2, pp. 18 - 25 2004.

2.   G. McGraw, "Software Security," *IEEE Security & Privacity*,
pp. 80-83, 2004.

3.   B. R., "The Risks to System Quality Investing in Software
Testing Series, Part 3."

4.   I. Sommerville, "Ingeniería de Software," P. Education, Ed., 6
ed. México, 2002.

5.   D. M. Verdon, G., "Risk analysis in software design,"
IEEESecurity & Privacy Magazine, vol. 2, pp. 79-84, 2004.

6.   G. McGraw, "From the ground up: the DIMACS software
security workshop," *IEEE Security & Privacy Magazine*, vol.
1, pp. 59-66, 2003.

7.   B. M. Potter, G., "Software security testing," *IEEESecurity &
Privacy Magazine*, vol. 2, pp. 81-85, 2004.

8.   J. A. Whittaker, "Software's invisible users," *IEEE Software*,
vol. 19, pp. 84-88, 2001.

9.   H. W. a. C. Wang, "Taxonomy of security considerations and
software quality," *Communications of the ACM*, vol. 46, pp. 75
- 78, 2003.

10.   K. R. M. Van Wyk, G., "Bridging the gap between software
development and information security," *Security & Privacy
Magazine IEEE*, vol. 3, pp. 75 - 79, 2005.

11.   G. E. McGraw, "Risk Management Framework (RMF),"
Cigital, Inc., 2005.

12.   C. Alberts, Dorofee, A., Stevens, J., Woody, C., "Introduction
to the OCTAVE Approach," vol. Software Engineering
Institute, 2003.

13.   C. Alberts and A. Dorofee, *Managing Information Security
Risk. The OCTAVE Approach*: Addison Wesley, 2005.

14.   J. Mañas, "Pilar. Herramientas para el Análisis y la Gestión de
Riesgos," 2004.

15.   D. P. P. Gilliam, J.D.; Kelly, J.C.; Bishop, M.;, "Reducing
software security risk through an integrated approach,"
*Software Engineering Workshop, 2001. Proceedings. 26th
Annual NASA Goddard*, pp. 36 - 42 2001.

16.   H., *Failure Mode and Effect Analysis. FMEA from Theory to
Execution*, Second Edition ed.

P3P Semantic Checker of Site Behaviours

Robson Eduardo Grande[1] and Sérgio Donizetti Zorzo
Federal University of São Carlos, Computing Department
Zip Code 676 - 13565-905, São Carlos, Brazil
{robson_grande,zorzo}@dc.ufscar.br,
WWW home page: http://www.dc.ufscar.br

Abstract. The interactive use of the web between users and service providers introduces a privacy problem that involves the undesired disclosing of user personal information, mainly with the presence of personalization that needs this type of information. Also there are many manners to face it, but the Platform for Privacy Preferences (P3P) is one that provides a variable level of privacy for the user's browsing. However, the P3P only introduces a privacy contract between the site and the user, without guarantees that it will be obeyed by the site. Then a semantic checker can be added to the P3P architecture to compare the contract with the site attitude and to increase the trustworthiness on the P3P contract. Some experiments are accomplished and the results are displayed to show the present situation of the privacy policies of the sites, and we discuss what it implies in the data gathering and what is gained with the use of the semantic checker.

1 Introduction

The interface implementation in e-commerce applications must consider two aspects: the marketing necessities and the user privacy. For both aspects user's personal data has a great worth. On one side, providing competitive advantages in the market through the marketing and, on the other hand, presenting a bigger user confidence with regard to his disclosed data. This user confidence is recognized as an important item to bring to the success of an online marketing, and consequently to increase purchases and sales in the web and to improve the e-commerce markets.

The personalization application is one of the strongest competitive advantages in the market. It has become an indispensable instrument to the progress of the services and online businesses. The idea of receiving personalized services from visited web sites is sufficiently attractive, besides very well accepted by the users. In accordance with Kobsa [1], clients need to feel that possess a personal and unique relationship

[1] Robson Eduardo Grande receives financial support from CAPES.

Please use the following format when citing this chapter:

Grande, R.E., Zorzo, S.D., 2006, in IFIP International Federation for Information Processing, Volume 213, Network Control and Engineering for QoS, Security, and Mobility, V, ed. Gaïti, D., (Boston: Springer), pp. 41–53.

with the enterprises, and to confirm this is presented a research that shows that sites offering personalized services achieved an increase of 47% in the number of new clients.

Meanwhile, so that personalization to be applied it is necessary the information collection originated in several provenance, which can be gotten explicitly or implicitly.

An individual that sends explicitly information is obviously aware of the sending of it. On the other hand, the implicit gathering of information is the resultant data acquisition from the user browsing observation, and he can be or not aware of its existence. Information obtained by this method contemplates the e-commerce interaction data and the clickstream [2] [3] data, which makes possible the creation of user profiles based in user interests, browsing patterns, preferences and others.

But, while the user data gathering can help in the marketing of e-commerce sites, it can prejudice the marketing too. Depending on the form that the gathering method and analysis process of user data are accomplished it can characterize a privacy invasion, whereas the user can loose the control of his personal information [4].

This privacy lack results to a user confidence loss, as from this he stops accessing certain services fearing that personal information, which has a considerable value for him, is disclosed or has a malicious use. This can be confirmed by Teltzrow [5] that says 64% of web users haven't accessed some time a web site, or they haven't bought something from it because they don't know how their information would be used. Also 53% of the users don't trust in commercial web sites that gather data, 66% of them don't register in online sites fearing that their information may be used inappropriately, and 40% of them falsify data when registering online [6].

Moreover, privacy is considered to be intrinsically related with the control that an individual has over determined information [4]. In this way, it must be inherent in trustworthy transactions, in another way a privacy lack will contribute to cause a fault of the business model of the electronic commerce.

An increase of the user control perception causes an increase of adoption of services and products based on the web. The user control perception is provided by bigger information disclosing of the collected data use that is made, and the receiving of something worthy in return stimulates the data disclosing by the user. Jutla [6] reports that 51% of web users desire to disclose personal data to receive something worthy in return and, a research shows that 90% of users want to be asked after permission before their information is used or gathered [5].

The question is to find an equilibrium point between personal information gathering and user privacy. Nevertheless, to find this equilibrium point becomes difficult because the privacy is subjective, in this case each one has its privacy discernment.

Several mechanisms utilized to guarantee the user privacy have consequences in their access form, producing degrees of reachable personalization. In this way they can denigrate the personalized service availableness.

The 3P Platform, that have been used in a pretty crescent and extensive way [7], is interesting to become possible the privacy level modulation in accordance with the user preferences, and in this way adapting better to the user characteristics. Also, to the use of this platform isn't necessary to make many modifications, since basically it includes an automatic method of privacy policy reading. Add to that, the privacy policies have a big user acceptance, 76% of users think privacy policies are very important and 55% of them believe that it turns the personal information disclosing more comfortable [5].

Notwithstanding, this platform presents a low level of trustworthiness in the semantic aspects of the manipulated data. In this manner, it is proposed a semantic checker looking at the increment of the trustworthiness degree in the P3P tool. The user trustworthiness is incremented by comparing the P3P privacy policies with the site's behavior. Tests are accomplished and their results show that some sites write P3P policies correctly, and the inclusion of the checker can obey the other sites to improve the construction of their policies.

This work introduces in the second section several access forms to the user data with privacy. In the third section we present the 3P platform mechanisms and its limitations. The fourth section presents the Semantic Analyzer. The fifth section shows the experiments and results obtained and finally the sixth section describes the conclusions and future works.

2   Privacy Mechanisms

As manners to face the problem of privacy in the web, many proposals exist that can be divided in two basic forms of approach. One of these forms aims at the introduction of architectures or mechanisms, tries to keep the anonymity of the user, or makes difficult the identification of him. The next mechanisms follow this line of approach.

Cookie crushers or cookie filters are the most common of them. They provide a way of controlling or not permitting the cookie existence in the user computer, avoiding that personal information can be stored to be recovered subsequently.

Theoretically cookie [8] is used to store in the user computer the estate of his browsing in a determined site. The cookie content is created by web server. The sites utilize this information piece to characterize the user profile, gathered through analysis methods of browsing as clickstream.

Clickstream, also known as clickpaths, is the route that the user chooses when he clicks or browses by a site. This information is used to determine user profile in his browsing.

The anonymity is wanted by several users that don't permit that any personal information is discovered, thus avoiding any privacy problem and identification of the user identity. Three mechanisms are presented as examples of this type of approach. Anonymizer [9] is a web proxy that forwards the user requisitions and applies certain methods to mask them as requisitions from the proxy.

Onion Routing [10] is constituted of one or more routers and each one works as a proxy that applies certain methods to improve the privacy and to forward randomly to the next router or to the destiny site in question. This routers net is built dynamically, it is fault tolerant and works to avoid eavesdroppers by making difficult to determine the user requisitions source.

In Crowds [11], each user contributes hiding the real origin of a requisition, with the member co-operation of a group. Randomly and dynamically a requisition can be forwarded to a member of a Crowd group or to the site destiny, and it isn't possible to make backtracking search to determine the origin user because each user requisition changes the routing process to create a different path.

Another approach to permit privacy during the user browsing is using pseudonyms. It consists basically in to create fictitious names to users to disguise the user identity permitting personalization, as soon as web sites are able to determine user profiles without link them to the user real identity. An example of this type of mechanism is the JPWA (Janus Personalized Web Anonymizer) [12]. It acts as an intermediary entity (proxy) between the user and the web site generating automatically nicknames when users want to access determined services, executing the authentication process. If the real identity of a pseudonym is discovered, all the user actions in the past will be automatically exposed.

Managing Anonymity while Sharing Knowledge to Servers (MASKS) [13] is another approach to protect the user privacy permitting personalization based in the pseudonyms idea. It hides the user identity under masks or pseudonyms. These pseudonyms are associated by some way to a group of similar requisitions. These groups are defined in accordance with user interests exhibited during the interaction with a web service by making requisitions in name of a group, contrary to an individual user, thus not disclosing the user identity. The user requisition is designed to a group and not to a user because the requisition represents the user interest in a specific moment. The MASKS doesn't provide privacy when users send explicitly their information to sites.

All the presented mechanisms show some limitations in preserving the privacy or permitting personalization. Those mechanisms that protect all the user privacy don't permit personalization, and those that permit personalization have faults to protect the user privacy, or they have some problems in the security aspects.

3   P3P

Another line of approach introduces the idea to police the sites or to inform the user about the privacy policies that are adopted by them, communicating the information that is gathered. According to this criterion are presented the following systems.
One of them is a tool that provides information related to context about privacy and personalization options [14]. It is a support system to the user navigation exhibiting a situational communication dialogue when the user information is gathered.

P3P [15][16] inserts a way to manage the user browsing through of a standardized method to disclose how the user information is gathered, how they will be utilized and the sharing of them to third parts. This management is made through the P3P privacy policy checking by a user agent.

P3P inserts a contract between sites and users, defining a protocol that permits the site administrators to publish a site privacy policy. Add to that, a user agent is defined by the platform that reads automatically this privacy police, verifying if it combines with the user privacy preferences or user security configurations, because the majority of the users pay attention poorly to the privacy policy readings [5].

Web sites are qualified to express their privacy actions by the 3P platform in a standard format. This standard format consists in indications made and based in the P3P vocabulary to express the privacy behavior of each web site. These indications are made by a XML codification with name spaces from P3P vocabulary to provide information that defines the site privacy policies, informing which information is obtaining and which form is using to obtain it, where and how long the information will be stored, who is the responsible and the information gathering purpose. The P3P vocabulary é planed to be descriptive of the site behavior, but not to be simply an obedience indicator to a particular law or a conduct code.

The privacy policies of a site must have a reference with their respective and specific particularities, permitting to determine the policy range in determined site region.

The policy reference is a codification in XML with name spaces that can specify the policy to an entire site, portions of a site or to a unique web document. It also links the site parts to its respective policies, shows the exact location of the file that contains the P3P privacy policies, defines the access methods to which the policy is applicable and the time period to which it claim that is considered to be valid.

By any means the P3P reference file location must be known to find the file, to begin the analysis, and to know the P3P privacy policy location. To his, four mechanisms can be used to indicate the policy reference file place: a well known location (/w3c/p3p.xml), HTTP headers can be used to point to a policy reference file through the creation of a new answer header, a HTML or SHTML link tag can be used to obtain the policy reference file.

The user preferences inform the way how the user agent must act when analyzing a privacy policy of a site.

The user P3P agent works as a tool that acts co-operating with the browser. It can be a plug-in added to the browser, a proxy server, or built in the web browsers.

The user agent looks for a reference of a policy reference file in the HTTP header, HTML or SHTMLK link tags and by the well known location. With the reference file the agent can obtain the privacy policy respective to the URL the user requested and can begin to analyze the policy by comparing it with the user privacy preferences. This analysis process results in an indication with symbols, sounds or generating alerts to the user.

P3P Limitations

According to the P3P specification there is one limitation. It's argued that the user should have control of his privacy instead of to trust completely in privacy policies of web sites [13]. Add to that, this is a great problem with the P3P because it can't guarantee sites will act following their policies, considering that P3P is only a document describing the privacy policy of a site.

In this way the site can be obtaining additional data that is specified by the privacy policy, and the user doesn't have guarantees of what information is collected. Add to that, this is passed in way that the user doesn't perceive, whereas he trusts on the signalizing of the user agent that makes the automatic policy analysis.

Laws and auto-regulatory programs that protect the user privacy can be verified during the P3P policy assimilation, and, thus imposing certain obedience to the policy correctness related to the site. Such laws are only a way to influence web sites to be sincere in the building of its policies. However, these laws don't guarantee that every web site will apply it.

To guarantee that the P3P policies are obeyed is necessary to insert some checker that can't be handled by the sites, it executes a verification of the privacy policy faithfulness considering the sites behavior, and returns a guarantee seal.

4 P3P Semantic Checker

The Semantic Checker presented in this work objectifies to extend the 3P Platform. It adds a bigger trustworthiness to the user browsing by the conference of the privacy policy correctness proposed by the 3P platform. The conference of the privacy policy correctness is made by inserting a semantic analyzer to the P3P agent user that makes a P3P privacy policy checking. This checking is made comparing the site behavior with it privacy policy, and this behavior is represented by the site source code that comes to the user browser.

It must be localized in the user computer, trying to increase the security of this checker proposed. With this guarantee that the site doesn't have access to the checker and, thus the site can't corrupt it to produce a false result to the user. If it produces a false result it will be deceiving the user, coming back to the original situation where there weren't privacy guarantees.

After that the user information is collected there isn't possibility of knowing the destiny that will be given to it. Thus, the privacy policy checking with the site behavior is only possible at the verification of user data gathering, and without this approach only rests the trustworthiness on the privacy policy as the unique way of to police the site attitudes with the collected information, or to belief on the law codes [16].

At the implicit gathering, the information collectors utilize ways that can't be identified by some mechanic analysis method, or they don't follow a pattern to be identified. The cookies can be identified, seeing that they are stored in the user computer through a http requisition. However, they aren't a form of information gathering, but a form of storage of information gathered, and their content can't be understood.

The analysis of explicit gathering is the way that better shows the site behavior at the user computer view. This type of gathering can be observed in the html page source code that the user accesses. The data requisition, which is made to the users, is accomplished by html elements of data entrance. Also, the html code is very used to the construction of Web pages, it is generated by the majority of languages of dynamic pages as ASP, PHP, JSP and others, and it is embedded in the JavaScript code.

To find the places where the user information is obtained is necessary to look for by the form tags in the page source code in question. Each data entrance field in each form in the site source code represents a data entrance that the user can enter his information to be sent to the site, and the set of these input fields results in the information set that the user send explicitly to the site. To accomplish the analysis is necessary to find each one of these data entrance fields e to compare with the respective P3P policy to verify if, through the page, the site is obtaining some information over that the policy specifies.

The checker can be added as a module to the user agent, accomplishing the checking every time that the user does a page requisition, which can be visualized by the figure 1. In the figure the first communication that is accomplished with the site server is to obtain the privacy policy, with it the agent can make the comparison with the user preferences. In the second communication the server sends the requested page, and the semantic checker accomplishes the analysis with the source code of this page and the P3P privacy policy.

The privacy policy validation can be made before or after that the agent makes the comparison between the policy and the user preferences, resulting in an additional signalization to the user or even to influence the result that the agent signalizes.

Therefore the semantic checker functioning is made of the following form, incorporated at the 3P platform, which can be visualized by the figure 1.

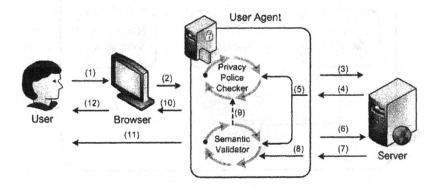

Fig. 1. A Diagram that represents the insertion of the semantic checker to the P3P Platform architecture.

In a page requisition made by the user in his browser (1) in an architecture that uses P3P, the user agent intercepts the requisition (2). Initially it looks for (3) (4) a P3P privacy policy to analyze the site policies with the user preferences (5). With the analysis made, the agent can signalize to the user positively (11), permitting that the user can access the page (6) (7) (10) (12), or negatively, letting to the user to take the decision in accessing or not the page.

The checker makes a semantic analysis with the privacy policy obtained (5) and the source code (8). By this analysis is created a signalization that can be incorporated to the signalization that the user agent produces (11), or can be refined by the agent as an additional criterion in its policy analysis process (9).

A functioning architecture of semantic checker is presented by the figure 2. At it, three entrances can be identified, html source code file and the respective URL (1), privacy policy reference file (2) and P3P privacy policy file (3).

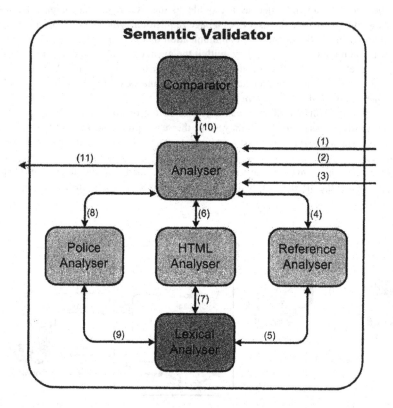

Fig. 2. Semantic Checker Architecture and functioning – through the html source code analysis of the site and of its privacy policy is generated a result to the policy approbation.

By the entrances at the figure 2 will be begun the policy analysis by the Analyzer. First is necessary to find the respective page privacy policy according to its URL (4), to this is utilized a lexicon analyzer to recognize the reference file elements (5). At the end of this process it is returned the policy name that must be used.

Determined the respective policy, the data entrance elements are obtained, which are identified by the *input* fields (6). Also it is used the lexicon analyzer to recognize the html elements and to be able to found them (7). The privacy policy data elements also will be obtained (8) using a lexicon analyzer to identify them by the *data* fields.

Obtained the both elements, is accomplished a comparison of each input field of the html source code with the privacy policy elements to investigate is the field is specified by the policy (10). Depending on this comparison made, a negative or positive result can be returned (11).

The figure 3 presents a sequence diagram of a user's page requisition. The sixth arrow represents the semantic checker action added to the P3P, and the others arrows represent the user requisitions and the P3P answers without the checker functioning inclusion.

Add to that, each information entrance field needs to be delimited by the site privacy policy, and the fields of data entrance in the site source code needs to have some binding with the respective elements of its P3P specification, which in the case of this initial implementation, the link is the html field to have a name equals to the P3P policy specification.

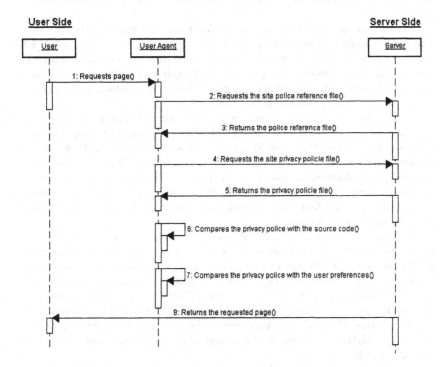

Fig. 3. Sequence diagram of an example of semantic checker execution in a page requisition.

However, this proposed link between names restrings the page construction. But, the proposal suggested is initial and utilized more to test. A proposal more suitable is to create an attribution file together with the P3P policy to be utilized to accomplish the verification of the input fields. This additional brings flexibility to the owners of the sites at the creation of entrance fields.

5   Experiments and Results

The experiments are accomplished trying to present a situation of how the sites and their respective P3P privacy policies are.

The research consisted in to make a process closed to the mechanism of the semantic checker, obtaining each source code of each page and its respective privacy policy. It was made a comparison between the data element names of the policy and the input element names of the page, signalizing if some element wasn't delimited by the policy.

The result of the automatic analysis was the same as the result that was hoped, no one page that had text entrance elements and was analyzed passed by the verification with positive signalization, whereas the analysis is based in the comparison of names.

But, in a manual analysis of the gathered data some evidences could be observed. This manual analysis consists in to observe the input elements obtained with their respective data elements. In this observation was approached also the comparison between the name means of the gathered input fields and the means of the data elements obtained, and thus to try understand how was constructed the privacy policy and the site page to relate them in some way.

Initially were accessed 100 compliant sites with the 3P Platform. The addresses of these sites were obtained from a listing in *http://www.w3.org/P3P/compliant_site*. In a sampling of 100 sites only 57 could be analyzed, the others 43 had some problem that made impossible their access or the use of their P3P privacy policy: the site was in construction, it wasn't found, the access was forbidden, there were problems in the syntactic construction of the P3P policies, the policies weren't found or the policy reference files weren't found, seeing that the reference file was looked for in the well known location.

With these 57 correct sites 120 pages were obtained so that their html source codes were analyzed. By the analysis, 33 pages of 120 didn't have any input element of data entrance, and thus they weren't utilized to the verification. Therefore, with a sampling of 87 pages was obtained the following graphic presented in figure 4.

The research only approaches the explicit information gathering, the dynamic data specification [16] wasn't considered, as *dynamic.http*, *dynamic.clickstream* or *dynamic.cookies*. The cookie content doesn't follow a construction pattern: each site builds it in a different way, needing knowledge of all site behavior and source code to predict its value.

The 87 pages were classified in six categories, in accordance with how they presented their privacy policies, and each category represents a percentage of the 87 pages.

The "A" category delimits the pages that have a P3P privacy police and doesn't describe any one of their input fields of their html source codes.

The "B" category delimits the pages that have policies specified in a generic way all or a big part of their input fields. It describes only what is made with any data that is collected by the page, or also it can be a generic specification as *user.business-info* or *user.home-info*.

The "C" category delimits the pages that have a privacy policy that specifies each input element of the form in their html codes.

The "D" category delimits the pages that have privacy policy that specifies only some input fields of the source code.

The "E" category delimits the pages that have names of input fields in the html code that their meaning can't be understood or they have a very generic meaning, as loesung1, sp-q or word.

The "F" category delimits the pages that have some input field names in the html code that can be understood and they are specified by the privacy policy.

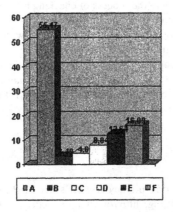

Fig. 4. Graphic that presents the experiment results classified in categories of P3P privacy policy situation.

Also it was observed that the majority of the pages, close to the totality, specified the dynamic data gathering. Even to those policies that informed nothing to the explicit data gathering. This evidences that the P3P compliant sites are aware in specify the implicit information gathering, but they specify poorly the input fields at html source code.

Therefore, in general terms can be concluded that 44.82 percent of the pages, almost half of the pages that utilize the 3P platform specify with more details in majority of their fields of explicit information gathering. This shows that the mechanism can be used as a tool to improve the user trustworthiness by verifying.

6 Conclusions

Among all the experiment results made, it can be observed that the totality of the sites compliant with the P3P policy don't satisfy the restrictions to the execution of the checker. It was also observed that more than half of the sampling of these 100 sites complaints with the 3P platform don't look for to specify in detail the data that is obtain from the users.

The insertion of this checker in the 3P platform increases the user trustworthiness guaranteeing that all the data that is gathered explicitly is specified by the P3P privacy policy. The checker would be an additional reinforcement to the sites that use P3P and detail their specification of data gathering, and would force the others to detail the elements of the information gathered. Thus, over increasing the trustworthiness in the privacy policies, also would improve the construction of the P3P policies, with more details in the site specifications.

The next step is to improve the process of checking by retiring the restriction that each html entrance field must have the same name as in its respective P3P privacy policy, this can be made by using a file stored together with the privacy policy that makes the linking between the names, as suggested before.

As evidenced, this proposal considers the explicit data gathering, which is analyzed in the site source code. However a cookie analysis can be added to the checking process, the cookie presence is identified by the HTTP communication, but its content can't be understood or analyzed.

References

1. A. Kobsa (2001). Tailoring privacy to user's needs. Proc. Of 8th International Conference on User Modeling. http://www.ics.uci.edu/~kobsa/papers/2001-UM01-kobsa.pdf.

2. R. E. Bucklin, J. M. Lattin, A. Ansari, D. Bell, E. Coupey, S. Gupta, J. D. C. Little, C. Mela, A. Montgomery, J. Steckel, "Choice and the Internet: from Clickstream to Research Stream", U.C. Berkeley 5th Invitational Choice Symposium, Mareting Letters, 13(3), 245 -258, Last Revised February 10, 2002.

3. A. L. Montgomery, S. Li, K. Srinivasan, and J. C. Liechty, (2004) "Modeling ONline Browsing and Path Analysis Using Clickstream Data", Marketing Science, Vol 23, No. 4, p579-595.

4. Privacilla, (October 11, 2005); http://www.privacilla.org.

5. M. Teltzrow and A. Kobsa (2004) "Communication of Privacy and Personalization in E-Business". Proceedings of the Workshop "WHOLES: A Multiple View of Individual Privacy in a Networked World", Stockholm, Sweden. http://www.ics.uci.edu/~kobsa/papers/2004-WHOLES-kobsa.pdf.

6. D. Jutla, and P. Bodorik, (2003) "A Client-Side Model for Electronic Privacy". 16th Bled eCommerce Conference and Transformation. June 2003.

7. P. Kumaraguru, and P. Cranor, "Privacy in India: Attitudes and Awareness". In Proceedings of the 2005 Workshop on Privacy Enhancing Technologies (PET2005), 30 May - 1 June 2005, Dubrovnik, Croatia.

8. D. Kristol, and L. Montulli, "HTTP State Management Mechanism". Bell Laboratories, Lucent Technologies. Epinions.com, Inc. October 2000. RFC 2965. http://www.ietf.org/rfc/rfc2965.txt.

9. Anonymizer, Inc. (2004) "Anonymizer Enterprise Network Privacy/Security Appliance". Technology Overview. www.anonymizer.com.

10. D. Goldschlag, M. Reedy, and P. Syversony, (1999) "Onion Routing for Anonymous and Private Internet Connectinos". January 1999. www.onion-router.net/Publications/CACM-1999.pdf.

11. M. K. Reiter, and A. D. Rubin, (1997) "Crowds: Anonymity for Web Transactions". AT&T Labs – Research. avirubin.com/crowds.pdf.

12. E. Gabber, P. E. Gibbons, Y. Matias, and A. Mayer (1997) "How to Make Personalized Web Browsing Simple, Secure, and Anonymous". Bell Laboratiories, Lucent Technologies. http://www.bell-labs.com/project/lpwa/papers.html.

13. B. G. Rocha, V. A. F. Almeida, L. Ishitani, and W. Meira Jr., (2002) "Disclosing Users' Data in an Environment that Preserves Privacy". Workshop On Privacy In The Electronic Society.

14. A. Kobsa, and M. Teltzrow, (2005). "Contextualized Communication of Privacy Practices and Personalization Benefits: Impacts on Users' Data Sharing and Purchase Behavior". PET 2004.

15. L. F. Cranor, (2003) "'I Didn't Buy it for Myself' Privacy and Ecommerce Personalization", WPES'03 (Washington DC, USA, October 30, 2003), AT&T Labs-Research.

16. Platform for Privacy Preferences Project, P3P Public Overview. http://www.w3.org/P3P/.

A Sliding Window Based Management Traffic Clustering Algorithm for 802.11 WLAN Intrusion Detection

Wenzhe Zhou[1], Alan Marshall[1], ,and Qiang Gu[2]
1 School of Electrical & Electronic Engineering, Queen's University,
Belfast, UK
{w.zhou, a.marshall}@ee.qub.ac.uk
2 ECIT, Queen's University, Belfast, UK
qiang.gu@ee.qub.ac.uk

Abstract. This paper introduces a novel Management Traffic Clustering Algorithm (MTCA) based on a sliding window methodology for intrusion detection in 802.11 networks Active attacks and other network events such as scanning, joining and leaving in 802.11 WLANs can be observed by clustering the management frames in the MAC Layer. The new algorithm is based on a sliding window and measures the similarity of management frames within a certain period by calculating their variance. Through filtering out certain management frames, clusters are recognized from the discrete distribution of the variance of the management traffic load. Two parameters determine the accuracy and robustness of the algorithm: the Sample Interval and the Window Size of the sliding window. Extensive tests and comparisons between different sets of Sample Intervals and Window Sizes have been carried out. From analysis of the results, recommendations on what are the most appropriate values for these two parameters in various scenarios are presented.

1   Introduction

Today 802.11 WLANs are widely used in different areas such as home, enterprise, and military due to their convenient nature. However, attacks against 802.11 WLANs are more feasible than against fixed networks as malicious users can easily access the wireless links. Furthermore, research has shown that the security mechanisms such as WEP, WPA and 802.11i provided to protect the WLAN MAC Layer are not completely safe [1] [2] [3]. Even the newly ratified 802.11i standard [4] is vulnerable to certain active attacks such as Denial-of-Service (DoS) and Man-In-The-Middle (MITM) due to the unencrypted management frames and EAPOL (Extensible Authentication Protocol Over Local Area Network) frames [5].

Please use the following format when citing this chapter:

Zhou, W., Marshall, A., Gu, Q., 2006, in IFIP International Federation for Information Processing, Volume 213, Network Control and Engineering for QoS, Security, and Mobility, V, ed. Gaïti, D., (Boston: Springer), pp. 55–64.

Expert security systems are essential in order to address the vulnerabilities of 802.11 WLANs. During the past decade, data mining approaches have been used to improve security because they have the advantage of discovering useful knowledge that describes a user's or program's behaviour from large audit data sets. A good example is intrusion detection, which has been used to protect computer systems as a first line of defense. Next generation Intrusion Detection Expert Systems (NIDES) represents an IDS based on statistics that measures the similarity between a subject's long-term and short-term behaviours [8]. In [9] S.Chebrolu applied Bayesian Networks (BN) and Classification and Regression Trees (CART) approaches in fixed networks to model Intrusion Detection Systems (IDS) with high accuracies of detecting certain intrusions. In [10] C.Kruegel implemented the Bayesian Network approach in IDS to reduce false alarms. To date these approaches have not been applied to implement IDS in the lower protocol layers of WLANs.

Recent research has shown that active attacks exhibit certain fingerprints in terms of the patterns of management frames [6]. By clustering and analyzing certain features of the management traffic (e.g. frame types, source/destination addresses) in the network, an intrusion detection system can recognize and predict the abnormal events. This paper focuses on the clustering of the 802.11 management frames. Our work contributes in three ways: firstly, it specifically addresses the security issues in 802.11 WLANs and uses the characteristic features of management traffic to analyze intrusions; secondly, our algorithm statistically measures the similarity of the management traffic clusters between a long-term and a short-term performance. This meets the requirements of the NIDES systems. Thirdly, we perform a series of test to decide the most appropriate parameters (window size and sample interval) and their optimum values for cluster recognition. This paper is organized as the following: section 2 introduces the background theory and experiment set-up; section 3 introduces the sliding window algorithm for intrusion detection in 802.11 WLAN; section 4 analyzes the choice of parameters for the sliding window algorithm; section 5 gives the conclusion and future work.

2   Background & Challenges

The 802.11 management frames are responsible for the access control, which is expressed by the 802.11 state machine [7]. These management frames are: beacon, probe request, probe response, authentication, association request, association response, reassociation request, reassociation response, disassociation and deauthentication. When stations (STAs) search for connections, join or leave the WLAN, they send out management frames to the access point and negotiate about the access. Research shows that as events (e.g. scanning, joining, leaving, or an active attack) occur in the WLAN, corresponding clusters of management frames are formed [6]. Each event has an individual cluster pattern. By observing the management frame clusters, an IDS can detect the events in a WLAN, and by analysing the pattern of a cluster, the IDS can tell the type of event occurring. In this paper, we focus on how to detect the clusters. The challenges are: how to define the similarities of the clusters? How to decide the border of a cluster? And how to separate one cluster from another?

We have set up a WLAN with five clients, one attacker and one sniffer to observe the traffic in the WLAN [6]. We injected two types of attacks into the network. Figure 1 shows the complete WLAN traffic trace. The trace file includes the following four events with six clusters: a link problem, a DoS attack, the DoS recovery, and an MITM attack.. From the figure we can see that when events occur, the number of management frames will increase. The "frame density" can be regarded as the number of frames in each time period. From a more abstract point of view, the change of the management frame density shows the occurance of events. Thus we introduce the variance of number of management frames in each sample time point to describe the similarities of the management frame clusters. The average number of frames A can be expressed as:

$$A = \frac{\sum_{i=0}^{n} X_i}{n} \tag{1}$$

And the variance can be expressed as:

$$\delta = \sqrt{\frac{\sum_{i=0}^{n} (X_i - A)^2}{n}} \tag{2}$$

In the above two equations, Xi is the frame number in each sample time point, n is the total frame number during the chosen period of time. The observation of a cluster also includes the contrast between the "past" and the "present" management traffic density in the network. The comparison shows the change in density. The challenges are: (i) how to define the time period of the "past" and the "present"? This can be interpreted as how to decide the value of n in equations (1) and (2) and (ii) how to define the sampling time point. Another challenge is how to describe the comparison with a machine understandable language? In the following section, we introduce our Management Traffic Clustering Algorithm (MTCA), which is based on a sliding window approach.

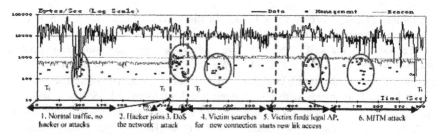

Fig. 1. The complete WLAN traffic trace

3   The Management Traffic Clustering Algorithm (MTCA)

Figure 2 shows the sliding window algorithm. The algorithm contains two parameters: the Window Size (WS) and the Sample Interval (SI). There are two counters calculating the SI and the WS, the SI Counter (SIC) and the WS Counter (WSC). In figure 2, the sliding window body is originally positioned at time t_0. When the SIC counts to the first SI, the sliding window heads forward one SI. At the same time, the original window decreases one SI at the bottom so that the total window size always remains the same length. Thus, the sliding window body moves to a new position at time t_1. As the algorithm keeps running, after n-1 sample intervals, the sliding window will move to new position at time t_{n-1} as shown.

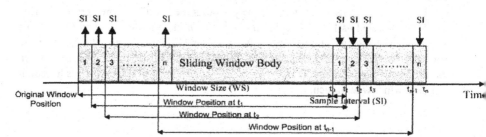

Fig. 2. Sliding Window Algorithm

The sliding window approach meets the requirements discussed in section two for the management frame cluster detection. Firstly, it can easily define the "past" and "present" time periods. We can use the window size WS to represent the "past" time period, its value determines how much importance one wishes to place on past events. The sample interval is used to represent the "present" time period; its value determines how much importance one wishes to place on the present events.

In order to cluster the management traffic in the network, we are concerned with the similarity inside the clusters, that is, the change of the management traffic density.. The change of management traffic density can be represented by comparing the average density during the time period of the window size and the density during the time period of the sample interval. As described in section two, the average number of frames and the variance of the numbers of frames per time unit can be used to represent the similarity inside of a cluster. We define:

$$WS = K \times SI \tag{3}$$

Where K is the number of sample intervals inside of the sliding window. The value of K decides the how many samples are in the sliding window body. In the following analysis, we use WT_i to represent the total traffic load in the window body at time t_i, ST_i to represent the traffic load in the ith sample interval. For window position at time t_n, we can express the traffic load WT_n as:

$$WT_n = WT_{n-1} + ST_n - ST_{n-1-K} \tag{4}$$

Thus, we can obtain the average number of frames per sample interval AT_n and the variance of the number of frames per sample interval δT_n in the sliding window body at time t_n as:

$$AT_n = {WT_n}/{K} = (WT_{n-1} + ST_n - ST_{n-1-K})/K \tag{5}$$

$$\delta T_n = \sqrt{\frac{\sum_{i=n-K}^{n}(ST_i - AT_n)^2}{K}} = \sqrt{\frac{\sum_{i=n-K}^{n}(ST_i - (WT_{n-1}+ST_n-ST_{n-1-K})/K)^2}{K}} \tag{6}$$

We set the sample interval as 0.5s and 20 samples ($K=20$) in the window body (WS = 10s). From equations (5) and (6), we cluster the management frames using the variance of the number of management frames in each sample interval as shown in figure 3. The management traffic includes: Beacon frame, probe request, probe response, association request, association response, authentication, deauthentication, disassociation.

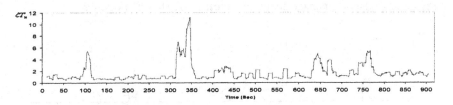

Fig. 3. Management traffic clustering using the sliding window algorithm

The challenge is therefore to detect abnormal events from this trace. Employing a simple threshold scheme can cause erroneous results (e.g. false alarms) because normal events such as the joining of a new client can also cause management traffic clusters, Additionally, some of the abnormal events cause similar clusters to normal events. Also, events can last for unpredictable time periods, for example, the time for a client to joint the network depends on the link quality. Therefore it is also difficult to base a threshold scheme on the duration of events. An alternative approach is to detect *all* the events occurring in the network and then classify them. In order to do this we need to obtain a discrete distribution of the management frames so that we can regard each separate group as one cluster. We assume that clusters are separated from each other by periods of zero variance.

The beacon frames are continuously sent by the access point. The number of beacon frames and the BSSID field can be used to tell the existence of rogue access points. We can filter out the beacon frames and store the useful information such as the BSSID, the number of beacons, the AP's MAC address in additional space for further cluster recognition purposes. The resultant management traffic can then be clustered as shown in figure 4.

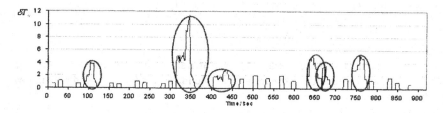

Fig.4. Management traffic clustering without beacon frames

We highlight the six clusters which are supposed to represent the four events. The other groups are normal WLAN events such as clients scanning for new connections. When STAs scan for new connections, they send out probe requests and receive probe responses. The probe frames carry the information about the SSID the STA wish to associate with and the information for synchronization. They don't cause any change to the STA's state machine, but they do provide information to those STAs who wish to search for a new connection. Again, we can filter out the probe frames and also store them as additional information for further cluster recognition purposes, the resultant management traffic clusters are shown in figure 5.

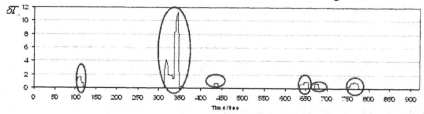

Fig.5. Management traffic clustering without beacon and probe frames

Figure 6 shows the state flow of the MTCA. When the algorithm starts, it transfers to the IDLE state where it remains until triggered by events. When new frames arrive, the algorithm transfers to the FILTER state. If the new frame is a beacon or a probe frame, the FILTER state will transfer to the ADD_storage state which stores certain information about the frame. Otherwise the FILTER state goes back to the IDLE state. If the time for sample interval expires, the algorithm then goes to the SIFrame Count to accumulate the number of the arriving management frames during the sample interval. If the time for the window size expires, it will transfer to the WS Count state to accumulate the total number of management frames occurring during the window size period. The variance is then calculated and the algorithm returns to the IDLE state.

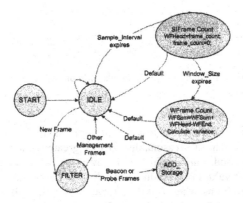

Fig.6. MTCA State Flow

4   Determination of Parameters

There are two parameters in the MTCA: the window size and the sample interval. The value of the WS decides the portion of the "past" traffic the algorithm takes into account, and the value of the SI decides the portion of the "current" traffic. From the point of view of IDS, a small sampling time will introduce many false alarms; a large sampling time will reduce the system's reaction time and thus some events may be missed. The size of the window should satisfy the following constraints:

(i)   The window should be long enough so that the algorithm can compare the "past" and the "current" traffic load;

(ii)   The window should not be too long so that the "past" part of the traffic will not have an overlarge influence on the "current" traffic.

If we consider the behaviour of abnormal events, the shortest attack can be completed within one second. For example, the deauthentication DoS attack we injected in the experiment sends out on average seven deauthentication frames per second. When the victim received the deauthentication frames, it dropped the connection immediately and started searching for new connections. Yet the attacker continued sending the deauthentication frames so that the victim kept dropping the connection and couldn't get a chance to reconnect with the AP. Thus, we set the sampling time SI less than one second. The choice of window size can be regarded as choosing the value of K, that is, the number of the samples under different sample intervals. We ran 20 tests for each sample interval with different numbers of samples (K) per interval. Figure 7 shows the number of false alarms generated for each case.

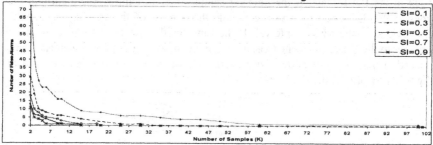

Fig.7. False alarms under different Sample Intervals and number of samples

All the five curves have the same feature: the more samples used, the fewer false alarms are received. This is reasonable since a greater number of samples will generate a longer period, during which more events can be completed. The results also show that larger values of SI reduce the false alarms more rapidly. For SI=0.1s, there are zero false alarms when $K \geq 100$; however, for SI=0.9s, the corresponding zero false alarm point is reached at $K \geq 11$. From the point view of decreasing the false alarms, the larger the sample interval, the fewer false alarms we will get. However a longer sample interval also increases the time to detect events.

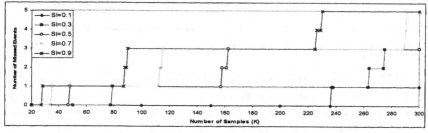

Fig.8. Missed Events under different Sample Intervals and number of samples

The other problem in the choice of parameters is the events which will be missed. Events lasting for a short time period can easily be missed by a large window size and sample interval. We have run more than 100 tests for all five SI values with different numbers of samples. Figure 8 shows the number of missed events under different sample intervals and number of samples. The x-axis starts from 20 which means when the number of samples is less than 20, there are no missed events from any of the sample intervals. When SI=0.1s, there is only one missed event when the number of samples ≥ 237; at the other extreme, when SI=0.9s there is one missed event when the number of samples ≥ 28, and five events are missed when there are 230 samples.

There is therefore a trade-off between the false alarm rate and the probability of missed events. From the point view of security, false alarms are more tolerable than missed events because one missed event could be fatal to the whole system. When choosing the sample interval, we should avoid the 'end' values (i.e. 0.1s and 0.9s); the rest of the choices are SI=0.3s, SI=0.5s and SI=0.7s. For a very busy network which has users frequently joining or leaving it, a smaller sample interval SI=0.3s is preferable since the time between two events is small, a small sampling point would be more accurate for the events; but more false alarms will occur. For a network which is not busy (lightly loaded), we can choose SI=0.7s as we can get less false alarms. The number of samples should be varied depending on the choice of SI. Table 1 shows the range of K for different sample intervals. For SI=0.3s, when K is between 33 and 78, the system will have no false alarms or missed events. For SI=0.5s, when K is between 20 and 47, the system will have no false alarms or missed events; similarly, for SI=0.7s, K should be between 15 and 34. We have also run several sets of tests on other trace files from attacks on both busy and lightly loaded networks. The results showed that the following ranges of K are practical. Generally, when the window size is around 10 seconds, we obtain the best results. From inspection of this we can chose SI=0.5s and the number of samples to be 20, this set of values causes zero false alarms or missed events over a wide range of network loadings.

Table 1. Range of K for different Sample intervals

K	Zero FalseAlarms	Zero MissedEvents
SI=0.3	>=33	<=78
SI=0.5	>=20	<=47

5   Conclusions & Future work

In this paper, we introduce our novel methodology for detecting anomalous events in 802.11 WLANs, the Management Traffic Clustering Algorithm (MTCA). This algorithm is based on a sliding window approach to identify the clusters of management traffic. We use the variance of the number of frames δT_n to represent the similarities inside a cluster. We implemented our theory on a trace file obtained from our experiment described in detail in [6], and obtained a distribution of δT_n. The algorithm filters out beacon frames and probe frames in order to obtain a discrete distribution of δT_n. From the experimental trace six clusters are identified which represent four network events: a link problem, a deauthentication DoS attack, a DoS recovery, and an MITM attack. Analysis of the choice of window size and sample interval for the MTCA is also presented. From consideration of the minimum attacking period, the sample interval should be less than one second. The false alarms and the missed events are two main design criteria. False alarms are more tolerable than the missed events in an intrusion detection system. Nevertheless there is a trade-off between each criterion. From anlaysis of a range of network traces we chose SI=0.3s for a very busy network to avoid missed events and SI=0.7s for a

WLAN which is not busy in order to reduce the of false alarms; pragmatically, we use SI=0.5s as the most reasonable value. For the choice of window size, we obtain the lowest false alarms and missed events when the window size is around 10 seconds.

Future work will focus on the recognition and classification of the complete range of events in 802.11 WLAN. This will involve determining the management frame cluster patterns produced by each type of WLAN attack. The cluster models will then be used to aid real-time analysis and prediction of both normal and anomalous events occurring in WLANS.

References

[1] A.Arbaugh, N.Shankar, J.Wang, and K.Zhang, "Your 802.11 Network has No Clothes", In First IEEE International Conference on Wireless LANs and Home Networks, December, 2001.

[2] N. Borisov, I.Goldberg, and D.Wagner. Intercepting Mobile Communications: "The Insecurity of 802.11", In the Seventh Annual International Conference on Mobile Computing and Networking, July 2001

[3] R.Moskowitz, "Weakness in Passphrase Choice in WPA Interface", http://wifinetnews.com/archives/002452.html, November, 2003

[4] IEEE 802.11i specification. http://standards.ieee.org/getieee802/download/802.11i-2004.pdf

[5] A.Mikhailovsky, K.Gavrilenko and A.Vladimirov, "Wireless Hacking: Breaking Through",   December   2004, http://www.awprofessional.com/articles/article.asp?p=353735&seqNum=8&rl= 1

[6] W.Zhou, A.Marshall and Q.Gu, "A Novel Classification Scheme 802.11 WLAN Active Attacking Traffic Patterns", Las Vegas, US, WCNC 2006.

[7]   IEEE   802.11-1999   specification. http://standards.ieee.org/getieee802/download/802.11-1999.pdf

[8] Debar H, Becker M, Siboni D. "A neural network component for an intrusion detection system." Proceedings of 1992 IEEE computer society symposium on research in security and privacy. Oakland, CA; May 1992.

[9] S.Chebrolu, A.Abraham, and J.P.Thomas, "Feature deduction and ensemble design of intrusion detection systems", Computers & Security, Volume 24, Issue 4, June 2005.

[10] C.Kruegel, D.Mutz, W.Robertson and F.Valeur, "Bayesian Event Classification for Intrusion Detection", in Proceedings of the 19th Annual Computer Security Applications Conference (ACSAC), Las Vegas, NV, December 2003.

Secure SCTP against DoS Attacks in Wireless Internet *

Inwhee Joe

College of Information and Communications
Hanyang University
Seoul, Korea
iwjoe@hanyang.ac.kr

Abstract. The Stream Control Transport Protocol (SCTP) is a new transport layer protocol that has been designed to provide reliable transport over the Internet. While the Transport Control Protocol (TCP) is the most popular transport protocol for the Internet, it falls short with regard to security, more specifically resilience to Denial-of-Service (DoS) attacks, such as SYN attacks. The need for resilience to DoS attacks is obvious, and SCTP provides for this resilience via its improved handshake mechanism and the Cookie feature. This paper discusses the SCTP simulation with particular emphasis on resilience to DoS attacks. As revealed by our detailed simulation study, the increased DoS resilience comes with increased overheads. While DoS resilience is extremely critical, reducing overheads in the resource-constrained wireless environment also assumes paramount importance. Hence we propose secure SCTP with an innovative Cookie mechanism using a combination of cache and INIT packet repetition to minimize the communication overhead and simultaneously to maximize security associated with SCTP's DoS resilience for wireless Internet.

1 INTRODUCTION

The Stream Control Transport Protocol (SCTP) [7] is a new transport-layer protocol that is being designed to provide reliable and secure transport of a variety of applications over IP networks. While the Transport Control Protocol (TCP) as its counterpart is the most popular and widely used transport protocol in the IP networks [3], SCTP not only provides the features offered by TCP but also has additional important characteristics. Examples include SCTP's novel features such as multi-homing and multi-streaming, built-in "protocol-hooks" to provide resistance to DoS (Denial of Service) attacks as well as the capability of supporting various ordering types (i.e., strict ordering, partial ordering and un-ordered delivery types).

In this paper, we use simulation techniques to investigate and analyze the SCTP's DoS feature in the wireless Internet. To this end, we have constructed

---

* This work was supported by grant No. IITA-2005-C1090-0501-0022 from the ITRC Support Program of the Ministry of Information and Communication.

Please use the following format when citing this chapter:

Joe, I., 2006, in IFIP International Federation for Information Processing, Volume 213, Network Control and Engineering for QoS, Security, and Mobility, V, ed. Gaïti, D., (Boston: Springer), pp. 65–74.

detailed simulation models of SCTP to generate DoS-attack scenarios in a wireless Internet model consisting of wireless workstations connected by a wireless LAN as a preliminary simulation study. Our detailed simulation analysis has helped reveal the overheads/bottlenecks associated with SCTP's DoS scenarios and to arrive at an innovative Cookie mechanism (via a combination of cache and INIT packet repetition) to minimize the overhead and to maximize security at the same time.

The remainder of this paper is organized as follows. Section 2 presents the SCTP simulation and resulting scenarios developed using OPNET as well as overhead and delay-analysis. Section 3 proposes secure SCTP with an improved Cookie mechanism (based on an innovative combination of cache and INIT packet repetition) to help reduce the DoS related overheads and thereby render SCTP an extremely viable solution in the resource-constrained wireless Internet environment. Section 4 concludes the paper.

2 SCTP SIMULATION

First, we will compare TCP and SCTP briefly in terms of connection estalishment. In TCP, the 3-way handshake sequence is used to set up TCP connections. To open a connection, the TCP client initiates a connection establishment procedure as an active opener by sending a SYN packet to the TCP server. The SYN packet carries connection initialization information like the initial value of the sequence number. Then, the TCP server waits for an acknowledgment (ACK) from the TCP server, indicating that the SYN packet has been received. After receiving the SYN packet, the TCP server sends its SYN packet along with the acknowledgment, indicating that it is also ready to accept the connection as a passive opener. Finally, the TCP client sends its ACK packet in response with the SYN/ACK packet from the TCP server. Once this exchange is complete, the connection is fully established and data can be transferred through this connection.

In case of TCP, whenever a connection establishment request arrives, the TCP server just allocates for each connection all the resources including memory for the transmission control block (TCB), before it verifies the TCP client. Assume that there is an intruder, trying to attack the TCP server by sending a bunch of SYN packets. Since TCP implementations limit the number of connections due to the resource problem, it could cause the server to use up memory and resources handling new connection requests. As a result, the TCP server reaches its limit so that it cannot accept any new incoming connections, leading to the state of the denial of service (DoS).

On the other hand, SCTP relies on the 4-way handshake sequence instead of the 3-way handshake of TCP, where a cookie mechanism is incorporated into the sequence to guard against some types of DoS attacks. To start an association (or connection in the TCP terminology), the SCTP client initiates the 4-way handshake by sending an INIT packet to the SCTP server. The INIT packet carries association initialization information including the initial sequence number and receiver window. Likewise, the SCTP client waits for an acknowledgment (ACK) from the SCTP server, indicating that the INIT packet has been received. After receiving the INIT packet, the SCTP server sends its INIT-ACK packet along with the Cookie as a variable parameter in it. The Cookie parameter contains the minimal TCB information required to create the association and a message authentication code (MAC). The MAC code is generated using a hash algorithm (e.g., MD5 or SHA-1 algorithms) with the input of the TCB information and a secret key.

When the SCTP client receives the INIT-ACK packet from the SCTP server, it puts the servers Cookie into a COOKIE-ECHO packet as it is and returns to the server. At the same time, if there is any data to send, it can be included in this packet for transmission efficiency. Upon reception of the COOKIE-ECHO packet, the SCTP server can validate the Cookie by checking the MAC code and uses it to rebuild the TCB. Since the SCTP client has been verified through the cookie mechanism at this point, the server allocates all the resources and memory right away. Then, the server sends a COOKIE-ACK packet to the SCTP client (optionally bundling any data with this packet for transmission efficiency). Once this last exchange is done, the association is fully established and data can be transferred through this association.

This section presents SCTP simulation using OPNET to demonstrate how SCTP performs in response to DoS attacks and also in normal situation compared to TCP, focusing on the connection establishment phase. As shown in Fig. 1, our network model is built on one wireless LAN (IEEE 802.11) as our preliminary study for a wireless Internet model, which contains 20 wireless workstations and one of them is an intruder. The Access Point (AP) in the wireless LAN is connected to the IP router and the File Server on the 100Base-T wireline LAN operating at 100 Mbps. The wireless workstations in the wireless LAN communicate with the File Server through the AP and the IP router.

To compare the security feature between TCP and SCTP in the scenario of DoS attacks, we develop two types of node models for the wireless workstation. The two node models differ in the transport protocol, namely one employs TCP and the other SCTP. The node model represents a wireless workstation with file transfer applications running as a client over TCP/IP or SCTP/IP according to the type of the node model. The wireless workstation supports one underlying wireless LAN connection at 1 Mbps. Likewise, we also develop two types of node models for the File Server, which represents a server node with file server applications running over TCP/IP or SCTP/IP.

The scenario is that the Intruder in the wireless LAN attacks the File Server by sending a large number of association or connection establishment requests (i.e., INIT packets for SCTP and SYN packets for TCP, respectively) with the forged IP source address, until the File Server has reached its limit on the number of connections (due to resource problems). In case of TCP, since the TCP server (File Server) allocates all the resources right away before it verifies the TCP client, it causes the server to very rapidly become unable to accept any new incoming connections, declaring itself as the DoS state. Even if this situation

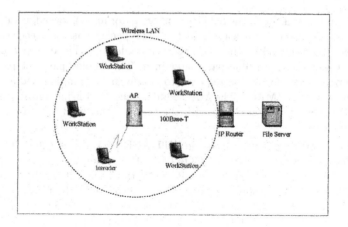

Fig. 1. Simulation Network Model

is cleared out after a period of time, the Intruder can send SYN packets fast enough so that it ensures to make the situation recur. The time period can be obtained using the current values of the TCP simulation parameters in OPNET, as shown in Fig. 2.

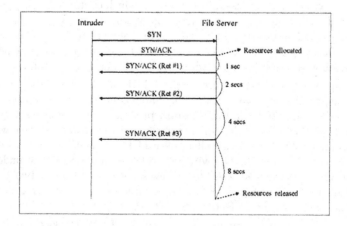

Fig. 2. Time Sequence Diagram for SYN Retransmission in TCP

When a SYN packet arrives from the Intruder, the File Server allocates all the resources right away and then sends to the Intruder its SYN packet with the acknowledgment, indicating that the SYN packet has been received successfully.

At the same time, the File Server starts a retransmission (RTO) timer whose value is set initially to 1 second in the TCP parameters with OPNET simulation. Since the Intruder uses a forged source IP address, the SYN/ACK packet from the File Server gets nowhere and therefore, there is no ACK for this packet. As a result, the retransmission timer on the File Server expires, and then it triggers a retransmission of the SYN/ACK packet to the Intruder using the same forged source IP address. At this time, the value of the retransmission timer is doubled to 2 seconds based on the TCP protocol.

Since the maximum number of retransmission attempts on connection establishment is restricted to 3 in the TCP parameters, the File Server gives up after 3 times of retransmission. At this point, it releases all the resources allocated before and reports an error to the upper layer. The value of the retransmission timer is doubled every time it expires, because there is no ACK packet received from the other side (Intruder). In summary, with the current values of the TCP simulation parameters in OPNET, it takes 15 seconds to clear out the whole situation once it starts from the time when the resources are allocated first. Also, there is a limit on the number of connections, which is 200 as a configurable system parameter. Therefore, if the Intruder sends more than 200 SYN packets within 15 seconds, then it causes the File Server to reach the limit, rendering it unable to accept any new incoming connections as the DoS state.

In the OPNET simulation, the Intruder is designed to generate SYN packets at the rate of 15 packets/s, which is faster than the rate of 200/15 packets/s above. The simulation results show that the File Server has entered the DoS state after it receives 200 SYN packets from the Intruder. On the other hand, since SCTP unlike its counterpart TCP allocates the resources only after the SCTP client is confirmed with the Cookie mechanism, the Intruder is prevented from "hogging" up system resources. Our simulation studies create the above scenario for the SCTP case and we validate via the OPNET-based simulation models developed in this work that SCTP indeed avoids this situation. Furthermore, unlike the TCP case, the SCTP system continues to accept new and valid incoming association requests. Finally, after a certain maximum number of retransmission attempts, the File Server gives up and reports an error to the upper layer. No resource-release phase is entered now since there were no resources allocated to begin with (to the intruding end station).

In fact, more increased security comes at the cost of more increased overhead in the transport layer, as shown in Table 1. In terms of the number of packets, TCP and SCTP have the same overhead based on the protocol behavior. However, if the packet size is considered in the overhead comparison, SCTP causes more overhead than TCP. To make the equal conditions, it is assumed that only mandatory parameters are used for both cases. Since there is no data carried in this connection setup phase, the TCP packet contains only the packet header of 20 bytes. In SCTP, the packet size is different according to the packet type. The INIT packet is 32 bytes and the INIT-ACK packet is 32 bytes plus a variable Cookie parameter, which is up to 156 bytes depending on the implementation. Since the bandwidth is a scarce resource in the wireless environment, the Cookie parameter should be minimized. In the next section, we present a novel efficient and secure Cookie mechanism for wireless Internet.

Table 1. Overhead Table for TCP vs. SCTP in DoS'Attack

	TCP SYN	SCTP INIT	TCP SYN/ACK	SCTP INIT-ACK
Number of Packets	1	1	4	4
Packet Size	20 bytes	32 bytes	20 bytes	32 bytes + Cookie

Even in normal situation, SCTP causes more overhead at the connection setup phase because of the 4-way handshake and Cookie mechanisms. To establish a connection, SCTP consumes 4 packets instead of 3 packets of TCP in terms of the number of packets. For the packet size, the total overhead is 60 bytes in case of TCP, because each TCP packet is 20 bytes and the 3-way handshake sequence is used. On the other hand, the total overhead in SCTP comes to 96 bytes plus twice the Cookie parameter, because the 4-way handshake sequence is used instead with the INIT packet of 32 bytes, the INIT-ACK packet of 32 bytes plus Cookie, the COOKIE-ECHO packet of 16 bytes plus Cookie, and the COOKIE-ACK packet of 16 bytes. Therefore, SCTP has 36 bytes plus twice the Cookie more overhead than TCP in terms of the packet size.

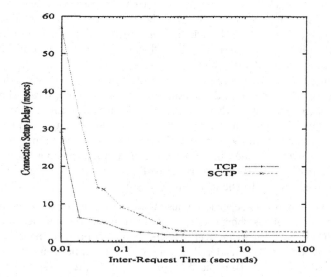

Fig. 3. Connection Setup Delay for SCTP vs. TCP in Normal Situation

We also measure connection setup delays for SCTP versus TCP as a function of offered load in normal situation over the simulated wireless network. The connection setup delay denotes the entire duration measured from the time a connection setup request packet is sent to the time the transport connection is established successfully. The offered load is defined as data traffic offered to the transport layer by the file transfer application on the client side by changing the mean value of the IRT (Inter-Request Time) according to the exponential distribution. In SCTP, it is assumed that the Cookie parameter is fixed as 32 bytes. In Fig. 3, the simulation results exhibit the exponentially increasing delay behavior on connection setup with the higher load for both SCTP and TCP, where the shorter IRT interval means the higher load. Since SCTP uses the 4-way handshake sequence, it causes more queuing delay at the higher load, compared to the 3-way handshake TCP. Under light load conditions, SCTP takes about 1 msec more delay than TCP and the simulation results approach the theoretical minimum delay values, which can be obtained by computing transmission times only (packet size/bit rate). Those minimum values are 1.5 msecs for TCP and 2.56 msecs for SCTP, respectively.

3 SECURE SCTP FOR WIRELESS INTERNET

Here, we propose secure SCTP with an efficient and secure Cookie mechanism using an innovative combination of cache and INIT packet repetition to minimize the communication overhead and simultaneously to maximize security for wireless Internet. In essence, since the transmission control block (TCB) information consumes a large bandwidth and contains sensitive connection information, the Cookie parameter is modified to exclude any TCB information inside for transmission efficiency and security purposes. Instead, the INIT packet is repeated to recreate the TCB information later just in case of the DOS attacks, and also the TCB cache is used to significantly reduce the connection set-up delays in normal situation. First, we will describe briefly how TCP and SCTP establish connections, before we get into the details of our proposed Cookie mechanism.

In TCP, the 3-way handshake sequence is used to set up TCP connections. To open a connection, the TCP client initiates a connection establishment procedure as an active opener by sending a SYN packet to the TCP server. The SYN packet carries connection initialization information like the initial value of the sequence number. Then, the TCP client waits for an acknowledgment (ACK) from the TCP server, indicating that the SYN packet has been received. After receiving the SYN packet, the TCP server sends its SYN packet along with the acknowledgment, indicating that it is also ready to accept the connection as a passive opener. Finally, the TCP client sends its ACK packet in response with the SYN/ACK packet from the TCP server. Once this exchange is complete, the connection is fully established and data can be transferred through this connection.

In case of TCP, whenever a connection establishment request arrives in the form of SYN packet, the TCP server just allocates for each connection all the resources including memory for the TCB without verifying the TCP client. Assume that there is an intruder, trying to attack the TCP server by sending a bunch of SYN packets (so called SYN attack). Since TCP implementations limit the number of connections due to the resource problem, eventually it could cause the server to use up all the resources. As a result, the TCP server cannot accept any new incoming connections, leading to the state of the denial of service (DoS).

On the other hand, SCTP relies on the 4-way handshake sequence instead of the 3-way handshake of TCP, where a "Cookie" mechanism is incorporated into the sequence to guard against some types of DoS attacks. To start an association (or connection in the TCP terminology), the SCTP client initiates the 4-way handshake by sending an INIT packet to the SCTP server. The INIT packet carries association initialization information including the initial sequence number and receiver window. Likewise, the SCTP client waits for an acknowledgment (ACK) from the SCTP server, indicating that the INIT packet has been received. After receiving the INIT packet, the SCTP server responds with its INIT-ACK packet along with the Cookie as a variable parameter in it. The Cookie parameter contains the minimal TCB information required to create the association and a message authentication code (MAC). The MAC code is generated using a hash algorithm (e.g., MD5 or SHA-1 algorithms) with the input of the minimal TCB information and a secret key [4].

When the SCTP client receives the INIT-ACK packet from the SCTP server, it puts the received Cookie into a COOKIE-ECHO packet as it is and sends the packet to the server. At the same time, if there is any data to send, it can be included in this packet for transmission efficiency. Upon reception of the COOKIE-ECHO packet, the SCTP server first validates the Cookie by the MAC code and its lifespan, and then uses it to rebuild the TCB information only if the Cookie is valid. Since the SCTP client has been verified through the Cookie mechanism at this point, the server can allocate all the resources and memory right away. Then, the server sends a COOKIE-ACK packet to the SCTP client (optionally bundling any data with this packet for transmission efficiency). Once this last exchange is done, the association is fully established and data can be transferred through this association.

The Cookie mechanism is employed to guard specifically against the DoS attacks flooding with INIT packets. Rather than allocating resources for the INIT packet, the server instead creates a Cookie parameter with the TCB subset in it and sends it back in the INIT-ACK packet. Since this packet goes back to the source address of the INIT packet, the Intruder with a forged IP address will not get the Cookie. Only a valid SCTP client will get the Cookie and return it in the COOKIE-ECHO packet. In this case, the SCTP server checks its integrity by the MAC code and its validity by the lifespan. If it is good, the server uses it to rebuild the TCB for this connection by allocating all the resources at this time, avoiding the DoS attacks as a result.

The Cookie parameter is defined in a Type-Length-Value format, because it is variable. The first two fields of Type and Length take 4 bytes, and the Value field of Cookie consists of 4 parts: TCB subset, MAC, Timestamp, and Life span. The TCB subset represents the minimal subset of TCB information necessary to recreate the TCB. Its size is variable up to 140 bytes, which is the entire TCB data. The remaining three parts of the Cookie parameter are fixed: 4 bytes of MAC, 4 bytes of Timestamp, and 4 bytes of Lifespan as typical size values. The Cookie creation timestamp and the lifespan are used together to check whether the received Cookie is stale or not, while the MAC code is used to check the Cookie integrity.

According to the 4-way handshake sequence of SCTP, the Cookie parameter is echoed between client and server in the INIT-ACK and COOKIE-ECHO packets. Since the Cookie parameter includes the large TCB data up to 140 bytes, such round trip causes a large overhead especially for wireless networks, where the bandwidth is a scarce resource. The proposed Cookie mechanism is to exclude the TCB data from the Cookie parameter to substantially reduce the communication overhead. At the same time, since the TCB information carries sensitive connection information like source identity and initial sequence number, the best way for security is to get rid of it completely so that this information may not be exposed at all to outside. Another point of our mechanism is to use a TCB cache in order to speed up the connection setup operation. That is, if there is a cache hit, there is no need to recreate the TCB in this case. Most of time, cache hits are expected in normal situation except for the DoS attacks or near-capacity situation. The TCB cache is implemented in S/W just like the buffer cache concept and the total number of TCB cache is the same as the limit on the number of connections.

To begin with, the TCB cache is initialized as an empty list. If the INIT packet is received, the SCTP server allocates a cache entry to create a new TCB based on the connection information from this packet. The source IP address and port can be used as an index key to the TCB cache in the cache pool. In response, the INIT-ACK packet is sent along with the Cookie parameter in it without the variable TCB part, as mentioned above. After that, the client sends the COOKIE-ECHO packet with the Cookie parameter as it is and the repeated INIT packet as well. Actually, the entire INIT packet does not have to be repeated and instead the client sends only a part of the INIT packet (e.g., receiver window, initial sequence number) required to recreate the TCB data on the server side just in case there is a cache miss. Later, when the COOKIE-ECHO packet arrives, first the SCTP server uses the index key to look up the corresponding TCB in the cache pool. If there is a cache hit, this TCB can be used directly as long as the Cookie is valid. Otherwise, a new TCB is created again using the repeated INIT information from the received COOKIE-ECHO packet.

To compare the overhead between the existing and the proposed Cookie mechanisms, the worst case scenario is assumed where the entire TCB data of 140 bytes is carried in the Cookie parameter for the existing case. The rest of the Cookie is the same for both cases and it takes up 16 bytes, because there are 4 bytes of the Type/Length fields plus 12 bytes of the Value field without the TCB part. In the existing mechanism, since the INIT-ACK and COOKIE-ECHO packets are exchanged along with the Cookie between client and server, the total overhead comes to 360 bytes for the Cookie mechanism. On the other hand, our new mechanism does not send any TCB data in the Cookie parameter and only a part of the INIT packet is repeated in the COOKIE-ECHO packet. Because the repeated portion of the INIT packet is 16 bytes without the first Type/Length fields, the total overhead in this case comes to 96 bytes for the Cookie mechanism, which means about 73% reduction of overhead compared to the existing scheme, resulting in a significant improvement. Moreover, since cache hits are expected most of time, the setup delay can also be reduced substantially.

4   CONCLUSIONS

In this paper, we have presented simulation studies of SCTP in wireless Internet, with particular emphasis on the DoS resistance feature. Observe that SCTP achieves DoS resilience via its improved handshake mechanism and Cookie feature. We also have discussed the overhead issue in return of more security and proposed one possible approach to minimize it. We have performed detailed simulations to not only demonstrate the network's resilience to intruder attacks while using SCTP, but to also provide a detailed analysis of the associated overheads and delays with regard to SCTP's DoS resilience feature, and comparisons with TCP. Additionally our detailed simulation study has furnished invaluable insights into the feature and helped in the derivation of a novel Cookie mechanism that judiciously combines cache and INIT packet repetition to minimize the overhead and to maximize security at the same time associated with SCTP's DoS resilience over wireless Internet.

References

1. S. Aidarous and T. Plevyak, "Telecommunications Network Management - Technologies and Implementations," IEEE Series on Network Management, 1997.
2. L. Coene, "Stream Control Transmission Protocol Applicability Statement," IETF Internet Draft, November 2001.
3. D. Comer, "Internetworking with TCP/IP," Prentice Hall Publications, 1995.
4. H. Krawczyk, et al., "HMAC: Keyed-Hashing for Message Authentication," IETF RFC 2104, March 1997.
5. A. Law and W. Kelton, "Simulation Modeling and Analysis," McGraw Hill Publications, Second Edition, 1991.
6. M. Mathis, et al., "TCP Selective Acknowledgment (SACK) Options," IETF RFC 2018, October 1996.
7. R. Stewart, et al., "Stream Control Transmission Protocol," IETF RFC 2960, October 2000.
8. I. Joe, "Secure Routing with Time-Space Cryptography for Mobile Ad-Hoc Networks," Proceedings of IEEE MILCOM, October 2005.

Design of an Adaptive-Rate Video-Streaming Service with Different Classes of Users[1]

I.V. Martín, Mónica Aguilar-Igartua, and Jorge Mata-Díaz

Telematics Engineering Department, Technical University of Catalonia
(UPC), Jordi Girona 1-3, 08034, Campus Nord, Barcelona, Spain.
{isabelm, maguilar, jmata}@ entel.upc.es

Abstract. The provision of end-to-end Quality of Service (QoS) for multimedia services over IP-based networks is already an open issue. To achieve this goal, service providers need to manage Service Level Agreements (SLAs), which specify parameters of the services operation such as availability and performance. Additional mechanisms are needed to quantitatively evaluate the user-level SLA parameters. This work is focused on the evaluation and assessment of different design options of an adaptive VoD service providing several classes of users and fulfilling the SLA commitments. Based on a straightforward Markov Chain, Markov-Reward Chain (MRC) models are developed in order to obtain various QoS measures of the adaptive VoD service. The MRC model has a clear understanding with the design and operation of the VoD system.

1 Introduction

During the last years, Video-on-Demand (VoD) applications for the transmission and distribution of video have experienced a growing development and acceptance from the users. Video-streaming systems have a special relevance in wired and wireless networks. In these systems, the video is distributed for its reproduction in real-time [1]. The video server of a video-streaming system stores a set of movies that can be requested by any client. If the connection request is accepted, a session is initiated; then a multimedia stream flows through a set of heterogeneous networks from the video server to the client terminal.

In end-to-end Quality of Service (QoS) scenarios, QoS measures such as packet loss, packet delay and jitter must be guaranteed when the connection is accepted. These real-time guarantees required by the VoD systems could be achieved using QoS differentiation between traffic classes over heterogeneous networks. On the

[1] This work has been financed by the Spanish investigation projects SECONNET (CICYT-TSI2005-07293-C02-01) and ARPA (CICYT-TIC2003-08184-C02-02)

Please use the following format when citing this chapter:

Martín, I.V., Aguilar-Igartua, M., Mata-Díaz, J., 2006, in IFIP International Federation for Information Processing, Volume 213, Network Control and Engineering for QoS, Security, and Mobility, V, ed. Gaïti, D., (Boston: Springer), pp. 75–88.

other hand, with the aim of reducing the huge amount of information generated by the video source, loss compression techniques are applied. The most common coding techniques are H.26x and MPEG standards [2]. The price to pay for a high compression level is a degradation level in the image quality.

The adaptive VoD services employ a set of policies for dynamic resource allocation. It is accomplished by means of signalling protocols used between the service and the network. Thus, related to the bit rate variability of the flow, the service raises renegotiations to the network in order to modify the allocated resources during the session. These renegotiations are performed at the temporal-scale of the scenes in a video sequence. In this way, the amount of network resources reserved during the session are reduced substantially and a more efficient exploitation of these resources is achieved [1, 3, 4]. However, in congestion situations the service adapts the transmission bit rate to the available network resources applying a higher compression level or managing the enhanced layers when scalability techniques are employed [1]. Thus, the final QoS provided to the customers of these streaming services depends on the available network resources.

Both the service providers and the customers are indeed interested in tools which quantify the performance of these systems from their points of view. To facilitate the required evaluations, these tools should provide feasibility to incorporate modifications into the system in an easy way. Further, these tools also must admit a computational evaluation. Analytical tools are the most appropriate mechanisms to facilitate the required evaluation. This kind of analytical tools help to address some of the typically required main objectives: to maximize the use of network resources, to fulfil the QoS offered to the users and to define billing metrics. Likewise, these tools could compute diverse parameters in order to specify, to manage and to control the fulfilment of the Service Level Agreements (SLAs). The management of SLAs is a current challenge into the multimedia services area. There are diverse recent proposals about SLA management (e.g. [5, 6]), although none of them specifies how to quantitatively evaluate the user-level SLA parameters.

In particular, we are interested in computing *a priori* the QoS offered to the user of adaptive video-streaming services, where video sources are capable to adapt their output bit rate to time-varying network conditions. Some proposals of design and evaluation of adaptive VoD systems are presented in [3, 7, 8, 9, 10]. Most of them use either simulation models or real platforms to carry out the performance evaluation of these systems. These evaluation techniques hinder the system analysis and also they make difficult the study of several design options. In addition, some analytical proposals do not regard the interaction between the different video sources sharing the network resources. In [11] we proposed a generic methodology to develop Performability models [12] for VoD systems. This methodology solves the lacks above mentioned. The applicability of this method is based on the characterization of the coded multimedia flows and the channel behaviour. This characterization requires suitable markovian models of both, the flows and the channel. Besides, an analytical model for a VoD service was developed in [11] applying this generic method. Further, in [13], we obtained two new analytical models which reduced the states space to characterize the resources reserved by a group of users. Therefore, the computational cost of the evaluations was substantially reduced. These models provide accurate results for the measures of user-level QoS parameters such as the image quality, reserved resources, or effectively-used resources.

In the present work we construct analytical models to analyze the performance of a VoD service for different configuration parameters. Firstly, we define different QoS user-profiles to evaluate the measures of user-level QoS parameters when only one of these classes of user is accepted. After that, we analyze the interaction between users' classes, i.e. when there are users belonging to more than one QoS profile in the system. Finally, we analyze the trade-off between service providers' profits and a variable pricing policy which depends on the video quality perceived by the customers.

The rest of the work is organized as follows. Section 2 describes the VoD system under evaluation. A background of the previous works presented in [11] and [13] are summarized in section 3. In section 4 we assess some design options of VoD services providing several classes of users and fulfilling the SLA commitments. Finally, conclusions and future work are presented in section 5.

2   The System Description

Figure 1 depicts the VoD system analysed in this work. Video sequences of movies have previously been coded using the VBR MPEG-II algorithm and then stored in the video server. When any customer of the VoD service demands one of these sequences, a connection is established if the video service has enough resources to provide the contracted user's profile, i.e. the agreements specified in the service contract. In many IP QoS-aware networks, the RSVP (Resource reSerVation Protocol) is employed as signalling protocol to manage resource reservation requests [14]. Video-streaming services send RSVP requests to the network in order to renegotiate the required resources of the video-stream transmitted. The description of these resources is specified by means of the *Traffic Specification* (TSpec) parameters carried in the PATH messages of the RSVP. The RSVP requests are associated with the scene changes of the video sequence. The TSpec of each RSVP request is set according to the complexity of scene. Thus, different network resources are requested over the whole transmission of a sequence. Moreover, this renegotiation process yields to changes of the available network resources due to the interaction between the multiplexed connections. With the aim that the video sources are capable to adapt their output bit rate to the time-varying network resources, each available sequence has a set of MPEG flows coded with different quantization step (Q). Then, each available flow offers a different image quality according to Q [2]. For each accepted session, the transmitted stream will match with one of the different available coded flows of the requested sequence. This selection changes depending on the image quality contracted by the user and on the result of the reservation request produced by the end-to-end admission control of the RSVP-based system.

To carry out the system functions, three blocks have been designed as it is sketched in Fig. 1. These blocks are performed as follows. For each available flow, the *Statistical Planner* block has previously calculated and stored the TSpec parameters of each scene and the events of resources renegotiation in each sequence. When scene changes or variations of the available resources happen, the *Regulator/Negotiator* block decides which flow (Q_i) will be transmitted. To guarantee a minimum video quality, the minimum reservation needed to transmit the lower image quality flow must always be assured. The *Traffic Shaper* block extracts the variability introduced by the frame coding modes (Intra, Predicted and Bidirectional-Predicted) of the MPEG algorithm. In this way, the bit rate is smoothed and it is maintained constant (r_{GoP}) for a GoP (Group of Pictures) interval.

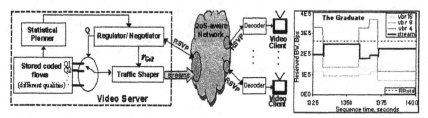

Fig. 1. System model for the VoD service.   **Fig. 2.** Required bit rate.

3   Background

3.1   Scene-based Markovian models for a video sequence

In order to efficiently characterize the network resources required by a constant-quality flow of a video sequence, we need to identify the groups of frames with same complexity or activity in the sequence. The identification process of these consecutive groups of frames has been called in the literature as *Segmentation* [15].

The segmentation of a video sequence results on series of groups of pictures with similar requirements of network resources [16]. These segments, also named scenes, define different complexity levels within the sequence. Through the classification of the scenes into activity levels, scene-based models have been proposed in previous works [17]. Some of the more relevant works have developed analytical models based on Markov chains. These models set the number of scene classes heuristically. Straightforward scene-based Markovian models represent scene changes by means of transitions between states, where states identify classes of scenes. For the sake of the simplicity, we will refer to each class of scenes as an activity level. An example of the Markovian scene-based model is shown in Fig. 3, where L activity levels are defined. The segmentation process of different constant-quality flows of the same movie gives rise to the same scene bounds. Consequently, for a set of video-flow models related to the same movie, the changes of scene occur at the same time. As an example Fig. 2 shows the bit rate required to transmit the sequence "The Graduate" coded with a quantification step Q equal to 4, 8 and 16. Fig. 2 remarks how these flows are time-tracked. Hereafter, we will indistinctly refer to a change of the activity level of the sequence as well as a change of the activity level in anyone of its coded flows.

3.2   Generic Method to Develop Analytical Models of VoD Systems

A generic method to construct Markov Reward Chain (MRC) models for VoD systems was proposed in [11]. Then, to carry out computations of QoS measures, the method of Randomization [18] was applied to the MRC. The generic modelling methodology presented there consists on 5 steps to obtain a MRC that statistically characterizes the network resources required by a connection and the resources amount available for this connection. Also, applying this methodology, an analytical model of a particular VoD system was derived in [11]. We proposed some modifications to this model obtaining new models which reduced the space of states and therefore provided a faster computation of expected results [13]. The reader can find the full explanation of this analytical model and the generic method in [11] and [13]. We summarize these models, using this method, as follows

In **Step 1**, a markovian model for each available fixed-quality video flow in the VoD system is derived in a similar way as it was developed in [3]. This model is composed by three states that define three activity levels (see section 3.1).

The Continuous-Time Markov Chain (CTMC) shown in Fig. 4 was derived in [11] applying **Step 2**. For the sake of the clarity, only 3 different constant image-quality flows have been depicted in the draw. Each column corresponds with the model of each available flow, which was obtained in step 1. This CTMC models the behaviour of a connection in the system, where e_f^a is a connection state where flow of quality f (1: worst quality... F: best quality) in the activity level a (0: regular, 1: medium, 2: high) is transmitted through the connection. The transitions between states reflect the scene changes and renegotiation decisions that have been designed in the VoD system. In addition, in this example while the stream remains in the same activity level, the system periodically tries to improve by sending requests for the next better image-quality. We call this process *polling of improvement*. The transition rates in this CTMC depend on the required resources and on the available resources. In order to formally express these dependencies, two boolean factors are defined:

$$\alpha(e_f^a) = \begin{cases} 1 & \text{, if } RSV(f,a) \leq RS_{available} \\ 0 & \text{, otherwise.} \end{cases} \text{ and} \tag{1}$$

$$\beta(e_f^a, e_g^b) = \begin{cases} 1 & \text{, if } RSV(f,a) \geq RSV(g,b) \\ 0 & \text{, otherwise.} \end{cases}, \tag{2}$$

where $RS_{available}$ is the amount of available resources for the connection and $RSV(f, a)$ is the amount of network resources that the system reserves for the connection when the server transmits a flow of quality f in activity level a

Let $\psi(e_f^a, e_g^b)$ be the transition rate from state e_f^a to state e_g^b for a connection. These rates in the CTMC, related to increments or decrements of the activity level in the video sequence, are formulated by means of equations which depend on the rates $\lambda_{a,b}$ and on the factors β (see [11]). Finally, transitions owing to the *polling of improvement* are formulated as a function that depends on the poll rate λ_p and on the factor α. Note that the factors α and β provide the general characterization of the adaptive VoD service by means of the proposed CTMC. Different behaviours for the renegotiation mechanism can simply be designed using these factors. When several connections are being served, $RS_{available}$ vary throughout time. In this case, it is mandatory to know the state of all the connections that interact with the one under analysis. This state leads to know the amount of resources available for the connexion under analysis, $RS_{available}$.

In **Step 3**, to achieve the goal of knowing the state which represents the rest of all the connexions except the one under analysis, we developed a model for those N accepted sessions. Firstly, the state of all the connections with a same QoS profile is defined. In this homogeneous case, each connection is characterized with the same parameter values of the generic connection model that has been described in step 2. Let $S^* = \{ (n_1^0, n_1^1, n_1^2), (n_2^0, n_2^1, n_2^2), \dots, (n_F^0, n_F^1, n_F^2) \}$ be the system state, where n_f^a is the number of connections transmitting a flow of quality f in activity level a. Let $S_{+(g,b)}^{-(f,a)}$ be a system state with one more connection transmitting a flow of quality g in activity level b and one less connection transmitting a flow of quality f in activity level a, regarding state S^*. If all transmissions are uncorrelated, only transitions from state S^* to state $S_{+(g,b)}^{-(f,a)}$ can occur. Then, the transition rates $\Psi\left(S^*, S_{+(g,b)}^{-(f,a)}\right)$ are expressed as a function of rate ψ multiplied by n_f^a. Where, generalizing (1) for N connections and with a conservative admission control, the factor $\alpha(S^*)$ is expressed as:

$$\alpha(S^*) = \begin{cases} 1 & \text{, si } \sum_{\forall f} \sum_{\forall a} n_f^a \cdot RSV(f,a) \leq RS_{total} \\ 0 & \text{, otherwise.} \end{cases} \tag{3}$$

To develop the heterogeneous customers' situation, the simpler way is to redefine the system state as the joining state of all the user-classes, that is: $S = \{S^1, S^2, \dots, S^C\}$.

Step 4 is applied to evaluate the performance of a session in the system with other N accepted sessions. Let $\left\{e_f^a, S\right\}$ be a system state, where e_f^a describes the state of the connection under evaluation and S characterizes $RS_{available}$. The state S may be described e.g. as the one obtained in step 3, where RS_{total} is the total amount of resources available for the VoD service which could be either a constant value or a variable amount characterized by any Markovian model of channel capacity.

The analytical models that were obtained applying this methodology provide accurate results for measures of the VoD system performance. Nevertheless, as the number of users N grows or the number of classes of users C grows, the computational cost of these models increases combinatorially [19]. To address this issue, in [13] we proposed a way to reduce the number of states that characterize the amount of resources reserved by the other N sessions accepted in the system, $RS_{available}$. We observed that, for any video sequence, the probability to achieve the highest activity level was very low for the model with three activity levels (see Fig. 3). Based on this observation, we proposed to maintain the same regular activity level (level 0) and to establish just one state to define jointly the medium (level 1) and high (level 2) activity levels to model the resources reserved by each available flow of the sessions that were not under analysis. We called to this new level as level 1*. The transition rates between level 0 and level 1* are the same ones that between level 0 and level 1 in the analytical model with three levels. The resources required to be in level 1* are calculated as the average of $RSV(f, 1)$ and $RSV(f, 2)$ (see equation (4) in [13]).

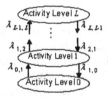   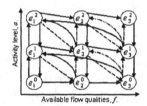

Fig. 3. Scene-based Markovian model.   **Fig. 4.** Generic model of an accepted connection.

4   Evaluation of Different Design Options in the Video Service

Section 2 describes the general operation of the VoD system under analysis. However, there still are open options to configure the final video service offered to the customers. Many QoS measures of these adaptive VoD services can be evaluated using our analytical model as it has been summarized in section 3. We also can easily compare the system performance under these different design options. Some of these design options are: the set of coded flows with different video qualities for each film; the resources assignment policy and the admission control policy for each user-class.

Service providers must design these sets of coded flows according to the QoS that they want to offer to each class of user. The question is to decide how many flows of different qualities are going to be arranged and which are going to be the most proper video qualities of these flows to satisfy the QoS requirements of each class of user. Service providers can design different user classes, i.e. different user profiles with different QoS characteristics. All the connections from the different user classes are interacting and sharing the system resources. Therefore, the quality perceived by each user-class depends on the proper design of the VoD operation. Service providers must carry out the design fulfilling the SLA parameters of each user class. Even though we seek to accomplish the committed levels of QoS when designing the system, the service provider also asks for maximizing his/her profits. Hence, not only must we set a charging policy to attract customers, but also we must consider all the factors that produce a cost for the service provider to supply that service to the customers. On the one hand, an adaptive charging policy that varies according to the received video quality throughout time may be very interesting for the customers. On the other hand, the designing options to configure the service have a straight influence on the costs that the service providers must assume to provide the VoD service.

In this section we assess some design options and configurations in our VoD system when there are different classes of user, i.e. the heterogeneous situation. In addition, we evaluate a simple cost function for the service provider that depends on the reserved resources. Also we evaluate a variable pricing policy to charge customers in a dynamic way that depends on the video quality perceived by the users.

4.1 Designing the Set of Video Flows Available to Each User-Class Maximizing the Service Provider's Profits

The basic configuration parameters of the VoD system used here are the same ones used in [13]. Likewise, the designed user profile makes that each accepted connection can access to all the available resources, without distinction among the users or the classes of user. However, in the present work another admission control has been designed and evaluated. Now, a new connection request is accepted if the amount of resources is sufficient to transmit the minimum quality (RSV_{min}) for all the connections. The quality will be lowered for the already accepted connections, if it is necessary. This VoD system only guaranties the resources for the flow with minimum quality. As a consequence, this admission control is more permissive, it maximizes the number of accepted users even though they may notice a high level of QoS degradation.

Several measures of the QoS offered to a customer of the VoD service have been computed, such as the PSNR, the failure time, the transmitted bit-rate and the reserved BW. The expected mean value of these measures for an observed user and the standard deviation among all the users, have been evaluated. For space reasons only some of them are shown here. The computation of these measures from the analytical models has been done using the MRC solution proposed in [19].

First of all, we examine the performance of the VoD system with only a class of user. The transmitted sequence is "The Graduate", and the stored flows have been coded with quantization step Q equal to 4, 8 and 16. We will refer to these flows as *vrb4* (highest video quality), *vbr8* and *vbr16* (lowest video quality), respectively. Table 1 summarizes the values of the *RSV* parameters (reserved resources) used for the analytical model of the different classes of user. We call *class0* to the *exigent* user-class which has available the two flows with higher quality (*vrb4*, *vbr8*), *class1* to the *tolerant* user-class which has available the three flows (*vrb4* and *vbr8* and *vbr16*), and *class2* to the *conformist* user-class which has available the two flows with lower quality (*vbr8* and *vbr16*). Remember a minimum bandwidth must be reserved to assure the transmission of the lower image quality flow of the requested movie. We call RSV_{min} to this minimum reserve. RSV_{min} is determined by *vbr8* for *class0* and by *vbr16* for *class1* and *class2*. As *vbr8* has a higher quality than *vbr16*, RSV_{min} is higher for *class0* than for *class1* or *class2*. We also may design another *class3* that arranges the highest quality and the lowest quality flows (*vrb4* and *vbr16*). In fact, this option is inefficient. We could verify that the *mean* PSNR was lower in *class3* than in *class1* for the same reserved BW in both classes, as Fig. 9 in [13] shows.

Table 1. Estimated required resources, *RSV* [bits/GoP].

				Class1	
	Class0		Class2		
	Vbr8	Vbr4	Vbr16	Vbr8	Vbr4
level 2	702793.41	1033529.9	364476.06	501597.41	1033529.9
level 1	702793.41	724278.90	364476.06	392237.95	717029.09
level 0	702793.41	702793.41	364476.06	364476.06	504715.88

Figure 5 depicts the *Mean PSNR* provided to a user and the *Mean Bit Rate Reserved* to each accepted sessions, when there is only one of the three user classes (*class0*, *class1*, *class2*) in the system. These figures are represented as a function of the total BW assigned to the VoD service and with the number of accepted streaming sessions (N) as a parameter. For each N, the curves start at the minimum BW required to accept the Nth session in the VoD system. For example, the curves pointed out as **N1_class1** correspond to N=1 user of *class1*, where the value of RSV_{min} is 1.5 Mbps (=364476.06 bits/GoP, see Table 1). Discontinuities in the analytic curves are produced as a result of the discretization of the activity levels of the flows. For more details please refer to [11] and [13]. These curves prove the fact that *class0* users have assured a high PSNR, *class2* users are limited to a low PSNR while *class1* users experiment a wider range of PSNR that depends on the available resources. The reserved BW to a *class0* user or a *class2* user is almost constant (3 Mbps for *class0* and 1.6 Mbps for *class1*). Users of *class1* use well the resources because they always take up the available bandwidth, as the black line from Figure 5 shows.

A service provider could already use these results to design the VoD service with a single class of user. On the one hand, from a particular VoD service the service provider could estimate the QoS parameters that he/she could offer to the customers. On the other hand, the service provider may design a VoD service given a certain level of QoS required for the customers. However, if the service provider wants to give service to different user profiles, these figures would be just a rough reference of the system performance. The reason is that the behaviour of users from one class influence on the QoS of the other classes. In this case, it is necessary to evaluate the system model when different classes of user are simultaneously accepted in the system.

Figures 6 to 8 present measures of PSNR and Profits, when heterogeneous users of *class0*, *class1* and *class2* can be accepted in our VoD system. The total bandwidth that the provider has available to offer the service is 12 Mbps. We evaluate a simple function of variable benefits: The revenues are adjusted to the video quality effectively transmitted to the users and the service provider's costs depend on the reserved resources. Many more complex billing functions can be evaluated as well. They could consider different factors, e.g. different charges and costs. As an example, [20, 21] show billing functions based on fixed and variable costs due to the connection setup and the consumed bandwidth, respectively. Any proposed policy trades off performance degradation with monetary incentives to improve user benefit and network revenue. To facilitate the performance evaluation considering the costs, we define a monetary unit [u] equivalent to the price to pay for the transmission of the whole movie with the flow of maximum quality (Q=4). The cost C that the service provider must assume depends on the reserved resources; Here we have set C equal to $2 \cdot 10^{-5}$ [u] per reserved Mbit. The price that each user would pay has been estimated using our analytical model applying a set of assigned rewards equal to 0.0023692, 0.003948667 and 0.000789733 [u] per each GoP transmitted for flows *vbr4*, *vbr8* and *vbr16*, respectively. This leads to pay 1[u], 0.6[u] or 0.2[u] for the transmission of the whole flow *vbr4*, *vbr8* or *vbr16*, respectively.

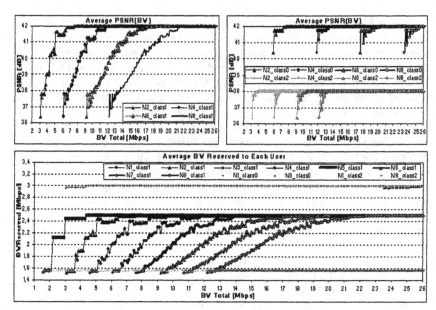

Fig. 5. Mean BW reserved and mean PSNR provided to a single class. The available quality flows are: Q=4 and 8 (*class0*); Q=4, 8 and 16 (*class1*); Q=8 and 16 (*class2*).

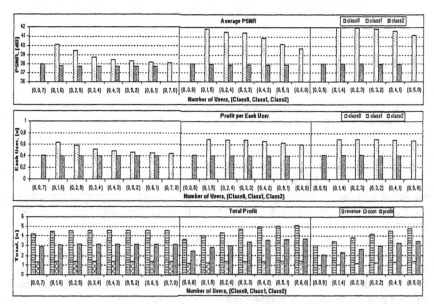

Fig. 6. PSNR provided to a customer and service provider's profits. Users of *class1* and *class2* interact in the VoD system. There are 7, 6, 5 accepted users (from left to right).

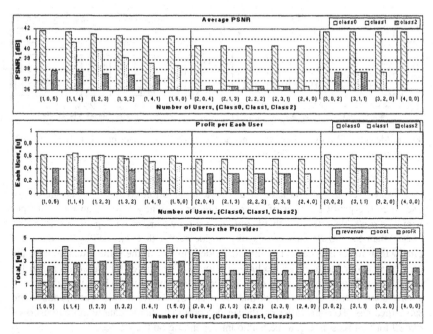

Fig. 7. Mean PSNR provided to a customer and profits for the service provider. Users of *class0*, *class1* and *class2* interact in the VoD system. There are 1, 2, 3 and 4 accepted users of *class0*.

Figure 6 presents some of the measures that we have calculated when there is no accepted user of *class0* in the VoD system. This way, the system capacity is 7 users. The results are shown for 7, 6, 5 (from left to right) users in the system. Measures for *class2* users are independent of the number of accepted users of *class1*. These values are almost constant and close to those of maximum quality e.g. PSNR=38dB, *Profit_per_user*=0,4[u]. On the contrary, measures for users form *class1* are quite degraded when a new user from *class2* or *class1* enters the system. Nevertheless, measures (including profits) for *class1* are always the same or better than for *class2*.

Figure 7 shows the performance evaluation for the number of users equal to the system capacity when there are 1, 2, 3 and 4 accepted users of *class0* (from left to right). We can notice that the PSNR of *class1* and *class2* is not much degraded when there is only one user of *class0*. Nevertheless, when there are 2 users of *class2*, the system is quite congested producing a notable degradation in the video quality offered to the users of any class. Alternatively, if the capacity of the system is decreased in one user less, the PSNR offered to the users improves, as Fig. 8 shows. Further, the service provider's profits increase in spite of having a user less than before. The reason is that the profit per user is higher than before, i.e. 0.4u/*class2*, 0.6u/*class1* now and 0.3u/*class2*, 0.3u/*class1* before. However, a lower system capacity decreases the access probability for new users.

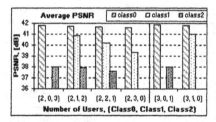 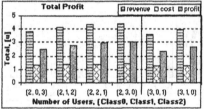

Fig. 8. Mean PSNR provided to a customer and profits for the service provider. There are 2, 3 accepted users of *class0*, (from left to right).

Figure 7 clearly shows another undesirable situation. When there is one *class0* user then the profit per user of *class1* is higher or faintly lower than the profit per user of *class0*. Nevertheless, that is unfair because we are providing a lower PSNR to *class1* than to *class0*. This incongruity is due to the fact that RSV_{min} is higher for *class0* than for *class1* i.e. to transmit the coded flow with the same video quality, the service provider has to reserve a higher amount of resources for *class0* user than for *class1* user. That affects in the cost for the service provider, which is higher when giving service to users of *class0* than to users of *class1*, despite both produce the same incomes. To cope with this, the service provider should charge more to users of *class0* for that reason, e.g. a fixed amount depending on the RSV_{min}.

5   Conclusions and Future Work

Many QoS management frameworks available in the literature need mechanisms and procedures to quantitatively evaluate the user-level SLA parameters. The generic methodology which we proposed in [11] utilizes the characterization of the available constant-quality flows to develop a model for adaptive video-streaming services. Models obtained with this methodology capture the dynamism of the transmitted stream taking into account the interaction among all the users accepted in the system. Employing this methodology, we have obtained evaluations of an adaptive VoD system when several QoS customer profiles are considered. We have assessed some VoD system design options, avoiding operating states where the QoS requirements are not fulfilled or the efficiency is not suitable. On the other hand, we have estimated the QoS parameters which the service providers could agree with their customers. Also, we have evaluated an adaptive pricing scheme for the customers and its trade-off with the service provider's profits. In particular, we have analysed the service provider's profits when we limit the number of accepted users of each class. As future lines of research, we are analysing another design aspects, such as: the algorithm of segmentation applied on the video sequences stored in the VoD server and different policies to assign resources to each user-class. We are developing general criteria to select the set of coded flows that the service provider will arrange to offer the service.

References

1. D. Wu, Y.T. Hou, W. Zhu, Y. Zang, and J.M. Peha, Streaming Video over Internet: Approaches and Directions, IEEE Trans. on Circuits and Systems for Video Technology **11**(3), 282-300 (2001).
2. M. Ghanbari, Video Coding: An Introduction to Standard Codecs (IEE Telecommunications Series 42), IEE Publishing, (1999).
3. L.J. De la Cruz and J. Mata, Performance of Dynamic Resource Allocation with QoS Guarantees for MPEG VBR Video Traffic Transmission over ATM Networks, Global Telecomunications Conference, IEEE GLOBECOM'99, vol. **2**, pp. 1483-1489 (1999).
4. P. Manzoni, P. Cremonesi, and G. Serazzi, Workload Models of VBR Traffic and Their Use in Resource Allocation Policie, IEEE/ACM Trans. on Networking **7**(3), 387-397 (1999).
5. G. Cortese, R. Cremonese, P. Fiutem, S. D'antonio, M. Esposito, S.P. Romano, and A. Diaconescu, CADENUS: Creation and Deployment of End-User Services in Premium IP Networks, IEEE Communications Magazine **41**(1), 54-60, (2003).
6. IST Project: TAPAS- Trusted and QoS-Aware Provision of Application Services, (2001) http://www.newcastle.research.ec.org/tapas/
7. G.M. Muntean and L. Murphy, A New Adaptive Multimedia Streaming System for All-IP Multi-Service Networks, IEEE Transactions on Broadcasting **50**(1), 1-10 (2004).
8. A. Lombardo and G. Schembra, Performance Evaluation of an Adaptive-Rate MPEG Encoder Matching IntServ Traffic Constraints, IEEE/ACM Trans. on Networking **11**(1), 47-65 (2003).
9. C. Luna, L. Kondi, and A. Katsaggelos, Maximizing User Utility in Video Streaming Applications, IEEE Transaction on Circuits and Systems for Video Technology **13**(2), 141-148 (2003).
10. R.S. Ramanujan, J.A. Newhouse, M.N. Kaddoura, A. Ahamad, E.R. Chartier, and K.J. Thurber, Adaptive streaming of MPEG video over IP networks, Proceedings 22nd Annual Conference on Local Computer Networks, IEEE, pp. 398-409, (1997).
11. I.V. Martín, J.J. Alins-Delgado, M. Aguilar-Igartua, and J. Mata-Díaz, "Modelling an Adaptive-Rate Video-Streaming Service Using Markov-Rewards Models", Proc. of the First International Conference on Quality of Service in Heterogeneous Wired/Wireless Networks (QSHINE04), IEEE, pp. 92-99, Dallas, Texas, USA, (2004).
12. J.F. Meyer, Performability Evaluation of Telecommunication Networks, in: Teletraffic Science for Cost-Effective Systems, Network and Services, edited by M. Bonnati, ITC-12, pp. 1163-1172, Elsevier Science Publishers B. V. (North Holland, 1989).
13. I.V. Martín, J.J. Alins-Delgado, M. Aguilar-Igartua, and J. Mata-Díaz, Performability Analysis of an Adaptive-Rate Video-Streaming Service in End-to-End QoS Scenarios, 16th IFIP/IEEE Distributed Systems: Operations and Management, LNCS **3775**, 157-168 (2005).
14. Y. Bernet et al., RFC 2998: A Framework for Integrated Services Operation over Diffserv Networks, (2000).
15. U. Sarkar, S. Ramakrishnan, and D. Sarkar, Study of long-duration MPEG-trace segmentation methods for developing frame-size-based traffic models, Computer Networks **44**(22), 177-188 2004).
16. Min Wu, R.A. Joyce, Hau-San Wong, Long Guan, and Sun-Yuan Kung, Dynamic Resource Allocation via Video Content and Short-Term Traffic Statistics, IEEE Transactions on Multimedia 3(2), 186-199 (2001).
17. A. Mashat and M. Kara, Performance Evaluation of a Scene-based Model for VBR MPEG Traffic, Performance Evaluation IFIP WG7.3 **36**(1), (1999).
18. B. R. Haverkort, R. Marie, G. Rubino, and K. Trivedi (eds), Performability Modelling: Techniques and Tools, (John Wiley & Sons, ISBN: 047149195-0, 2001).

19. R. Vallejos and M. Barria, Evaluation of Moments of Cumulative Reward in Repairable Systems, Universidad Técnica Federico Santa María Technical Report (unpublished), (2005).
20. A.S. Elmaghraby, A. Kumar, M.M. Kantardzic, and M.G. Mostafa, Bandwidth Allocation in a Dynamic Environment Using a Variable Pricing Policy, 7th International Symposium on Computers and Communications (ISCC'02), IEEE, pp. 589-594, (2002).
21. A. Krishnamurthy, T.D.C. Little, and D. Castañon, A Pricing Mechanism for Scalable Video Delivery, Multimedia Systems 4(6), 328-337 (1996).

A Novel Architecture for Utility Driven Management

Issam Aib[12], Raouf Boutaba[1], and Guy Pujolle[2]

[1] Networks and Distributed Systems Laboratory,
University of Waterloo, Canada,
iaib@bcr2.uwaterloo.ca
[2] Lip6 Laboratory, University of Paris 6, France

Abstract. In this paper, we specify and implement a framework for utility driven generation and scheduling of management actions based on Business context and Service Level Agreements (SLAs). SLAs are compiled into low level management policies; as well as sets of performance metrics and utility functions. These are subsequently used to drive the scheduling of the low level policy actions. Each action is associated with a utility participation value based on parameters relevant to the contract(s) it is related to; as well as the run-time context of its triggering and execution times. A Web hosting company case study is used to illustrate the benefit of taking into account business level implications when scheduling the execution of management tasks. We measure the overall business profitability as a pondered linear function of other business metrics such as overall raw financial profit and overall customer satisfaction. Finally, we discuss the difficulties and challenges related to the correct estimation of utility costs associated with the low level management/control actions.

Key words: Utility Driven Management, Service Level Agreement, Policy based Management

1 Introduction

With the increasing number, complexity and frequency of IT related decisions, the mechanisms to determine the optimal utilization of IT resources must become an integral part of automated IT Operations. Given the timescales involved, the decision making process has to be implemented through management rules (policies) whose objective is to maximize the business profit (value) of the services offered by the IT system.

We propose a management approach [2] which stems from the observation that however successful an enterprize might be with its adoption of a management solution, it must be remembered that its IT infrastructure is aimed at the provision of a service which is exchanged for economic value. Therefore, it is extremely important to make the low-level management capability clearly

Please use the following format when citing this chapter:

Aib, I., Boutaba, R., Pujolle, G., 2006, in IFIP International Federation for Information Processing, Volume 213, Network Control and Engineering for QoS, Security, and Mobility, V, ed. Gaïti, D., (Boston: Springer), pp. 89–99.

aware of business level considerations. Low-level configuration and management actions are either triggered by events and system states or manually issued by a system administrator. We consider the use of policies to model this behavior reasonable as it does not lure out the generality of our approach. The reason is that any automatic action or rule can always fit within the Event Condition Action (ECA) paradigm. Hence, we model the dynamics of an IT system through a dynamic set of ECA rules that govern all of its behavior. Manually enforced actions make no exception as they fall too within the ECA rule set where the event part is something like "admin-decision".

In our framework low-level configuration and management policies are generated from the set of contracts (SLAs) the IT provider has concluded as well as his own Business objectives and high level management policies. Our study does not concern itself with how these low-level configuration and management actions are actually generated. We are rather interested in how to monetize and maximize the business level utility at run-time through the appropriate scheduling of low level actions. Each action is associated with a utility (or penalty if negative) participation value based on parameters related to the contract(s) it is related to and the run-time context of its triggering and execution times. We compare this new business-level utility-driven scheduling to the default mode which is the simple FIFO execution of actions as soon as they are triggered. We show that our technique would always result in a better performance and more optimized value for the overall Business Profit of the IT provider.

2 Related Work

Driving IT management from business objectives is quite a novel proposition. In [6][7], Buco et. al. present a business-objectives-based utility computing SLA management system. The business objective(s) that they consider is the minimization of the exposed business impact of service level violation, for which a high-level solution is presented in [15]. However, the Management by Business Objectives component of the Framework presented in this paper goes far beyond just using impact of service level violations. It provides a comprehensive method for IT management that can take into account strategic business objectives; thereby, going a long way towards the much needed synchronization of IT and business objectives. For a more detailed discussion of MBO capability applied to the incident management domain see [5].

In another respect, the area of SLA-driven management has been closely interested in the subject of SLA modeling. WSLA [10][11] from IBM research and WSMN [12][13] from HP Labs analyze and define SLAs for Web Services by building new constructs over existing Web Services formalisms. [13] specifies SLOs within SLAs and relates each SLO to a set of Clauses. Clauses provide the exact details on the expected service performance. Each clause represents an event-triggered function over a measured item which evaluates an SLO and triggers an action in the case the SLO has not been respected. In [4], an FSA

(Finite State Automata) is defined for SLA state management in which each state specifies the set of SLA clauses that are active. Transitions between states can be either events generated by an SLA monitoring layer or actions taken by parties in the SLA.

Keller A.and Ludwig H. [10][11] define the Web Service Level Agreement (WSLA) Language for the Specification and Monitoring of SLAs for Web Services. The framework provides differentiated levels of Web services to different customers on the basis of SLAs. In this work, an SLA is defined as a bilateral contract made up of two signatory parties, a Customer and a Provider. Service provider and service customer are ultimately responsible for all obligations, mainly in the case of the service provider, and the ultimate beneficiary of obligations. WSLA defines an SLO as a commitment to maintain a particular state of the service in a given period. An action guarantee performs a particular activity if a given precondition is met. Action guarantees are used as a means to meet SLOs. [9] adds on this work by proposing an approach of using CIM for the SLA-driven management of distributed systems. It proposes a mapping of SLAs, defined using the WSLA framework, onto the CIM information model. Finally, [8] considers a direct application of WSLA within UCEs.

The GSLA model we propose for SLA specification [1] has the novelty of considering each contracted service relationship as a set of parties playing an SLA game in which each party plays one or more roles to achieve the SLA objectives. GSLA party behavior is captured into a unique semantic component; modeling a role that the party plays. SLOs are specified for each role and enforcement policies are generated to meet them. These policies need not be specified at contract sign time, they can change according to run-time circumstances. Ultimately, roles represent a high-level representation of a set of low-level enforcement policies which are generated, enabled, disabled, and removed as a whole and help keep a consistent relationship between what is high-level behavior and its corresponding low-level actions.

Finally, the use of policies for the management of utility computing infrastructures has been recently addressed by Akhil et al. [14] from HP Labs where policy is used to assist in service deployment. We consider this component as part of the policy deployment and resource configuration component of the PDP.

3 The Business Driven Management Framework (BDMF)

The main objective of the business driven management (BDMF) framework is to drive the management of IT resources and services from the business point of view. Most of the times, when tradeoff-kind of decisions are to be made, the IT managers have a feeling for which is the option available to them that guarantees the minimum cost or least disruption to the service. But unless the impact of carrying out the chosen course of action onto the business layer is understood, one may run the risk of solving the wrong problem optimally. Because of this, the BDMF was designed according to the principle of making information that pertains to the business visible from the IT and vice versa.

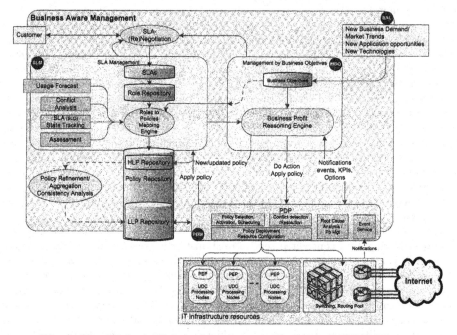

Fig. 1. The Business Driven Management Framework (BDMF)

As presented in fig. 1, the BDM architecture is divided into two main layers. On the top is the business aware layer (BAL), which is intended to host the long term control of the IT infrastructure based on the business objectives and market strategy of the IT provider. Beneath it is a resource control layer (RCL) which hosts the real time logic for the reactive short term control of the IT infrastructure.

The Business Management Layer is responsible for optimizing the alignment of IT resources usage with the objectives of the utility provider based on a set of business objectives defined and audited over relatively long periods of time (monthly, quarterly, etc.). Business objectives are the reflection of the utility provider's business strategy and range over diverse key performance indicators, which can be related to service operations, service level agreements, or any other business indicators.

Business relationships contracted by the utility provider are formalized by SLAs and modeled using the GSLA information model [1]. Using the GSLA, each contracted service relationship is modeled as a set of parties playing an SLA game in which each party plays one or more roles to achieve the SLA objectives. Each role in the SLA is associated with a set of Service Level Objectives (SLOs) to be achieved; as well as a set of intrinsic policies related to the role behavior per see. A special engine, we call the Role-to-policies mapping engine, translates Roles, SLOs and rules into a set of enabling policies. These policies are further refined to lower level policies (LLPs) that enclose all the low level logic required to correctly drive the utility resources. Note that the automation of the translation per see is still an open research problem which is out of the scope of this paper. For our use case we use a pre-established mapping between SLA templates and their manually generated enforcement policies.

Business objectives affect the way SLAs are defined and managed at the resource control layer. So whenever a business objective is changed, added, or removed, important impact takes place at the long term time scale on the SLA database.

Low level policies (LLPs) are dealt with by the Policy Decision Point (PDP) module [3] of the resource control layer. Part of the PDP's task is to monitor and respond to system events and notifications by selecting, activating, and scheduling the enforcement of the appropriate policies at the appropriate utility resources. The PDP contains also sub-components for policy run-time conflict detection, root cause analysis, generation of the set of options available in the presence of some incident or problem, as well as a the generate of appropriate configuration flows in order to enforce active policies.

As it is impossible to define policies upfront to cover all run-time events, it will happen that LLPs may not be sufficient to deal with certain conditions. In those cases, our PDP passes up the control to the BDM. Given the various options, the BDM will select the one that will maximize the value to the utility provider. That is, the option that will result in the closest alignment to the business objectives. Such interactions offer also the opportunity for the architecture to learn and refine the policy repository.

4 A utility computing web hosting use case

We consider a Utility Computing Provider, named UCP, which offers web hosting services to client companies. UCP offers a generic SLA template as described in fig. 2. For simplicity, we assume that UCP provides two different web hosting packages each with different QoS assurances and pricing. These are advertised as two SLA types, SLA-T1 and SLA-T2, which are actually instances of the generic SLA of fig. 2. The SLA instances are depicted in table 1.

UCP is free to enforce those SLA types the way it wants as long as it is able to meet its customers' requirements. In our case a set of ECA rules (policies) are generated for each SLA type. The detail of this is explained after describing the overall management architecture.

C is provided a Web-Server Service with schedule SC
Capacity is of CP simultaneous connections
Initial storage capacity is S GB
C is monthly charged $ a x Capacity +
b x Storage.initial + c x Storage.Extra.Average
Monthly availability of the hosted service will be A%
 Otherwise, refund C RA% of period PR
Any service unavailability will be fixed within at most MinTTR min
Otherwise, C will be refunded RMTTR of period RMTTRPR
Average time to process any customer service request over a month period will be less than ART ms
 Otherwise, credit C RRT% of period RRTPR
IF C fails to pay the monthly charge for MaxM successive months the contract becomes void.

Fig. 2. Generic UCP SLA Template

Table 1. Template SLA instances of the Generic UCP SLA

Param	SLA-T1	SLA-T2
SC	SC	SC
CP	2000	5000
S	0.5	1
a	0.1	0.15
b	5	5
c	10	10
A	99	99.9
RA	100	100
RAPR	breach period	month
MinTTR	∞	20
RMTTR	NA	100
RMTTRPR	NA	breach period
ART	300	200
RRT	20	80
RRTPR	month	month
MaxM	3	6

It is interesting to notice that the deduction of the appropriate set of parameters and the number of SLA templates UCP desires to offer is a complex issue that depends not only on UCP's IT infrastructure but also on the market state and its evolution. Through simulations, it is possible to get a feeling of which templates it can more "safely" go with.

4.1 Business Metrics

Although T1 and T2 SLA types (Sec. 4) are specified over two service parameters, namely availability and service latency, they each define different service levels and have different penalties.

In our use case, we assume that UCP defines two Business Level metrics as input to it its overall Business Profit Function: *RP* representing the raw financial profit in some monetary unit, and CS, a measure of overall customer satisfaction.

The Business Profit Function Ψ represents a measurement of the overall utility gained and is defined as:

$$\Psi = \alpha \times RP + \beta \times CS \qquad (1)$$

$$RP = \delta \sum_{s \in SLASet} RP(s) \qquad (2)$$

$$CS = \sum_{i \in TemplateSet} \gamma_i \sum_{s \in T1SLASet} CS(s) \qquad (3)$$

α, β, γ_i, and δ represent pondering wheighs that are tunable to reflect the importance the IT operator (UCP) gives to each business indicator (metric). Simulations can be used to determine and tune these values.

Customer importance is translated by the existence of pondering factors related to each type of SLA. A more fine grained view of Customer importance involves per customer importance pondering factors. These factors are calculated based on Customer history (profit generated from that customer, service importance, etc.)

RP, although it involves a whole computation tree, is relatively easy and more accurate to measure compared to CS. The latter business indicator is less evident to measure as it generally depends on a relatively subjective appreciation of the customer of the overall service performance and might vary from customer to customer even with the same service performance. For the sake of keeping the use case simple enough, we assume that Customer Satisfaction is calculated as follows:

For the first month of service usage, customer satisfaction (CS) is measured by the number of experienced service failures with a maximum of $\%FedUp$ at the occurrence of which the customer becomes completely unhappy with the provided service ($CS = 0$).

$$CS_1 = 1 - \frac{1}{FedUp} Min\left(Nb\left(SLOFailures\right), FedUp\right) \qquad (4)$$

On the following evaluation periods, the relationship becomes:

$$CS_{n+1} = \beta CS_n + (1 - \beta)$$
$$\left(1 - \frac{1}{FedUp} Min\left(Nb\left(SLOFailures\right), FedUp\right)\right) \qquad (5)$$

This means that Customer Satisfaction is a pondered sum of the last customer satisfaction experience and the number of experienced Service Failures majored by the predefined threshold $FedUp$.

4.2 Generation of configuration policies

In order to enforce each contracted SLA, the utility provider translates the set of Service Level Objectives (SLOs) it has to guarantee into a set of access control and management policies that are stored into the policy repository.

Given that the UCP Roles-to-policies mapping engine knows that a UCP web server resource instance can serve up to 500 clients without reducing the contracted QoS, we understand from the policy set of Fig. 3 that the UCP considered the "lazy policy" of per-need provisioning to meet its SLAs. Whenever there is a need, an additional web server instance is installed and provisioned for customers. For brevity, we include the generated policy set of SLA-T2.

T2-SLA{...Role T2-SLA.UCP-Role{

```
SLO1 = WS.Capacity.Max = "5000"
SLO2 = WS.Availability.Month.Average.Percent ≥ 99.9%"
SLO3 = MinTimeToRepair( WS.availability) ≤ 20 min
SLO4 = WS.SingleRequest.Duration.Month.Average ≤ 200 ms
WSThreshold = 80%;
WS.SingleInstance.capacity = 200
policy P21= on SLA.Schedule.deployTime do (WS.installNew (WS.Config, WS.SingleInstance.capacity)
policy P22= on WS.installed do ConfigureAccessRights(C)
policy P23= on WS.installed do SwitchFabric.AssignQoSTag (WS.TrafficID, EF)
policy P24= on (WS.load == WSThreshold)
do WS.installNew (WS.Config, WS.SingleInstance.capacity )
when (WS.NbInstances * WS.SingleInstance.capacity ≤ WS.Capacity.Max )
priority = AboveNormal
policy P25= on (Web-Server.InstanceFailure)
do WS.installBackup (WS.Config,WS.SingleInstance.capacity )
priority = 5 (Critical)
policy P26= on WS.load¡WSThreshold-20% do WS.LastInstance.free()
policy P27= on fail(SLO2) do C.Credit(C.Charge)
policy P28= on fail(SLO3) do C.Credit ( C.Charge * duration(fail(SLO3) ) / Time.Month.Duration)
policy P29= on fail(SLO4) do C.Credit ( 0.8 * C.Charge )
policy P210= on fail (C-Role.Policy-1, 6) do TerminateContract ( C-SLA )}}
```

Fig. 3. Generated SLOs and Policies for UCP-T2 Role

4.3 Runtime conflicts

by analyzing the sets of generated policies for SLA-T1 and SLA-T2 it is possible to expect the occurence of runtime conflicts between each subset of elements of the policy set $\{p21, p24, p25, p12, p14, p15\}$. This happens when the UCP provider accepts to signs as much number of SLA-T1 and SLA-T2 SLAs so as the statistical average of their resource consumption meets the actual available system capacity. Hence, the system needs to work with cases where it might become in shortage of resources.

Default priorities between the generated policies will give policies belonging to SLA-T2 priority over those belonging to SLA-T1. The reason is that SLA-T2 customers bring more money per allocated resource and have also more stringent QoS requirements. However, at runtime and depending on the SLO state of each SLA it might happen that at some point in time policies of SLA-T1 instances become more important to execute otherwise their respective SLOs will fail and generate real loss for the provider while if executed to the expense of delaying SLA-T2 policies will not generate penalties as long as there is still time for their respective SLOs to fail. This is an example of a runtime policy conflict which cannot be dealt with at compile time.

When the PDP is confronted here with a run-time policy conflict, it needs the assistance of the MBO for a wiser (business-driven) decision as a run-time policy conflict is generally symptom of service degradation that the PDP cannot measure correctly. The PDP hence sends a set of options for the MBO to decide which to apply.

The MBO engine will normally take into consideration service and business level parameters related to (i) SLAs (current total time of service unavailability, time to recover from unavailability, penalty amounts, Expectation of the evolution pattern for the number of customers for each SLA (to decide whether to allocate resources or just do not if the congestion period is expected to be temporary); and (ii) Current customers satisfaction indicators. In our implementation, it currently evaluates the impact of SLO failure on the BPF and decides by minimizing the overall impact on it.

It is clear that it is not necessarily the FIFO treatment of active policies which will lead to the best business profit. When the PDP knows that there will be inevitably a degradation of service (that might lead or not to some SLO violation) the MBO answers about the best options (strategy) to follow so as to achieve minimal degradation of the business profit function.

4.4 BDMF Simulation Testbed

In order to validate our framework, we designed a java based discrete event simulation system which features the main components of BDMF. The system is composed of three major packages:

- A base package of a process-based discrete event simulation system.
- Package edu.bdmf which implements all the components of BDMF.
- A testbed package which actually implements our running example.

The edu.bdmf package is the core component of the implementation. It builds on the base discrete process-based simulation package and features the core of a policy based management system supported by the high-level features of BDMF. These include the support for SLA specification according to the GSLA model [1], definition of business objectives; specification of metrics at resource, service and up to the overall business profit function; as well the connection with the BPF maximization (impact minimization) engine by determining which decision making algorithm to apply with regards to the scheduling of active policies (actions).

The generic SLA (sec. 2) of our running example is implemented as a java class with the associated attributes as class parameters. The two SLA templates we used are subclasses of it. A similar reuse technique is used in the Roles [1] and policy specifications. For example, policy p21 of SLA template T2 and p12 (not shown here) of SLA T1 are the same and hence specified using the same class.

˜ We compare the plain FIFO scheduling method, which launches triggered policy actions in the order of their arrival, to the second scheduling method employs a greedy approach to BPF maximization by selecting each time the policy which at the time being is expected to lead to the best positive participation (or least negative participation) to the BPF.

The simulation shows no difference between the two techniques as far as the set of available server units has not been exhausted. However, When the system operates in congested conditions either by increasing the number of contracted SLAs or the end customer connection rate, the greedy BPF maximization scheduling technique shows its power by succeeding to keep the BPF always at a better value than the plain FIFO method. The gain interval tends to reach a maximum value after which the two functions tend to converge to the same loss levels.

5 Conclusion

This paper presented the BDMF management framework which extends policy-based management with a wider scope decision ability that is informed and driven through the business objectives and the contractual obligations of the enterprise supported by the IT systems being managed.

We described preliminary results of the implementation of the BDMF framework on the base of a discrete process-based event simulation system. These include the utility generation and scheduling of management actions based on business context and the set of service level agreements an IT operator has contracted. We used a web hosting company example to illustrate the system functionalities. The use case showed the importance of management actions scheduling for maximizing the business profit function of IT providers.

The BDMF simulation environment can serve as a basis for the analysis and validation of policy performance at run time. In addition, our implementation illustrates how class inheritance can serve as a powerful tool to reinforce reusability of SLAs, Roles, and Policies at both template and instance levels.

We believe that this work represents a first step towards management actions scheduling and execution based on high level business metrics. As a future work, we plan to further validate our framework through simulations using other business level objectives and different scheduling techniques.

References

1. I. Aib, N. Agoulmine, and G. Pujolle. A multi-party approach to SLA modeling, application to WLANs. In *Second IEEE Consumer Communications and*

Networking Conference (CCNC), pages 451 – 455. IEEE, Jan 3-5 2005.

2. I. Aib, M. Salle, C. Bartolini, and A. Boulmakoul. A business driven management framework for utility computing environments. In *proceedings of the Ninth IFIP/IEEE International Symposium on Integrated Network Management (IM 2005)*. IEEE, 16-19 May 2005.

3. E. B. Moore. Policy core information model (PCIM) extensions, rfc 3460, January 2003.

4. C. Bartolini, A. Boulmakoul, A. Christodoulou, A. Farrell, M. Salle, and D. Trastour. Management by contract: IT management driven by business objectives. In P. University of Evry, editor, *HP Open University Association (HPOVUA)*, volume 10. HPL, June 2004.

5. C. Bartolini and M. Sall. Business driven prioritization of service incidents. In *Utility Computing: 15th IFIP/IEEE International Workshop on Distributed Systems: Operations and Management, DSOM*, volume 3278 of *Lecture Notes in Computer Science*, pages 64–75. Springer-Verlag GmbH, Jan 2004.

6. M. Buco, R. Chang, L. Luan, C. Ward, J. Wolf, P. Yu, T. Kosar, and S. U. Shah. Managing ebusiness on demand SLA contracts in business terms using the cross-SLA execution manager SAM. In *ISADS '03: Proceedings of the The Sixth International Symposium on Autonomous Decentralized Systems (ISADS'03)*, page 157, Washington, DC, USA, 2003. IEEE Computer Society.

7. M. J. Buco, R. N. Chang, L. Z. Luan, C. Ward, J. L. Wolf, and P. S. Yu. Utility computing SLA management based upon business objectives. *IBM Systems Journal*, 43(1):159–178, 2004.

8. A. Dan, D. Davis, R. Kearney, A. Keller, R. P. King, D. Kuebler, H. Ludwig, M. Polan, Mike, Spreitzer, and A. Youssef. Web services on demand: WSLA-driven automated management. *IBM Systems Journal*, 43(1):136–158, 2004.

9. M. Debusmann and A. Keller. SLA-driven management of distributed systems using the common information model. In *Proceedings of the VIII IFIP/IEEE IM conference on network management*, page 563, 2003.

10. A. Keller and H. Ludwig. The WSLA framework: Specifying and monitoring service level agreements for web services. *Journal of Networks and Systems Management*, 11(1), 2003.

11. H. Ludwig, A. Keller, A. Dan, R. P. King, and R. Franck. Web service level agreement (WSLA) language specification. Technical report, IBM T.J. Watson Research Center, 2003.

12. V. Machiraju, A. Sahai, and A. van Moorsel. Web services management network: An overlay network for federated service management. In *Proceedings of the VIII IFIP/IEEE IM conference on network management*, 2003.

13. A. Sahai, V. Machiraju, M. Sayal, A. P. A. van Moorsel, and F. Casati. Automated SLA monitoring for web services. In M. Feridun, P. G. Kropf, and G. Babin, editors, *DSOM*, volume 2506 of *Lecture Notes in Computer Science*, pages 28–41. Springer, Nov. 16 2002.

14. A. Sahai, S. Singhal, R. Joshi, and V. Machiraju. Automated policy-based resource construction in utility computing environments. In *IEEE/IFIP NOMS*, 2004.

15. M. Salle and C. Bartolini. Management by contract. In *IEEE/IFIP NOMS*, 2004.

Multiobjective Multicast Routing
with Ant Colony Optimization

Diego Pinto and Benjamín Barán

Polytechnic School, National University of Asunción

P.O. Box CC 2111 - Paraguay

{dpinto,bbaran}@pol.una.py

http://www.fpuna.edu.py/

Abstract. This work presents a multiobjective algorithm for multicast traffic engineering. The proposed algorithm is a new version of MultiObjective Ant Colony System (MOACS), based on Ant Colony Optimization (ACO). The proposed MOACS simultaneously optimizes the maximum link utilization, the cost of the multicast tree, the averages delay and the maximum end-to-end delay. In this way, a set of optimal solutions, known as Pareto set is calculated in only one run of the algorithm, without a priori restrictions. Experimental results obtained with the proposed MOACS were compared to a recently published Multiobjective Multicast Algorithm (MMA), showing a promising performance advantage for multicast traffic engineering.

1 Introduction

Multicast consists of simultaneous data transmission from a source node to a subset of destination nodes in a computer network [1]. Multicast routing algorithms have recently received great attention due to the increased use of recent point-to-multipoint applications, such as radio and TV transmission, on-demand video, teleconferences and so on. Such applications generally require optimization of several quality-of service (*QoS*) parameters such as maximum end-to-end delay and minimum use of bandwidth resources in a context of traffic engineering.

When a dynamic multicast problem considers several traffic requests, not only *QoS* parameters must be considered, but also load balancing and network resources must be taken into account. In order to avoid hot spots and to balance the network load, a common approach is to minimize the utilization of the most heavily used link in the network (α) or maximum link utilization [2]. At the same time, cost minimization of the tree of each multicast group, which is given by the sum of the cost of the used links, is also desired. It is known that the complexity of computing the minimum cost tree for a given multicast group is NP-hard [3]. Then, this paper presents a new MultiObjective Ant Optimization System (MOACS) [4], which finds a set of optimal solutions by simultaneously minimizing the maximum link

Please use the following format when citing this chapter:

Pinto, D., Barán, B., 2006, in IFIP International Federation for Information Processing, Volume 213, Network Control and Engineering for QoS, Security, and Mobility, V, ed. Gaïti, D., (Boston: Springer), pp. 101–115.

utilization, the cost of the tree, the maximum end-to-end delay and the average delay. In this way, a whole Pareto set of optimal solutions can be obtained in only one run of the proposed algorithm.

The remainder of this paper is organized as follows. Section 2 describes related works. A general definition of an Optimization Multiobjective Problem is presented in Section 3. The problem formulation and the objective functions are given in Section 4. The proposed algorithm is explained in Section 5 while a brief description of MMA algorithm is given in Section 6. The experimental environment is shown in Section 7 and experimental results are present in Section 8. Finally, conclusions and future works are presented in Section 9.

2 Related work

Several algorithms based on ACO consider multicast routing as a mono-objective problem, minimizing the cost of the tree under multiple constrains. In [5] Liu and Wu proposed the construction of a multicast tree, where only the cost of the tree is minimized using degree constrains. On the other hand, Gu et al. considered multiple parameters of QoS as constrains, minimizing just the cost of the tree [6]. It can be clearly noticed that previous algorithms treated the Traffic Engineering Multicast problem as a mono-objective problem with several constrains. The main disadvantage of this approach is the necessity of an *a priori* predefined upper bound that can exclude good trees from the final solution. In [3], Donoso et al. proposed a multi-tree traffic-engineering scheme using multiple trees for each multicast group. They took into account four metrics: (i) maximum link utilization α, (ii) hop count, (iii) bandwidth consumption and (iv) total end-to-end delay. The method minimizes a weighted sum function composed of the above four metrics. Considering the problem is NP-hard, the authors proposed a heuristic algorithm consisting of two steps: (1) obtaining a modified graph, where all possible paths between the source node and every destination node are looked for, and (2) finding out the trees based on the distance values and the available capacity of the paths, in the modified graph. Crichigno and Barán [7] have proposed a Multiobjective Multicast Algorithm (MMA), based on the Strength Pareto Evolutionary Algorithm (SPEA) [8], which simultaneously optimizes the maximum link utilization, the cost of the tree, the maximum end-to-end delay and the average delay. This MMA algorithm finds a set of optimal solutions, which is calculated in only one run, without *a priori* restrictions.

3 Multiobjective Optimization Problem

A general *Multiobjective Optimization Problem* (MOP) [9] includes a set of n decision variables, k objective functions, and m restrictions. Objective functions and restrictions are functions of decision variables. This can be expressed as:

$$
\begin{aligned}
\textit{Optimize} \quad & y = f(x) = (f_1(x), f_2(x) ..., f_k(x)). \\
\textit{Subject to} \quad & e(x) = (e_1(x), \ e_2(x), \ ... , e_m(x)) \geq 0, \\
\textit{where} \quad & x = (x_1, x_2, ..., x_n) \in X \text{ is the decision vector,} \\
\textit{and} \quad & y = (y_1, y_2, ... , y_k) \in Y \text{ is the objective vector.}
\end{aligned}
\tag{1}
$$

X denotes the decision space while the objective space is denoted by Y. Depending on the kind of the problem, "*optimize*" could mean minimize or maximize. The set of restrictions $e(x) \geq 0$ determines the set of feasible solutions $X_f \subseteq X$ and its corresponding set of objective vectors $Y_f \subseteq Y$. The problem consists in finding x that optimizes $f(x)$. In general, there is no unique "best" solution but a set of solutions, none of which can be considered better than the others when all objectives are considered at the same time. This derives from the fact that there can be conflicting objectives. Thus, a new concept of optimality should be established for MOPs.
Given two decision vectors $u, v \in X_f$:

$$f(u) = f(v) \quad \text{iff:} \quad \forall i \in \{1,2,...,k\}: f_i(u) = f_i(v)$$

$$f(u) \leq f(v) \quad \text{iff:} \quad \forall i \in \{1,2,...,k\}: f_i(u) \leq f_i(v) \tag{2}$$

$$f(u) < f(v) \quad \text{iff:} \quad f(u) \leq f(v) \wedge f(u) \neq f(v)$$

Then, in a minimization context, u and v comply with one and only one of the following three possible conditions:

$$u \succ v \ (u \text{ dominates } v), \quad \text{iff:} \quad f(u) < f(v)$$

$$v \succ u \ (v \text{ dominates } u), \quad \text{iff:} \quad f(v) < f(u) \tag{3}$$

$$u \sim v \ (u \text{ and } v \text{ are non-comparable}), \quad \text{iff:} \quad f(u) \nless f(v) \wedge f(v) \nless f(u)$$

Alternatively, for the rest of this work, $u \triangleleft v$ will denote that $u \succ v$ or $u \sim v$. A decision vector $x \in X_f$ is non-dominated with respect to a set $Q \subseteq X_f$ iff: $x \triangleleft v$, $\forall v \in Q$. When x is non-dominated with respect to the whole set X_f, it is called an optimal Pareto solution; therefore, the *Optimal Pareto set* X_{true} may be formally defined as:

$$X_{true} = \{x \in X_f \mid x \text{ is non-dominated with respect to } X_f\} \tag{4}$$

The corresponding set of objective vectors $Y_{true} = f(X_{true})$ constitutes the *Optimal Pareto Front.*

4 Problem Formulations

For this work, a network is modeled as a direct graph $G = (V, E)$, where V is the set of nodes and E is the set of links. Let:

$(i,j) \in E$	:	link from node i to node j; $i, j \in V$.
$c_{ij} \in \Re^+$	:	cost of link (i,j).
$d_{ij} \in \Re^+$	:	delay of link (i,j), in ms.
$z_{ij} \in \Re^+$	:	capacity of link (i,j), in Mbps.
$t_{ij} \in \Re^+$	:	current traffic of link (i,j), in Mbps.
$\phi \in \Re+$	:	traffic demand, in Mbps.
$s \in V$	:	source node of a multicast group.
$N_r \subseteq V\text{-}\{s\}$	:	set of destinations of a multicast group.
T	:	multicast tree with source in s and set of destinations N_r.

Also, let $p(s,n) \subseteq T$ be the path that connects the source node s with a destination node $n \in N_r$. Finally, let $d_{p(s,n)}$ represent the delay of the path $p(s,n)$, given by the sum of the link delays that conform the path, i.e.:

$$d_{p(s,n)} = \sum_{(i,j) \in p(s,n)} d_{ij}$$ (5)

Using the above definitions, a multicast routing problem for Traffic Engineering may be stated as a MOP that tries to find the multicast tree T that simultaneously minimizes the following objective functions:

1- *Maximum link utilization of the tree*:

$$\alpha_m = \underset{(i,j) \in T}{Max}\{\alpha_{ij}\}$$ (6)

where $\alpha_{ij} = (\phi + t_{ij})/z_{ij}$.

2- *Cost of the multicast tree*:

$$C = \phi * \sum_{(i,j) \in T} c_{ij}$$ (7)

3- *Maximum end-to-end delay of the multicast tree*:

$$D_m = \underset{n \in N_r}{Max}\{d_{p(s,n)}\}$$ (8)

4- *Average delay of the multicast tree*:

$$D_a = \frac{1}{|N_r|} * \sum_{n \in N_r} d_{p(s,n)}$$ (9)

where $|N_r|$ denotes the cardinality of N_r.
The problem is subject to a link capacity constraint:

$$\alpha_{ij} \leq 1 \quad \forall (i,j) \in T$$ (10)

A simple example follows to clarify the above notation.
Example 1. Given the NSF network topology of Fig. 1 [7], the number over each link (i,j) denotes d_{ij} in ms, c_{ij}, and t_{ij} at a given time (in Mbps). NSF network consist of 14 nodes and for each link, $z_{ij}=1.5$ Mbps. Let suppose a traffic request arriving with $\phi=0.2$ Mbps, $s=5$, and $N_r=\{0, 2, 6, 13\}$. Fig. 1 shows a multicast tree (T) while Table 1 presents the objective functions calculated for this tree.

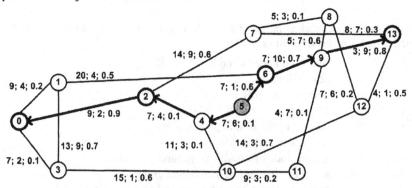

Fig. 1. The NSF Net. $\alpha_m=0.73$; $C=6.4$; $D_m=23$; $D_a=16.5$.

Table 1. Objective Functions Calculated for Example 1.

			Tree			
(i,j)	$(5,4)$	$(4,2)$	$(2,0)$	$(5,6)$	$(6,9)$	$(9,13)$
d_{ij}	7	7	9	7	7	8
c_{ij}	6	4	2	1	10	9
t_{ij}	0.1	0.1	0.9	0.6	0.7	0.8
z_{ij}	1.5	1.5	1.5	1.5	1.5	1.5
α_{ij}	0.2	0.2	0.73	0.53	0.6	0.53

	Delay paths
$d_{p(5,2)}$	$d_{5,4}+d_{4,2}=7+7=14$
$d_{p(5,0)}$	$d_{5,4}+d_{4,2}+d_{2,0}=7+7+9=23$
$d_{p(5,6)}$	$d_{5,6}=7$
$d_{p(5,13)}$	$d_{5,6}+d_{6,9}+d_{9,13}=7+7+8=22$

	Metrics of the solution Tree
α_m	$\alpha_{2,0}=0.73$
C	$\phi*(c_{5,4}+c_{4,2}+c_{2,0}+c_{5,6}+c_{6,9}+c_{9,13})=0.2*(6+4+2+1+10+9)$ $=6.4$
D_m	$d_{p(5,0)}=23$
D_a	$(d_{p(5,2)}+d_{p(5,0)}+d_{p(5,6)}+d_{p(5,13)})/|N_r|=(14+23+7+22)/4=16.5$

For the same example, Figure 2 presents in (a), (b) and (c) three different alternative solutions, for the same multicast group, to clarify the concept of non-dominance. Notice that each tree is better than any other in at least one objective.

It is important to notice, from the mathematical formulation that the four objective functions are treated independently and should be minimized simultaneously. They are not combined to form a scalar single-objective function through a linear combination (as weighted sum) nor are any of them treated as a restriction. This way, using the concept of dominance, a whole set of optimal Pareto solutions is calculated.

Table 2. "Optimal Pareto Set" and "Optimal Pareto Front" for Example 1.

	Optimal Pareto Set (Trees)	Optimal Pareto Front (Objective Vectors)			
		α_m	C	D_m	D_a
S_1	(5,6),(5,4),(4,2),(4,10),(2,0),(10,12),(12,13)	0.73	5	20	36
S_2	(5,6),(5,4),(6,1),(6,9),(4,2),(1,0),(9,8),(8,12),(12,13)	0.6	8.6	21.75	36
S_3	(5,6),(5,4),(6,1),(6,9),(4,2),(1,0),(9,13)	0.67	7.6	19.75	36
S_4	(5,6),(5,4),(6,9),(4,2),(9,13),(2,0)	0.73	6.4	16.50	23
S_5	(5,6),(5,4),(6,1),(4,2),(4,10),(1,0),(10,12),(12,13)	0.73	4	26.75	63
S_6	(5,6),(5,4),(6,1),(4,2),(4,10),(1,0),(10,12),(12,13)	0.6	6.2	23.25	36
S_7	(5,6),(6,1),(1,0),(0,3),(0,2),(3,10),(10,12),(12,13)	0.73	3.6	41	76
S_8	(5,6),(5,4),(6,1),(4,2),(1,0),(2,7),(7,13)	0.53	7	23.75	38
S_9	(5,6),(5,4),(4,2),(4,10),(10,12),(10,3),(12,13),(3,0)	0.6	5.2	24.25	4
S_{10}	(5,6),(5,4),(4,10),(10,3),(10,12),(3,0),(12,13),(0,2)	0.73	4.8	33	49

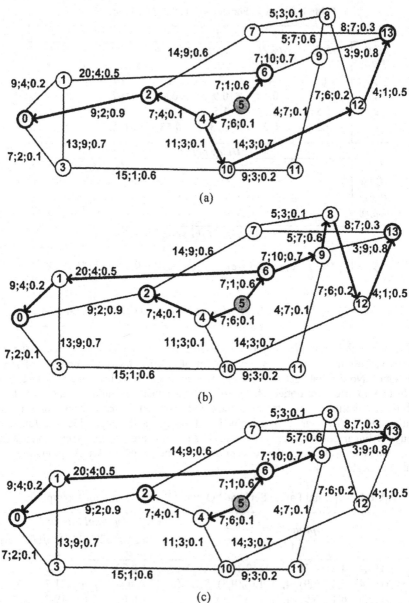

Fig. 2. The NSF Net. (a) to (c) show different Pareto solutions for the same multicast group of example 1.

For the presented example, the set of optimal Pareto set and corresponding objective functions are shown in Table 2. Notice that solution S_1 corresponds to Figure 2(a), S_2 corresponds to Figure 2(b) and S_3 corresponds to Figure 3(c).

5   Ant Colony Optimization Approach

Ant Colony Optimization (ACO) is a metaheuristic inspired by the behavior of natural ant colonies [10]. In the last few years, ACO has received increased attention by the scientific community as can be seen by the growing number of publications and different application fields [4]. Even though, there are several ACO variants that can be considered, a standard approach is next presented [11].

5.1   Standard Approach

ACO uses a pheromone matrix $\tau = \{\tau_{ij}\}$ for the construction of potential good solutions. The initial values of τ are set as $\tau_{ij} = \tau_0\ \forall(i, j)$, where $\tau_0 > 0$. It also takes advantage of heuristic information (known as visibility) using $\eta_{ij} = 1/d_{ij}$. Parameters α and β define the relative influence between the heuristic information and the pheromone levels [10]. While visiting node i, N_i represents the set of neighbor nodes that are not yet visited. The probability (p_{ij}) of choosing a next node j, while visiting node i, is defined by equation (11). At every iteration of the algorithm, each ant of a colony constructs a complete solution T using (11), starting at source node s. Pheromone evaporation is applied for all (i, j) of τ, according to $\tau_{ij} = (1 - \rho) \cdot \tau_{ij}$, where parameter $\rho \in (0; 1]$ determines the evaporation rate. Considering an elitist strategy, the best solution found so far T_{best} updates τ according to $\tau_{ij} = \tau_{ij} + \Delta\tau$, where $\Delta\tau = 1/l(T_{best})$ if $(i, j) \in T_{best}$ and $\Delta\tau = 0$ otherwise. Where $l(T_{best})$ represents and objective function to be minimized.

$$p_{ij} = \begin{cases} \dfrac{\tau_{ij}^{\alpha} \cdot \eta_{ij}^{\beta}}{\sum\limits_{g \in N_i} \tau_{ig}^{\alpha} \cdot \eta_{ig}^{\beta}} & \text{if } j \in N_i \\[4mm] 0 & \text{otherwise} \end{cases} \tag{11}$$

5.2   Proposed Algorithm

Following the *MultiObjective Ant Colony Optimization Algorithm* (MOACS) scheme [4], which is a generalization of the ACS [10], the proposed algorithm uses a colony of ants (or agents) for the construction of m solutions T at every generation. Then, a known Pareto Front Y_{know} [9] is updated including the best non-dominate solutions that have been calculated so far. Finally, the gathered information is saved updating a pheromone matrix τ_{ij}. Fig. 3 (a) presents the general procedure of MOACS. In general, if the state of Y_{know} was changed, the pheromone matrix τ_{ij} is re-initialized ($\tau_{ij} = \tau_0\ \forall(i, j) \in V$) to improve exploration in the decision space X_f. Otherwise, τ_{ij} is globally updated using the solutions of Y_{know} to exploit the knowledge of the best known solutions. Note that only the links of found solutions T in Y_{know} are used to update the pheromone matrix τ_{ij}. To construct a solution, an ant begins its job in the source node s. A non-visited node is pseudo-randomly [4] selected at each step. This process continues until all destination nodes of the multicast group are reached. Considering R as the list of starting nodes, K_i as the list of feasible neighboring nodes to the node i, D_r as the set of destination nodes already reached, the procedure to find a solution T is summarized in Fig. 3 (b).

```
Begin MOACS
    read G, (s,N_r), φ and t_ij
    initialize τ_ij with τ_0
    while (stops criterion is not verified)
        repeat (m times)
            T=Build Solution
            if (T ≺{T_y|T_y ∈Y_know}) then
                Y_know=Y_know∪T-{T_z|T≻T_z}  ∀T_z∈Y_know
            end if
        end repeat
        if (Y_know was changed) then
            Initialize τ_ij with τ_0
        else
            repeat (for every T ∈Y_know)
                τ_ij=(1-ρ).τ_ij+ρ.Δτ   ∀(i,j) ∈T
            end repeat
        end if
    end while
    return Y_know
end MOACS
```

(a)

```
Begin Build Solution
    T = {∅}; D_r = {∅}; R = R ∪ s
    repeat (until R = {∅} or D_r = N_r)
        select node i of R and build set K_i
        if (K_i = {∅}) then
            R = R – i  /*erase node without feasible neighbor*/
        else
            select node j of K_i /*pseudo-random rule*/
            T = T ∪ (i,j)   /*constructions of tree T*/
            R = R ∪ j    /*constructions list of starting nodes*/
            if (j ∈ N_r) then
                D_r = D_r ∪ j /*node j is node destination*/
            end if
            τ_ij=(1-ρ).τ_ij+ρ.τ_0 /*update pheromone*/
        end if
    end repeat
    Prune Tree T        /*eliminate nor used links*/
    return T            /*return solution*/
end Build Solution
```

(b)

Fig. 3. (a) General Procedure of MOACS and (b) Procedure to Build Solution.

where:

$$\Delta\tau = \frac{1}{\sum_{\forall T \in Y_{know}} (\alpha_m * C * D_m * D_a)}$$ (12)

and ρ ∈ (0, 1] represents trail persistence.

6   Multiobjective Multicast Algorithm

Multiobjective Multicast Algorithm (MMA), recently proposed in [7], is based on the *Strength Pareto Evolutionary Algorithm* (SPEA) [8]. MMA holds an evolutionary population P and an external Pareto solution set P_{nd}. Starting with a random population P of solutions, the individuals evolve to Pareto optimal solutions to be included in P_{nd}. The pseudo-code of the main MMA algorithm is shown in Fig. 4(a), while its codification is represented in Fig. 4(b).

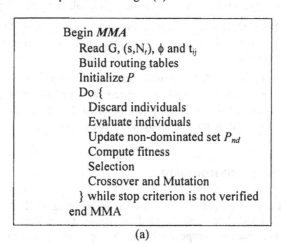

Begin *MMA*
    Read G, (s,N_r), ϕ and t_{ij}
    Build routing tables
    Initialize P
    Do {
        Discard individuals
        Evaluate individuals
        Update non-dominated set P_{nd}
        Compute fitness
        Selection
        Crossover and Mutation
    } while stop criterion is not verified
    end MMA

(a)

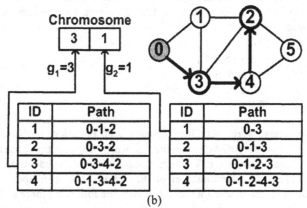

(b)

Fig. 4. (a) Pseudo-code of main MMA algorithm (b) Relationship between a chromosome, genes and routing tables for a tree with $s=0$ and $N_r=\{2, 3\}$.

The MMA algorithm begins reading the variables of the problem and basically proceeds as follows (see pseudo-code in Fig. 4(a)):

Build routing tables: For each $n_i \in N_r$, a routing table is built. It consists of the ψ shortest and ψ cheapest paths. ψ is a parameter of the algorithm. A chromosome is represented by a string of length $|N_r|$ in which each element (gene) g_i represents a path between s and n_j. See Fig. 4(b) to see a chromosome that represents the tree in Fig. 4(b).

Discard individuals: In P, there may be duplicated chromosomes. Thus, new randomly generated individuals replace duplicated chromosomes.

Evaluate individuals: The individuals of P are evaluated using the objective functions. Then, non-dominated individuals of P are compared with the individuals in P_{nd} to update the non-dominated set, removing from P_{nd} dominated individuals.

Compute fitness: Fitness is computed for each individual, using SPEA procedure [8].

Selection: Traditional tournament or roulette methods may be used [8]. In this works, a roulette selection operator is applied over the set $P_{nd} \cup P$ to generate the next evolutionary population P.

Crossover and Mutation: MMA uses two-point crossover operator over selected pair of individuals. Then, some genes in each chromosome of the new population are randomly changed (mutated), obtaining a new solution. The process continues until a stop criterion, as a maximum number of generations, is satisfied.

7 Experimental Environments

MOACS and MMA have been implemented on a 350 MHz AMD Athlon computer with a 128 MB of RAM. The compiler used was Borland C++ V 5.02.

In order to evaluate the proposed MOACS approach to a recently published algorithm as MMA [7], several test problems were used, but only two will be presented. Each test was divided into four sub-tests (or scenarios) where the networks are under different load level:

- low $(0 \le \alpha_{ij} \le 0.4)$,
- medium $(0.4 \le \alpha_{ij} \le 0.7)$,
- high $(0.7 \le \alpha_{ij} \le 0.9)$, and
- saturation $(0.9 \le \alpha_{ij} \le 1)$.

MMA parameters were: 40 chromosomes and mutation probability of 0.3, suggested in [7], while MOACS parameters were: 40 ant, 0.95 pseudo-random probability, 0.95 trail persistence. The runs stopped after 2000 generations.

For each sub-test an approximation of the Pareto Front corresponding to each multicast group is obtained using a procedure with the following three steps:

1) Each algorithm (MOACS & MMA) was run *ten times* to calculate average values.
2) A set solutions "Y" conformed by all solutions of both algorithms was calculated.
3) The dominated solutions were eliminated from "Y", and an approximation of "Y_{true}" was created.

7.1   Test Problem 1

The first test problem was the NSF network of Example 1, with ten multicast groups (MG) shown in Table 3.

The number of optimal solutions of the approximated Pareto Front Y_{true} is presented in Table 4, for each multicast group and load level.

Table 3. Multicast Groups for Test Problem 1.

MG*	$\{s\},\{N_r\}$	$|N_r|$
1	$\{0\},\{1,2,3,4,5,6,7,9,12,13\}$	11
2	$\{12\},\{0,1,2,4,5,6,8,9,11,13\}$	10
3	$\{0\},\{1,2,3,4,5,6,9,12,13\}$	9
4	$\{6\},\{4,8,10,11,12,13\}$	6
5	$\{4\},\{0,1,2,3,6,7,9,10,12,13\}$	10
6	$\{13\},\{0,1,2,3,4,5,6,7,8,9,10,11\}$	12
7	$\{12\},\{0,1,3,5,6,8,9,11,13\ \}$	9
8	$\{2\},\{0,4,5,7,9,10,12,13\}$	8
9	$\{5\},\{0,4,6,7,8,9,10,11,12\ \}$	9
10	$\{1\},\{0,7,8,9,12,13\}$	6

*MG = Multicast Group

Table 4. Number of Optimal Solutions in Y_{true} for each MG and load level for Test Problem 1.

MG	$|Y_{true}|$			
	Low	Half	High	Saturation
1	62	51	62	26
2	33	21	32	23
3	19	25	25	13
4	11	14	10	10
5	20	15	9	17
6	45	29	31	18
7	20	19	13	13
8	14	16	14	5
9	18	16	19	15
10	11	9	13	7

7.2   Test Problem 2

The second test was carried out using the NTT network topology [7] of Fig. 5, where a delay d_{ij} over each link (i,j) is shown. NTT network consists of 55 nodes and 144 links.

Multicast groups used in this test are shown in Table 5 and the number of optimal solutions of the approximated Pareto Front Y_{true} is presented in Table 6.

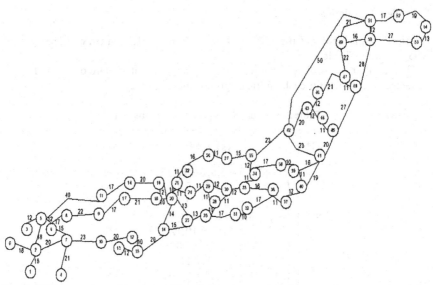

Fig. 5. NTT network used in test problem 2. Numbers over links represent propagation delay in ms.

Table 5. Multicast Groups for Test Problem 2.

MG	{s},{N_r}	$\lvert N_r \rvert$
1	{51},{0,3,4,8,13,15,16,22,30,31,40,41,44,47,50,54}	16
2	{48},{2,3,5,6,7,8,9,10,11,12,14,15,16,20,24,25,28,29,30,31,33,34,40,43,44,46,49,50,51,52,54}	31
3	{46},{0,3,5,6,7,12,14,15,16,17,20,23,24,26,28,29,31,32,34,35,37,39,47,48,50}	25
4	{26},{0,1,2,3,4,5,6,7,8,9,10,11,12,13,14,15,16,17,18,19,20,22,23,24,25,27,28,29,30,31,32,3334,35,36,37,38,39,40,41,42,43,44,45,46,47,49,50,51,52,53,54}	52
5	{36},{1,7,8,12,14,16,18,20,21,25,26,28,30,32,33,34,35,37,39,41,43,44,45,46,48,49,50,51,52,53,54}	31
6	{30},{0,5,10,12,15,25,29,31,36,42,44,46}	12
7	{13},{4,6,10,11,14,17,18,19,23,28,30,34,37,38,42,44,53}	17
8	{21},{0,1,3,4,5,6,7,8,9,10,11,12,13,14,15,17,18,19,20,22,23,24,25,26,27,28,30,31,32,33,34,35,36,38,39,41,42,43,44,46,47,48,49,50,51,52,53,54}	48
9	{51},{1,3,7,11,15,16,17,18,26,27,30,37,42,43,46,50,52}	17
10	{11},{1,4,5,6,9,10,12,15,16,17,19,20,22,23,27,29,30,31,32,34,35,36,37,38,39,40,42,43,45,4647,48,49,50,51,52,54}	37

Table 6. Numbers of Optimal Solutions Y_{true} for each MG and load level, for Test Problem 2.

MG	$|Y_{true}|$			
	Low	Half	High	Saturation
1	105	79	35	11
2	140	182	130	25
3	97	67	58	12
4	56	50	27	23
5	57	41	26	14
6	27	86	23	2
7	25	7	11	4
8	83	14	17	44
9	49	33	9	5
10	24	35	80	48

8   Experimental Results

Next, the experimental results for each test problem and different load levels are presented separately, comparing the results using the proposed MOACS to the corresponding results using MMA.

8.1 Test Problem 1

In these tests using the NSF network with 14 nodes and 42 links, it can be easily seen that in general MOACS outperforms MMA finding a larger number of Pareto solutions (see averages in Table 7). Only in column *"Average for each MG"* for multicast groups 4 (42 %) and 9 (49.25%) MMA may seem better than MOACS, but in the rest of the tests, MOACS is widely superior.

Table 7. Comparison of solutions in Y_{true} for each MG and load level, for Test Problem 1.

MG	Low		Medium		High		Saturation		Average for each MG	
	MOACS	MMA	MOACS	MMA	MOACS	MMA	MOACS	MMA	MOACS	MMA
1	80 %	1 %	96 %	0 %	86 %	0 %	100 %	0 %	90.50 %	0.25 %
2	27 %	1 %	28 %	21 %	3 %	44 %	100 %	0 %	39.50 %	24.50 %
3	95 %	1 %	96 %	0 %	88 %	2 %	94 %	0 %	93.25 %	0.75%
4	36 %	41 %	21 %	43 %	10 %	34 %	50 %	50 %	29.25 %	42 %
5	82 %	2 %	87 %	1 %	68 %	7 %	58 %	29 %	73.75 %	9.75 %
6	76 %	0 %	59 %	2 %	87 %	0 %	91 %	0 %	78.25 %	0.50 %
7	20 %	28 %	40 %	22 %	15 %	32 %	100 %	0 %	43.75 %	20.50 %
8	100 %	0 %	91 %	4 %	93 %	1 %	100 %	0 %	96 %	1.25 %
9	28 %	37 %	12 %	76 %	16 %	51 %	65 %	33 %	30.25 %	49.25 %
10	55 %	19 %	89 %	11 %	77 %	16 %	57 %	43 %	69.50 %	22.25 %
	Average for each Load Level								Global Average	
	60%	16%	62%	18%	54%	19%	82%	15%	*64.4%*	*17.1%*

8.2 Test Problem 2

In this seconds test, MOACS again demonstrates the best performance (see averages in Table 8). See in Table 8 column "*Average for each MG*", that only for multicast group 5 (15 %) MMA is superior. Also notice that in the "*Global Average*" MOACS calculated 40 % of Y_{true} solutions while MMA only found 3 %. Even more, considering "*Global Average*," MOACS achieved 67.2 % of Y_{true} solutions while MMA only reached 17.1 %.

Table 8. Comparison of Solutions with Y_{true} for each Multicast group and level load for test problem 2

MG	Low		Medium		High		Saturation		Average for each MG	
	MOACS	MMA	MOACS	MMA	MOACS	MMA	MOACS	MMA	MOACS	MMA
1	42 %	5 %	46 %	1 %	59 %	5 %	89 %	0 %	59 %	3 %
2	10 %	3 %	10 %	0 %	11 %	0 %	58 %	0 %	22 %	1 %
3	27 %	0 %	25 %	0 %	27 %	0 %	65 %	0 %	36 %	0 %
4	9 %	1 %	8 %	2 %	10 %	1 %	68 %	0 %	24 %	1 %
5	7 %	6 %	2 %	14 %	3 %	7 %	4 %	34 %	4 %	15 %
6	96 %	0 %	64 %	0 %	86 %	0 %	100 %	0 %	87 %	0 %
7	70 %	1 %	36 %	7 %	60 %	1 %	75 %	25 %	60 %	9 %
8	10 %	0 %	10 %	1 %	8 %	2 %	40 %	0 %	17 %	1 %
9	64 %	0 %	85 %	0 %	42 %	7 %	100 %	0 %	73 %	2 %
10	10 %	0 %	10 %	0 %	9 %	1 %	52 %	0 %	20 %	0 %
	Average for Load Level								*Global Average*	
	35 %	2 %	30 %	3 %	32 %	2 %	65 %	6 %	*40 %*	*3 %*

It can be concluded from Tables 7 and 8 that MOACS outperforms MMA for this type of MOP, finding a larger number of Pareto solutions.

From these experimental results, the following conjecture can be stated. ACO algorithms as MOACS build relatively good solutions using heuristic information (visibility) and avoiding not feasible solutions; therefore, in general, ACO algorithms are better suited for constructing good solution, compared to *Multiobjective Evolutionary Algorithms* – MOEAs [11] as MMA. However, the above algorithms are probabilistic; thus, MMA may eventually outperform MOACS, as shown in Table 8 (row 5 and column *Average for each MG*).

9 Conclusions

This paper introduces a new approach based on MOACS to solve the multicast routing problem. The proposed MOACS is able to optimize simultaneously four objective functions, such as, (1) maximum link utilization (α_m), (2) cost of the routing tree (C), (3) maximum end-to-end delay (D_m) and (4) average delay (D_a). This new proposal is able to solve a multicast routing problem in a truly multiobjective context, considering all four objectives at the same time, for the first time using an algorithm based on Ant Colony Optimization. The new approach calculates not only one possible solution, but a whole set of optimal Pareto solutions in only one run. This last feature is especially important since the most adequate solution can be chosen for each particular case without *a priori* restrictions that may eliminate otherwise good solutions. To validate the new approach, MOACS was compared to the MMA, a representative algorithm for solving the multicast routing problem in a truly multiobjective context, for Traffic Engineering. The experimental results showed that MOACS is able to find a larger number of Pareto solutions than MMA for different network topologies, different load level and various multicast groups, i.e. MOACS found better solutions in average than MMA.

As a future work, the authors will perform more tests over other network topologies and other metrics will be also considered to make sure that algorithms based on Ant Colonies are a promising approach for traffic engineering. At the same time, authors consider the study of convergence time for the proposed algorithm, as well as the control traffic load it causes.

References

1. A. Tanenbaum, Computer Networks, Prentice Hall 4° Edition, 2003.
2. Y. Seok, Y. Lee, Y. Choi, and C. Kim, "Explicit multicast routing algorithm for constrained traffic engineering", IEEE 7th International Symposium on Computer and Communications (ISCC'02). Italy, 2002.
3. Y. Donoso, R. Fabregat, and J. Marzo, "Multiobjective optimization algorithm for multicast routing with traffic engineering", IEEE 3rd International Conference on Networking (ICN'2004), Guadalupe, French Caribbean, March – 2004.
4. M. Schaerer, and B. Barán. "A Multiobjective Ant Colony System For Vehicle Routing Problem With Time Windows", IASTED International Conference on Applied Informatics, Innsbruck, Austria, 2003.
5. Y. Liu, and J. Wu. "The degree-constrained multicasting algorithm using ant algorithm" IEEE 10th International Conference on Telecommunications" 2003.
6. J. Gu, C. Chu, X. Hou, and Q. Gu. "A heuristic ant algorithm for solving QoS multicast routing problem" Evolutionary Computation, 2002. CEC '02. Volume 2, pp 1630-1635.
7. J. Crichigno, and B. Barán. "Multi-objective Multicast Routing Algorithm for Traffic Engineering" ICCCN'2004, California, USA, 2004.
8. E. Zitzler, and L. Thiele, "Multiobjective Evolutionary Algorithms: A comparative Case Study and the Strength Pareto Approach", IEEE Trans. Evolutionary Computation, Volume 3, No. 4, 1999, pp 257-271.
9. D. A. Van Veldhuizen. "Multiobjective Evolutionary Algorithms: Classifications, Analysis, and New Innovations", Ph.D Thesis, Graduated School of Engineering of the Air Force Institute of Technology, Air University, 1999.
10. M. Dorigo, and L. M. Gambardella. "Ant Colony System: A cooperative learning approach to the traveling salesman problem" IEEE Transactions on Evolutionary Computation, 1: 1, pp 53-66, 1997.
11. M. Guntsch and M. Middendorf. "*A Population Based Approach for ACO*". In Stefano Cagnoni, Jens Gottlieb, Emma Hart, Martin Middendorf, and Günther Raidl, *Applications of Evolutionary Computing, Proceedings of EvoWorkshops2002: EvoCOP, EvoIASP, EvoSTim*, Springer-Verlag ,vol. 2279, pp 71–80, Kinsale, Ireland, 2002.

A Survey of Application-level Multicast Group Communication and a Proposal for Intelligent Reflectors

Janine Kniess[1,2], Célio Vinicius N. Albuquerque [1]

1 Computer Science Institute, Federal Fluminense University (UFF)
Passos da Pátria Street, 156, São Domingos, Niterói – RJ, Brasil - Zip
Code 24.210- 240
{jkniess,celio}@ic.uff.br,
WWW home page: http://www.ic.uff.br
2 Computer Science Department, State University (UDESC)
Campus Universitário Prof. Avelino Marcante, Bom Retiro, Joinville-SC,
Brasil - Zip Code 89223-100
WWW home page: http://www.joinville.udesc.br

Abstract. The article proposes the state of the art in techniques and models designed to solve issues in application-layer IP multicast. Specifically, the issue of group communication for distributing video flows using reflectors to participants at a videoconference is considered. A proposed solution is introduced, involving an algorithm capable of dynamically discovering the appropriate reflector to meet a given client's needs. Simulations results show the efficiency of using reflectors in this type of application.

1 Introduction

As computer and network technologies have evolved, conditions have been created by which the transfer of multimedia data in real time can be supported. This means that the development of advanced applications, such as television and videoconferencing via the Internet, has become feasible.

Internet videoconferencing and TV belong to the category of group communication unlike others that are consisting of point-to-point conversations or file transfers. These new application often have a handful of sources and large number of receivers, and require large-scale video transmission. An efficient multicast service is required [1], since the use of multiple unicast channels is unfeasible in terms of bandwidth, and server processing, since the media, which are mainly audio and video, demand a variety of resources from the communications system.

Please use the following format when citing this chapter:

Kniess, J., Albuquerque, C.V.N., 2006, in IFIP International Federation for Information Processing, Volume 213, Network Control and Engineering for QoS, Security, and Mobility, V, ed. Gaïti, D., (Boston: Springer), pp. 117–126.

In traditional group communication, each node must have access to the native multicast service. Data travels over a data link once, and is replicated by intermediate routers in order to serve those clients who wish to receive the content. This approach is not scalable as it frequently floods the network with new trees of content distribution. Additionally, network-layer IP multicast is a restricted technology that is not yet widely deployed. Internet Service Providers (ISPs) are reluctant to deploy it because it is difficult to manage and because of the security issues involved with such an approach.

Recently, application-layer IP multicast has been used over the Internet to support multimedia applications. In this case, the end systems deploy and implement all group communication functions. Application-layer multicast improves the efficiency of one-to-many and many-to-many multi-destination communication and makes it possible for a huge reduction to be achieved in bandwidth requirements, proving advantageous in transmitting continuous media, especially high quality video.

Nevertheless, the features made available by application-layer multicast services are yet insufficient for the scaleable distribution of high quality multimedia data to a large number of clients [2]. In order to cope with the limitations in distributing advanced multimedia video applications, especially videoconferencing, media reflectors have been used.

In traditional video distribution systems, reflectors serve as proxies for the virtual multicast (or overlay) network that interconnect the participants in a multimedia conference located in different local networks. Reflectors allow for a more efficient use of the available bandwidth since packets (video, audio and data) are simply sent along data tunnels that link up two reflectors. Additionally, the topology of the reflector network takes into account the geography and bandwidth available at each link of the network, optimizing their available paths.

In view of the benefits gained by using reflectors for distributing multimedia data to multicast groups on the Internet, this article introduces an algorithm capable of dynamically encountering an adjusted configuration for the more appropriate reflector for one or more participants in a multicast group that wish to receive video content and the deployment of mobile agents located in machines close to the clients, which would serve temporarily as reflectors.

Experiments with reflectors performed in simulations are presented with the goal of demonstrating the reduction in the average delay in the delivery of video data packets as the number of reflectors is increased, or as these reflectors become more "intelligent"; i.e. a mobile reflectors replicating the code of the reflector server to a specific point in the network close to the client or group of participating clients. The most recent achievements in the area of application-layer multicast group communication are also presented; i.e. techniques and models.

The paper is organized as follows. Section 2 sets out the techniques for providing group communication services currently available, designed to circumvent the distribution problems encountered in multicast routing. Section 3 presents the main studies related into application-layer IP multicast. In section 4, the deployment of a video broadcasting multimedia application using application-layer multicast is presented. The same section also contains the results obtained in the simulation. Section 5 presents conclusions and future studies.

2   Alternative Techniques for Multicast Group Communication Services

The efficiency of a control technique for group communication depends upon its satisfying factors such as robustness, security, scalability, performance and dynamic reconfiguration to discover new transmitters or receivers. The techniques described in this section are designed to provide solutions for the limitations encountered in group communication using IP multicast.

Unicast/multicast reflectors and a individual data tunnels: As stated by [3] and [4], in this approach, a reflector acts as a gateway between a network with multicast capacity (e.g. Mbone [5]) and a set of unicast hosts. Each multicast packet in a network is delivered to each unicast host and other unicast hosts, creating tunnels between the reflector and the end hosts. One shortcoming of this model is that it creates hot spots in the network in the proximity of the reflector.

Permanent data tunnels: Tunnels are deployed at the routing level and make use of IP encapsulation. [6]. They require access to privileged information to be deployed and are not generally updated by the end host. The tunnels are totally integrated into the multicast routing and provide connectivity between all the possible multicast groups. Mrouted DVMRP [7] is the most widely used solution for this approach.

Gossiping-based solutions for peer-to-peer communication: Within the context of overlay networks, the gossiping technique as set out in [8] can be used for data distribution. Each member of the group periodically sends a message containing a list of their neighbors. Each node builds up knowledge about the members of the group by hops. Thus, one node can have complete knowledge about the group. For very large groups, the periodic messages can cause considerable overheads. Additionally, the view that nodes in a large group have of the group is restricted to their neighbors.

Communication routing services for a specific group: The main feature here is that the routing services for group communication are established inside one of the routers. The drawback is that this service cannot be distributed on demand by end users. Two models, XCAST [9] and DCM [10], provide solutions for the limited scalability inherent to this technique. AMRoute [11], DMRP [12] and MAODV [13] set out protocols which permit the use of IP multicast in mobile ad hoc networks.

Automatic Overlay Multicast: Here, the multicast support for the central routers is shifted to the end systems. The end systems deploy all the functionalities of the group communication. Other models presented in [6, 14, 15, 16], among others, have been developed with this principle as their basis.

2.2   Discussions and Prospects

The techniques described above can be used in environments where traditional multicast routing is entirely inappropriate, such as ad hot networks or in cases where there are a large number of small, dynamic groups. For this reason, many models have been developed based on these techniques. Given the advantages brought by overlay multicast, which include its simple configuration, flexible implementation and the customization of some attributes, such as data transcoding, error recovery, flow control, scaling, management and security of different messages, this technique has become the subject of much research and is being used as a basis for the development of new models.

In the following section, we present the state-of-the-art in multicast solutions that use overlay multicast. Within the scope of this work, this choice can be justified by the fact that this approach has achieved satisfactory results in video on demand applications, such as videoconferencing.

3   Related Work

A considerable number of projects have explored implementing multicast at the application layer. They can be classified into two broad categories: mesh-first (NARADA [15], CANs [17] and SCRIBE [7]) and tree-first protocols (Yoid [18], ALMI [14] and Host Multicast Tree Protocol (HMTP) [19]). In the tree-first protocols, the participants construct a covering tree and organize themselves around the same one. At the same time they keep links of control for some neighboring members of the tree and, use these links of control to reorganize the covering tree. On the other hand, in the mesh-first, the participants use periodic measured who allow detecting the best ways to organize themselves in a mesh through the selection of the best links. A definite time this mesh, applies a guiding algorithm multicasting to determine one or more trees of covering.

Yoid and HMTP defines a distributed tree building protocol between the end-hosts, while ALMI uses a centralized algorithm to create a minimum spanning tree rooted at a designated single source of multicast data distribution. One shortcoming of the model is that the centralized algorithm is entirely responsible for controlling the data path. If the algorithm fails in some way, all the operations related to the group may be put in jeopardy. The Overcast protocol [16] organizes a set of proxies (called Overcast nodes) into a distribution tree rooted at a central source for a single source multicast. In order to obtain specific content, a client is referred to a URL containing the address of the parent of the group, plus the name of the resource. The parent selects the most appropriate content server in the tree and redirects it to the client in a way that is transparent to the user.

The aim of the algorithm in an Overcast tree is to optimize the parent node's bandwidth for all the other nodes. In order to do so, the algorithm includes a new node as far as possible from the parent node, without affecting its bandwidth.

A distributed tree-building protocol is used to create this source specific tree, in a manner similar to Yoid.

NARADA, ALMI and CANs are designed for medium-sized groups. NARADA keeps a complete list of all the group members. NICE [20], HMTP, Overcast, and SCRIBE are designed for large-sized groups. The CANs protocol can be expanded to support large multicast groups. In CANs, heuristics are used to minimize the number of duplicate messages forwarded. This is achieved by the storage in cache of the message identifications received. Cache which obtained by storing the identifiers of the message received in a cache. Thanks to this, no duplicate message is forwarded. Some projects (CANs) and Pastry [21]) have also addressed the scalability issue in creating application layer overlays. CANs defines a set of end hosts implement a hash table on an Internet-wide scale for storing two member peers (i,j). The nodes are distributed into coordinate space, in which each member is the owner of their space. Patry is a self-organizing overlay network of nodes, where logical peer relationships on the overlay are based on matching prefixes of the node identifiers. Scribe is a large-scale event notification infrastructure that leverages the Pastry system to create groups and build efficient application layer multicast paths to the group members for dissemination of data on groups based on publish-subscribe. NICE also chooses overlay peers based on network locality which leads to low stretch end-to-end paths.

We summarize the above as follows: For both NICE and CANs, members maintain constant state for other members, and consequently exchange a constant amount of periodic refreshes messages. This overlay paths for NICE and SCRIBE, have a logarithmic number os application level hops, and path lengths in CANs asymptotically have a larger number os application level hops.

3.2   Analysis and Comparison of the Overlay Multicast Protocols Described

The models set out above have the main advantage of not requiring any support from network routers. Thus, overlay networks are particularly attractive for managing multicast group communication, as they improve scalability in terms of the number of concurrent groups, and allow for the creation of a robust communication system in a variety of different types of application (e.g. peer-to-peer and ad hoc networks). Other models which are no less relevant to application-layer multicast, but which are not included in this paper, can be found at, SHDC [22], ZIGZAG [23] and Bayeux [24].

In the simulation model presented below, we apply the ideas introduced in this article to construct a distributed multimedia application in C++ and show that the use of reflectors can reduce the mean end-to-end delay between nodes in the network that are receiving multimedia content. In this specific example, the content being transmitted is video.

4   Intelligent Reflectors: Simulation Model and Results

In order to simulate scenarios similar to the worldwide web, the network simulator ns-2 [25] was used together with the topology generator Georgia Tech Internetworking Topology Models (GT-ITM) [26]. This generates network topologies similar to the Internet. In this study, GT-ITM was used to generate a 100-node (1-100) transit-stub topology with one transit domain. The Transit-Stubs model does not currently support representation of the host systems. Thus, all nodes are of the same type and produces connected sub-graphs by repeatedly generating a graph according to the edge count, and checking the graph for connectivity.

We choose 4 groups of clients from this topology to make up the overlay network, which would in turn provide the multipoint communication through point-to-point channels. Any node in the network, with the exception of the reflectors (that they are selected with a circle), could act as a video distribution source. For the purpose of simulation, one chose the node of number 54 as source and nodes (14, 58, 63 and 93) as reflectors.

Figure 1 illustrates the topology generated using GT-ITM.

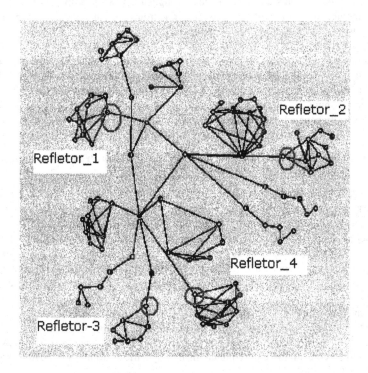

Fig. 1. Topology generated using GT-ITM

In the first simulation, just one reflector was used to forward a video stream using the IP multicast to the groups of clients. The same experiment was repeated, though each time new reflectors were added; in total, experiments were performed using 1, 2, 3 and 4 reflectors. In the experiments, the reflectors were the node closest to the backbone of the network, as shown in Figure 1. The simulator was configured to transmit a video stream at 2Mbps for a 15-minute period (900 s). The capacity of link is of 5 Mbps, the transmission delay is of 1.6 ms and the delay between links varies of 20 up to 490 (ms).

The graph in Figure 2 shows the results obtained for the average delay in the communication between the participant nodes for the different number of reflectors.

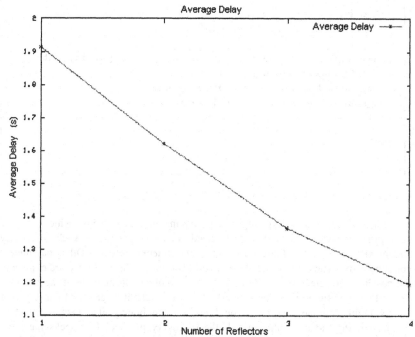

Fig. 2. Relation between average delay and the number of reflectors

This graph shows that as more reflectors are deployed in the network, the average delay is reduced. With reflectors, the video distribution source is not overloaded in terms of bandwidth, while the presence of reflectors makes the system more scalable and tolerant of failures.

In this study, it was observed that a support protocol for the dynamic discovery of reflectors was lacking. For example, in a videoconferencing system, users may be added and removed, and there are other features typical of group communication. This article explores the feasibility of using an algorithm which discovers the most appropriate reflector the moment a request is received by a client to receive video content. Figure 3 presents this algorithm.

```
//client requests access to the videoconference (join)
//search for the most suitable reflector in the reflector
//list ...
list<unsigned> ::interator i = listReflectors.begin();
while (i != listReflectors.end()){
//search for the reflector with the lowest load and
//ascertain whether the number of
//videoconference users has exceeded the maximum limit
```

```
if (value_Load <=(*ptr)->Load && maxUsers<=(*ptr)->MAX ){
...
//Add one channel to the reflector
init_reflect_sockets(channels);
...
//ascertain that the host is not already a participant
if!(inChannel(channel, verif)){
//add host to the communication channel
add_host_to_channel (channel,verif);
...}
...
}...
}
```

Fig. 3. Algorithm – Discovery most Appropriate Reflector

The reflector discovery algorithm dynamically ascertains which is the appropriate reflector to meet the client's needs, based on parameters such as capacity and maximum number of users present at the videoconference. Other parameters could be added, such as estimated delay and bandwidth. Currently, we are exploring the possibility of creating mobile reflectors, i.e. replicating the code of the reflector server to a specific point in the network close to the client or group of participating clients. In this case, new machines could install the mobile agent and act as reflectors to transmit the video. In this model, the discovery protocol first seeks the most suitable reflector, should the user be geographically very distant from the reflectors already established, or should they be unable to serve the client at the time that they make the request.

5   Conclusions and Future Studies

In this article, the latest achievements, techniques and models, in the area of application-layer multicast group communication have been presented. Furthermore, in section 3, this article proposes and shows the benefits of using reflectors to forward video streams for the practical deployment of application-layer video broadcasting. The results showing a reduction of the mean video delivery delay in the network are promising such as a reduced mean delay between the nodes in the network, are promising.

As a future improvement of this work to include the results of simulations using the reflector discovery protocol, how the clients subscribe the suitable reflector and the deployment of mobile agents located in machines close to the clients, which would serve temporarily as reflectors on an on-demand basis.

6   References

1. L. Costa, S. Fdida and O. Duarte, Hop by Hop Multicast Routing Protocol, ACM SIGCOMM'01, San Diego, CA, Aug. 2001.

2. F. Kon , R. H. Campbell and K. Nahrstedt, Using dynamic configuration to manage a scalable multimedia distribution system, Computer Communications Journal (Special Issue on QoS-Sensitive Distributed Systems and Applications), vol. 24, pp. 105-123, Jan, 2001.

3. R. Finlayson, The UDP Multicast Tunneling Protocol, work in progress, draft-finlaysonumtp- 07.txt, Sept. 2002.

4. P. Parnes, K. Synnes and D. Schefstrom, Lightweight Application Level Multicast Tunneling Using Mtunnel, Computer Communication, vol. 21, no. 15, Apr 1998.

5. K. C. Almeroth and K. Sarac, Monitoring IP Multicast in the Internet: Recent Advances and Ongoing Challenges, IEEE Communications Magazine. October 2005.

6. A. El-Sayed, V. Roca and Laurent Mathy, A Survey of Proposals for an Alternative Group Communication Service, IEEE Network, Jan 2003.

7. D. Thaler et al. IPv4 Automatic Multicast without Explicit Tunnels (AMT), work in progress: draft-ietf-mboned-auto-multicast-01.txt, Apr. 2002.

8. M. Castro, P. Druschel, A-M. Kermarrec and A. Rowstron, SCRIBE: A large-scale and decentralized application-level multicast infrastructure, IEEE Journal on Selected Areas in Communications (JSAC) (Special issue on Network Support for Multicast Communications), 2002.

9. R. Boivie et al. Explicit Multicast (Xcast) Basic Specification, work in progress, draftooms- xcast-basic-spec-03.txt, June 2002.

10. L. Blazevic and J.-Y. Le Boudec, Distributed Core Multicast (dcm): A Multicast Routing Protocol for Many Groups with Few Receivers, ACMSIG-COMM Computer Communications, vol. 29, no. 5, Oct. 1999.

11. M. Liu, R. Talpade, and A. McAuley, Amroute: Adhoc Multicast Routing Protocol, Technical Report. TR 99-8, CSHCN, (unpublished), 1999.

12. S-J. Lee, W. Su and M. Gerla, On-Demand Multicast Routing Protocol (ODMRP) for Ad Hoc Networks, IETF Internet Draft, work in progress, 2002.

13. S.-J. Lee et al. A Performance Comparison Study of Ad Hoc Wireless Mul-ticast Protocols, IEEE INFOCOM 2000, Mar. 2000.

14. D. Pendarakis, S. Shi, D. Verma and M. Waldvogel, ALMI: An application level multicast infrastructure. Proceedings of the 3rd, USENIX Symposium on Internet

Technologies and Systems (USITS '01), pp. 49-60, mar 2001.

15. C. Abad, W. Yurcik and R. H. Campbell, A Survey and Comparison of End-System Overlay Multicast Solutions Suitable for Network Centric Warfare, (December, 2005); http://www.citeseer.ist.psu.edu/735587.html.

16. J. Jannotti et al. Overcast: Reliable Multicasting with an Overlay Network, In Proc. Of OSDI, October 2000.

17. S. Ratnasamy, M. Handley, R. M. Karp and S. Shenker, Application-Level Multicast Using Content-Addressable Networks, Proceedings of the Third International COST264, isbn: 3-540-42824-0, pp. 14-29. 2001.

18. P. Francis, Yoid: Your own internet distribution, Technical report, ACIRI, (unpublished), (April, 2000); http://www.aciri.org/yoid.

19. B. Zhang and S. Jamin and L. Zhang, Host multicast: A framework for delivering multicast to end users, In Proceedings of IEEE Infocom, June 2002.

20. S. Banerjee, B. Bhattacharjee and C. Kommareddy, Scalable Application Layer Multicast, ACM SIGCOMM '02, Pittsburgh, PA, Aug. 2002.

21. A. Rowstron and P. Druschel, Pastry: Scalable, distributed object location and routing for large-scale peer-to-peer systems, IFIP/ACM International Conference on Distributed Systems Platforms (Middleware), pp. 329-350, November, 2001.

22. L. Mathy, R. Canonico and D. Hutchison, An Overlay Tree Building Con-trol Protocol, 3rd Int'l. Wksp. Networked Group Communication, Nov. 2001.

23. D. Tran, K. Hua, and T. Do, ZIGZAG: An Efficient Peer-to-Peer Scheme for Media Streaming, IEEE INFOCOM, 2003.

24. S. Zhuang et al. Bayeux: An Architecture for Scalable and Fault-Tolerant Wide-Area Data Dissemination, Proceedings of NOSSDAV, June 2001.
25. S. McCanne and S. Floyd, The Network Simulator-ns-2. (January, 2006); http://www.isi.edu/nsnam/ns.

26. E.W. Zegura, K. Calvert and S. Bhattacharjee, How to Model an Internetwork, IEEE Infocom, 1996.

Towards autonomic networking and self-configurating routers
The integration of autonomic agents

Thomas Bullot[1,2] and Dominique Gaiti[1]
(thomas.bullot@utt.fr) (dominique.gaiti@utt.fr)

(1) - ICD - FRE CNRS 2848, Université de Technologie de Troyes,
BP2060, 10010 Troyes cedex, France.
(2) - GINKGO-Networks, 8 rue du capitaine Scott 75015 Paris

Abstract. IP Networks, and particularly the Internet, were proposed to be a simple and robust support for heterogeneous communications. This implies that only basic controls have to be done by network elements. Connection management, along with transport, and more generally communication management, has to be done by the terminals. For example, error detection mechanisms, error recovery mechanisms with "Slow Start", are implemented within the transport protocol, managed by the terminals. However, integration of new services and increasing need for QoS require the network to be more and more flexible and adaptive. New algorithms and protocols are then proposed to address these issues, and include new configuration layers. Manual configuration of such network architectures is then very complex, if not impossible. We think that future core network elements will have to be more adaptive, but also more autonomic. Auto-configuration is indeed a necessary condition to integrate new services in the network. We believe that auto-configuration requires new knowledge provisioning and computing policies. This paper then presents an architecture of software agents, collaborative and autonomic. These agents are embedded inside the routers. Their role is to share local and situated knowledge, in order to control and optimize the existing control mechanism of the router.

1 Introduction

Since several years, evolution of networks includes the integration of new services. This achievement implies the setting of different features and tools. On one hand,

Please use the following format when citing this chapter:

Bullot, T., Gaiti, D., 2006, in IFIP International Federation for Information Processing, Volume 213, Network Control and Engineering for QoS, Security, and Mobility, V, ed. Gaïti, D., (Boston: Springer), pp. 127–142.

new control mechanisms (traffic engineering, QoS, security, etc...) are then proposed. On another hand, a new perspective of network evolution, more and more present in the discussions, is autonomy. It refers on creating a network that has self-configuring, self-healing, self-optimizing, and self-protecting features [IBM03], in order to adapt to new situations in the context.

To achieve these issues, the new mechanisms need a huge quantity of numeric and/or symbolic knowledge. Provisioning, computing and representation of this knowledge are for now achieved separately at a very low level by each existing control mechanism. We think that high level information cannot be provisioned at a larger scale by existing mechanisms, because this knowledge is complex, and it has to be more specifically provisioned.

This paper presents an architecture of software agents, collaborative and autonomic [FER99]. These agents are embedded inside the routers. Their role is to share local and situated knowledge, in order to control and optimize the existing control mechanism of the router. Our work is based and inspired by several papers in the literature, including [MES03] which proposes a multi-agent based architecture to share knowledge and control DiffServ; [MER03] which presents a 2 layer end-to-end adaptive monitoring mechanism based on collaborative agents. In a similar field, [BIE98] proposes to base the network management on a mobile agent system.

We first describe in section 2 the internal basis structure of an agent. In the third section are described the interfaces of this agent with its environment. In the end, last section proposes an application of this technology to control and optimize the routing algorithm OSPF, using high-level, local, and situated elements of knowledge. The steps of the conception of an agent are not detailed in this paper.

2   Basis structure of an agent

An agent is made of a decision core and several modules (fig. 1). Decision core is the kernel of the application. It is based on synchronous execution of several "behavior units", and is able to compute received data and observed data, in order to decide of an action.

Modules are the sensors and effectors of the agent. These are interfaces with the environment of the agent, which allows the behavior units to observe a given part of the functional environment (reading an element in a MIB, receiving inter-agent messages, etc...), and act on it (configuring equipments, send inter-agent messages, reporting events to the network operator, etc...).

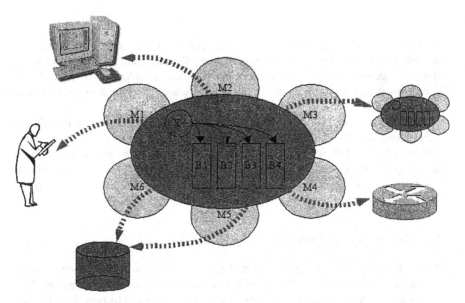

Fig. 1.   The agent within its environment

In this section the decision core and the modules mechanism are described in details.

2.1   Decision core

The decision core is based on one or more behavior units. These units are execution units, synchronized by an internal timer. They are executed in a given order, at a fixed rate.

There are three different kinds of behavior units:

- Observation and listening units, which are able to gather information about network elements and neighbor agents ;
- Computing units, which extract useful information from the data gathered by observation units, and compute a "good" decision for the network element configuration ;
- Action units, which apply actions decided by the computing units.

These are executed sequentially, in order to plan mechanisms over several behavior units. Decisions are taken after information was collected. Each one of these behavior units can access the modules they want. Actions decided by these units can use primitives of available modules ("send a message", "check a mailbox", "set a parameter", etc...). Each of these can access the controlled equipment, send messages to the neighbors, and update a remote database.

2.2 Modules

Modules are interfaces between an agent and its environment. Primitives are described and behavior units can access them. Development of these modules is strictly separated from the development of the application. It depends on environment (architecture, hardware, technical means, etc...) and on primitives to provide.

For example, the primitive « send a message » of a communication module can either: open a TCP connection with a neighbor to send an ACL message; send a simple string in UDP, without opening any connection; send an only Ethernet frame including the whole desired information; invoke a Java-RMI method on a remote agent; etc... There is a huge amount of possibilities. On the agent side, only the functionality is seen.

2.3 Needed support features

When building the different agent behaviors, one will need some basic functionalities (change a configuration parameter on the controlled equipment, send a message to a peer agent, etc...). These functionalities have to be provided to agents by the primitives of available modules. These modules, then, use some primitives in the controlled equipments (where the agent is embedded). If the agent, for example, has to be able to communicate with peers, it will need a communication module, which in turn will be based on available primitives in the equipment (a router with a UDP transport layer, for example).

3 Agent interfaces

These interfaces are classified in 3 categories (fig. 2): Agent-router interfaces, agent-agent interfaces, agent-human interfaces.

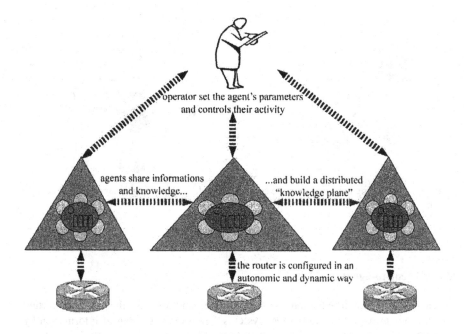

Fig. 2.   Interfaces between the agent and its environment

3.1   Agent-to-router interface

The agent-to-router interface is the most important interface: it allows the agent to control routing and QoS functions in the router.

This could be a local interface, if agents are embedded within routers (fig. 4); it could also be a remote interface, if agents cannot be embedded within routers (fig. 3). In any case, it can be based on IP-level protocols (telnet connection, SNMP, etc...).

Accessing the router parameters can be done in command lines via a telnet connection, or by consulting MIB databases. Generally, gathering data can be done within 2 modes: polling (active gathering of information from the router) or trap reception (alarm messages sent by the router when a threshold is reached).

Accessing the configuration always depends on the application. It could even not be necessary, when applications do not need to re-configure the router (i.e. monitoring applications). If it is necessary, it can be done in command lines via the router shell, or via specific configuration protocols like netconf.

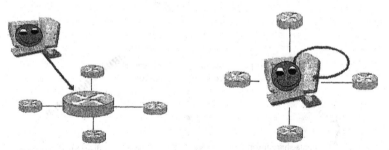

Fig. 3.   Deploying the agent : remote control   **Fig. 4.**   Deploying the agent : local control
agent   agent

3.2   Agent-to-agent interface

Agent-to-agent communication is a key issue, and one of the most important innovations provided by multi-agent systems. Transversal sharing of information by agents allows one to build a global distributed "knowledge plane". Each agent can build its own situated view of the network state. Addition of these different situated view results in what one can call a distributed knowledge plane. The situatedness of agent knowledge is a key point in our architecture: it ensures that our system can be scalable.

This transversal, peer-to-peer, and not hierarchical communication model is an answer to one of the most important issues in the domain of networks: how to build and maintain a global network state representation, without being stopped by scalability problems? Building in real time a unique and centralized view of the network is only possible in very small networks. On the contrary, if one accepts that this representation is not centralized, not always complete and deterministic; our architecture is a suitable answer.

In order to exchange data in a coherent way, a suitable representation of these data has to be adopted. On the suitability of this model will depend the efficiency of the application. It is necessary for example to find an adequate level of granularity.

Exchange protocols can also be a key issue of an application. Depending on the kind of protocol used, one can sometimes with very few messages exchange a huge amount of information. These protocols also have to be extremely robust: each agent has to be autonomic; it is a key quality of our system! The stability of an agent can never rely on the reception of a message. Every situation must be faced and managed. One should avoid explicit requests. Instead, one way information messages are preferred.

3.3   Agent-to-human interface

Technically, the agent-to-human interface is not a crucial interface. However, it's necessary for a human operator to observe and influence the evolution of the system. Monitoring facilities can be very precise, in order to allow a human operator to understand and validate or invalidate some of the agent-decisions in real time. On the contrary, it can be a very synthetic high-level monitoring, to observe the evolutions of the agents.

Agent configuration, in the same way, can either be very synthetic at a high level or more technical at a lower level. It should generally not be too precise, because if the agents are so difficult to configure as the network itself, utility of these agents is much reduced. Ideally, configuration of the agents should be down automatically by the agents themselves. To achieve this kind of auto-configuration skills, the agent has to be built to need as less information as possible. Its efficiency will always rely on the amount of information it's got to build a representation of the network, but it has to be working with very few information.

4   Automatic configuration of OSPF protocol using such agents

An example of agents applying on network functionality is auto-configuration of OSPF protocol.

OSPF is a dynamic routing protocol. As a routing protocol, it is a task achieved by all of the routers in the network. As it is dynamic, it should be done depending on the context and the local environment of nodes. Because of these 2 reasons, this example is a good application for our agent architecture.

The work of the agent consists in observing the current situation, and applying OSPF parameters reconfigurations, in real time.

4.1   Principles

OSPF is a dynamic routing protocol, which computes in real time all the routing tables depending on the weight affected to each interface. One route will be chosen to send packets from one point to another if the sum of the weights of each used interface in this route is minimal in the network.

Interface weights are then a key issue for choosing routes in OSPF. Choosing these weights is a complex issue. Many works refer to the general routing problem. [BER92] proposes a set of solutions to this problem, and [WAN99] studies different versions of this problem. The particular OSPF weight setting problem, on the contrary, has been proven to be NP-Hard [FOR00], and many heuristics has been proposed to address it. A generally accepted heuristic to choose these weights was proposed by Cisco [CIS98]: the weight of an interface should be proportional to the inverse of the capacity of that interface. Very capable interfaces are then more used than less capable interfaces. However, this heuristic doesn't take in account topology and current load of links, and sometimes causes misuse of small external links and overload of big main interior links.

A lot of works on the OSPF Weight Setting Problem [FOR00], and particularly using techniques based on artificial intelligence [ERI01], encountered a reasonable success [YE02], but it is often about off-line optimization techniques, based on such pieces of information that "demand matrix", which are very often unavailable.

How, then, to choose a "good" configuration of OSPF weights, at execution time, depending on topology and the current state of the system, without encountering scalability problems (i.e. with no centralized computing).

To address this issue, we propose our autonomic agent architecture. As far as we know, no work before has addressed this problem using multi-agent systems. At a fixed rate, agents observe the state of the different interfaces of their controlled router. They then broadcast a representation of that information to their neighbors. Each agent is informed of the load of its interfaces and of the state of its neighbors. It will then be able to recompute the weight of its interfaces.

4.2   Agents behavior

The implemented behavior can decide of 2 independent actions: on one hand, it can decide to change the weight of one of its interfaces; on the other hand, it has to decide what the new weight to set is. These decisions have to be separated, because changing a weight causes the whole network to be flooded with the topology with the new weights, and all the routing tables to be recomputed. It is important then to decide very rarely to change the weights. This decision can rely of different pieces of information as the new weight to set.

The choice of interface weights is based on the current load of these interfaces, and on the state of the routers directly linked to these. It's indeed very important, before deciding to redirect more traffic on an interface, to see if the adjacent router to this interface is already loaded or not.

In the following example (fig. 5), router-agent O has to choose OSPF weights of its interfaces. Available information is showed on the figure: the load of each one of its interfaces (cursors near each interface), and the state of nodes directly linked to these interfaces (color of the nodes). In this case, router-agent O has to set a weight to 3 interfaces, numbered from 1 to 3. For the interface 1, the current load of the interface is high, and the adjacent router (A) is in a "critical" state (red). Agent O's decision will then surely tend to increase the weight of this interface, in order to reduce the traffic passing through it. For interface 2, the load is high, but the state of the adjacent router (B) is "good" (green), so one can guess that the weight of this interface can remain the same. For interface 3, the load is low and the state of the adjacent router is "good", then the decision may be to decrease the weight associated to this interface.

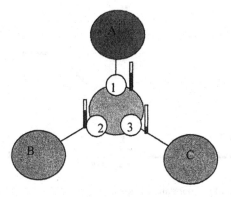

Fig. 5.   An example of a weight setting situation

On the contrary, deciding to effectively change the weights of the interfaces in a router (and, then, to reset the whole OSPF protocol in the network) does not rely directly on the load of interfaces, but on the global state of the router. This state takes in account the load of interfaces (max load, average load, etc...) and an evaluation of the state of environment (state of the neighbor routers). To avoid multiple OSPF resets at the same time in the same neighborhood, each agent sends an "I reset!" message to all its neighbors (on 1, or 2, or 3 hops). Multiple resets in a same neighborhood could indeed cause oscillation and strongly decrease the performance in the network. To avoid these problems, we also propose to take into account 2 kinds of influences: stabilizing influences and destabilizing influences. A positive state of the neighbors is a stabilizing influence. In the contrary, negative state of the neighbors is a destabilizing influence. Heavy load of an interface is a destabilizing influence, when light load of an interface is a stabilizing influence.

To avoid oscillation around a not-perfect-but-optimal configuration, we included within the agent behavior a habituation phenomenon. That means that a data has no sense by its own. Each data taken into account by the agent is pre-computed to compare it with previous identical data, to know if it is "particularly high", "normally high", "surprisingly high", etc... More precisely, each data is compared with its minimum, its maximum, and its average. This pre-computing is done by normalization (fig.6). Our normalization is done with the following system:

$Xnorm = [(X - Xmin)/Xavg]*0.5$ if $0 \le X < Xavg$

$Xnorm = 0.5 + [(X - Xavg)/Xmax]*0.5$ if $Xavg \le X < Xmax$

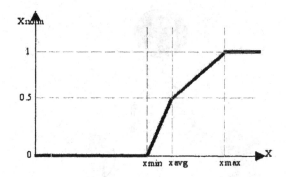

Fig. 6.   A representation of our normalizing operation

5   The simulation conditions

5.1   Motivations

The main motivation of this simulation is to show how the system works, and what its objectives are. This is definitely not a performance test, and one should take into account mechanisms, and not values. Values are given as a piece of illustration information. For the same reasons, the simulated traffic is uniform.

5.2   Data

The network topology used in our simulation (fig. 7) represents a network that is similar to the one of the British operator British Telecom. This topology has been chosen because it represents a network that is technically credible, highly meshed, with enough nodes. The nodes are distant enough (distance up to 5 hops between 2 nodes).

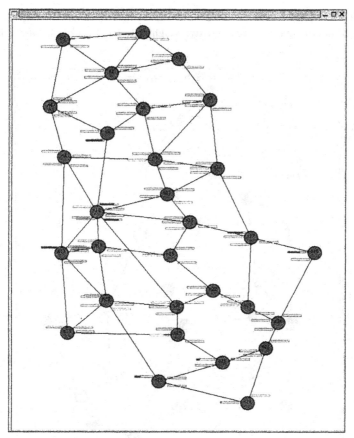

Fig. 7.   Topology used in this simulation

The traffic introduced is not even a nearly realistic traffic model. Every node in the model sends a uniform traffic stream to each other node in the network. The only aim is to overload the network, in order to push the agent system to try and find an optimal solution.

5.3   Simulation results

Given results are to study qualitatively. Our main evaluation criteria in a given instant is the number of overloaded interfaces at this instant. We just consider that, approximatively, the global load of the network is linked with the number of overloaded interfaces. This hypothesis is not exactly true, because an overloaded interface can reject a huge number of packets, when two overloaded interfaces can be just a little bit overloaded, and reject a very few packets... However, this is not the most common situation, and even if our results "only" show a very remarkable tendency of reducing the number of overloaded interfaces, one can think that we found a way to compute "good" weights in OSPF.

A first test allows us to observe the OSPF behavior without any agents (fig.8), configured following the Cisco heuristic: weight(interface) = 1/capacity(interface).

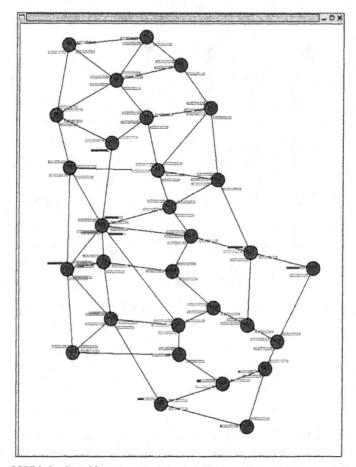

Fig. 8.   OSPF behavior without any agent

One can see that 6 interfaces are overloaded. One in node n5, two in node n10, one in node n13, one in node n17, and one in node n18. These interfaces are clearly overloaded, and the other interfaces are not.

When activating agents, one can observe a few transitive phases (fig.9). Duration of these phases is not studied here. Our aim in further studies will be to obtain duration of a transitive state that is proportional to the "stability" of the configuration (cf. stabilizing and destabilizing influences, in previous part). One data to study will also be the number of these transitive states. It has been told in previous parts that the cost of resetting OSPF is very high. It is capital to reduce the number of these resets at its minimum, and to converge as quickly as possible to a stable state.

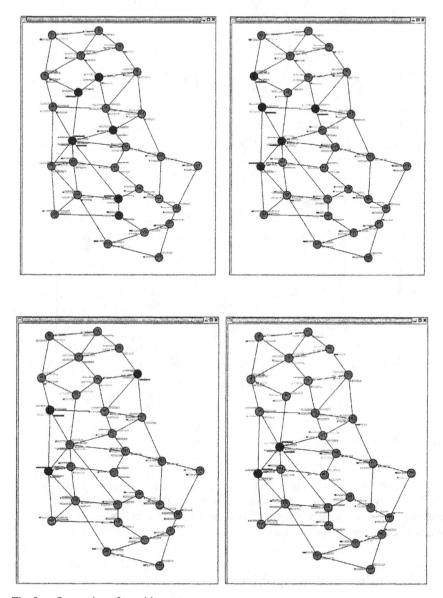

Fig. 9.   Succession of transitive states

Then, one can observe a succession of stable states. Stability of these states relies on the state of all agents in the network. Agents are influencing each other, and push to a stabilization of the global system. An example of a stable state is represented in fig. 10.

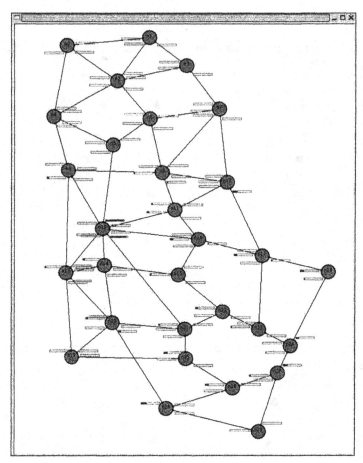

Fig. 10. An example of a stable state

One can observe on this example that, even if the situation is stable, not everything is perfect: the node n10 has two overloaded interfaces. Thanks the habituation phenomenon, the agent on node n10 considers that the situation is rather positive, and adopts a positive state.

6   Conclusions and perspectives

IP networks, and particularly the Internet, are supposed to be simple and robust. Integration of new differentiated services new functionalities implies adding new configuration layers. These new layers become quickly too complex, and require a huge amount of high-level knowledge, that cannot be provided by standard exchange protocols. As a consequence, new functionalities, not optimally configured, are either under-exploited or even not used at all.

Facing this result, we propose a simple and robust architecture of autonomic and collaborative agents, which role is to share local and situated information, in order to build a global distributed knowledge plane. In a distributed environment like a network, distributed computing approaches (from Artificial Intelligence) like multi-agent systems ideally fit. Sharing their situated views of the environment, agents are building locally a representation of their environment in order to decide elementary configuration actions. We assert that providing such high-level situated knowledge to the control mechanisms will open the way to new smart control heuristics. These heuristics shall be less deterministic, and more based on fuzzy/uncertain global knowledge.

We describe the application of our technology to a concrete issue: configuration of OSPF weights. To address this complex problem, our solution use a new set of heuristics, based on a situated representation of the local neighborhood (which is provided by our multi-agent system). This solution presents a convincing behavior. We manage to reduce drastically the number of overloaded interfaces, thanks to a simple, robust, scalable, and flexible new technology.

However, a lot of further studies are planned. As a first step, we will have to develop new test patterns. Even if qualitative tests provide appreciable information about the processes, we need to ensure that this technology allows us to get better performance within acceptable delays. We have to test our system with credible traffic models, and to observe the behavior of the system depending on the values of the parameters of the agents.

On another hand, new applications will allow us to try different techniques, in order to enhance our agent model. We particularly began to develop an alarm filtering and management application, which relies on more symbolic data and algorithms, when OSPF application was using more numeric data. We also improve with this new application new knowledge sharing mechanisms.

7   References

[FER99] Jacques Ferber, Multi-Agent Systems: An Introduction to Distributed Artificial Intelligence, Addison-Wesley Longman Publishing Co., Inc., Boston, MA, 1999

[MES03] Nada Meskaoui, Leila Merghem, Dominique Gaiti, Karim Y. Kablan, Diffserv network control using a behavioral multi-agent system, January 2003

[MER03] Leila Merghem, Dominique Gaiti, and Guy Pujolle, On Using Multi-agent Systems in End to End Adaptive Monitoring, Lecture Notes in Computer Science, Springer-Verlag GmbH, Volume 2839 / 2003, Management of Multimedia Networks and Services, Chapter: pp. 422 – 435

[YE02]   T Ye, HT Kaur, S Kalyanaraman, KS Vastola, S Yadav, Dynamic Optimization of OSPF Weights using Online Simulation – proceedings of IEEE INFOCOM, 2002

[FOR00] B Fortz, M Thorup, Internet traffic engineering by optimizing OSPF weights – PROC IEEE INFOCOM, 2000

[ERI01] M. Ericsson, M.G.C. Resende, and P.M. Pardalos, A Genetic Algorith for the Weight Setting Problem in OSPF Routing, Oct 2001

[BIE98] A Bieszczad, B Pagurek, T White, Mobile Agents for Network Management – IEEE Communications Surveys, 1998

[IBM03] AG Ganek, TA Corbi, The dawning of the autonomic computing era - IBM Systems Journal, 2003

[CIS98] T.M. Thomas, OSPF Network Design Solutions, Cisco Press, 1998

[WAN99] Y. Wang and Z. Wang, Explicit Routing Algorithms for Internet Traffic Engineering, proceedings of 8th Computer Communications and Networks, 1999

[BER92] D. Bertsekas and R. Gallager, Data Networks, Prentice Hall, 1992

Analysis of Individual Flows Performance
for Delay Sensitive Applications

Ricardo Nabhen[1,2], Edgard Jamhour[2], Manoel C. Penna[2] and Mauro
Fonseca[2]
1 Laboratoire d'Informatique de Paris 6
Université Pierre et Marie Curie
Paris – France
2 Pontifical Catholic University of Parana
Curitiba – Parana – Brazil
{rcnabhen,jamhour,penna,mauro.fonseca}@ppgia.pucpr.br

Abstract. SLA management approaches typically adopt provisioning strategies
based on aggregate traffic in order to support end-to-end delay requirements of
applications. They do not take into account individual flows needs in terms of
delay. However, this delay can be very higher than the one observed by aggregate
traffic, causing an important impact in network application performance. This
paper presents a study based on simulations that makes an analysis of the end-to-
end delay observed by individual flows. Several scenarios are used to evaluate
this performance and some metrics are proposed to investigate empirical relations
that show the end-to-end delay behavior when are analyzed individual flows, the
aggregate traffic and the network load.

1   Introduction

The necessity of quality of service (QoS) management in communication networks is
unanimity, as well as the use of Service Level Agreements (SLA) for its
implementation. The basis for quality evaluation is the specification of service level
parameters which are jointly agreed by customers and service providers. Thus, a SLA
establishes parameters and their levels that must be observed during service operation.
Real time applications (e.g., voice over IP – VoIP and video-conferencing) and
business critical applications are being considered in SLAs established between
Internet Service Providers (ISPs) and their customers. In this context, a SLA specifies
service level parameters, such as availability and mean time between failures, and
network performance parameters, typically, delay, delay variation, packet loss rate and
throughput [2].

The Differentiated Services (DiffServ) architecture allows IP services to be offered
in differentiated classes and has been considered as the main strategy for scalable QoS
deployment in the Internet. Its operation is based on traffic aggregation, where packets

Please use the following format when citing this chapter:

Nabhen, R., Jamhour, E., Penna, M.C., Fonseca, M., 2006, in IFIP International Federation for Information Processing, Volume 213, Network Control and Engineering for QoS, Security, and Mobility, V, ed.
Gaïti, D., (Boston: Springer), pp. 143–156.

are classified and marked to receive a specific per-hop forwarding behavior. Diffserv architecture delegates a complex job to edge nodes, including tasks such as classification, marking, policing and shaping, making core network operation simpler[1].

Two approaches have been used for QoS management in DiffServ networks. The first one is based on the use of admission control mechanisms. The idea is to deny admission of new traffic that could cause degradation of the performance level experienced by current (i.e., previously admitted) traffic. Several admission control strategies have been proposed which can broadly be classified in two methods: centralized and distributed [3]. Centralized methods involve a central entity, named Bandwidth Broker (BB), which is responsible for admission control decisions. Proposals presented in [4], [5] and [6] are examples of centralized mechanisms. Conversely, proposals presented in [7] and [8] adopt the distributed method, where admission control decisions are taken by edge devices or end systems [9]. Regardless of the adopted method, the proposed mechanisms vary widely with respect to their implementation details. It is usual to find proposals based on new signaling protocols or based on schemes to measure network load using probing packets. A main difficulty of admission control approach is the complexity it introduces in QoS management. Thus, a second approach is being considered in order to simplify it, which is based on overprovisioning network resources. Roughly speaking, it consists in keeping such a network configuration that supports bandwidth requirements at network peak rate, which means to provision more resources than required to support the average load rate. A practical rule seems to guide overprovisioning process: Provisioning twice the capacity as the peak aggregate load[10]. By following this empirical rule, SLAs involving network performance parameters, including delay, jitter, packet loss rate and throughput would be assured.

Despite of the chosen approach we can identify difficulties when considering SLA assurance for delay sensitive applications. First, in the case of admission control mechanisms, we didn't find any proposition that takes into account delay requirements. In fact, all revised mechanisms try to maximize bandwidth use, without considering the consequences on packet delay. Second, although the fundamental premise stated by overprovisioning approach, of keeping QoS management as simple as possible has a strong appeal, to restrict network traffic to fifty percent of network capacity can be an over simplification. In fact, under business perspective, service providers should try to maximize network resources use. Third, very few studies take into account individual flow requirements in order to handle fine-grained SLA involving delay parameters. As mentioned before, DiffServ operation is based on traffic aggregation, which renders management of individual flows performance a complex task. Finally, there certainly is a relationship between delay and network utilization level, but as far as we know, all studies just consider the mean percentage of bandwidth use, without considering its variation. We intend to explore the last two points in depth in our work.

Typically QoS management in DiffServ networks consider some method for sharing the available bandwidth in order to establish provisioning levels, but do not consider individual flows needs, more specifically, they do not consider end-to-end delay bounds. Regardless of the fact that the delay observed in aggregate traffic within high capacity backbones is not a relevant issue [11], we show in this paper that just establishing high overprovisioning levels can be not enough to ensure fine gain SLA commitments. Our concern is to consider deeply this issue, being able to answer more specific questions related to delay sensitive applications. For example, in a scenario that establishes a SLA where 97% of packets of each individual flow of a VoIP application in a DiffServ domain must observe a maximum end-to-end delay, we should be able to answer the following questions: Is it possible to guarantee this agreement just considering provisioning levels assigned to the aggregate traffic class? What is the relation between the aggregate traffic and its individual flows in terms of end-to-end delay? What are the main factors that affect individual flows performance in this context?

The use of bandwidth allocation in a per class basis for assuring QoS in DiffServ networks is a ubiquitous practice. The great majority of proposals limit the ratio of bandwidth allocation to assure quality for a given service class. However, there is no discussion about the time interval where this ratio should be computed. In our view, this is a fundamental issue if we want to control fine grain SLAs for delay sensitive application. In fact, unpredictable delay occurs due to packet queuing in IP routers, thus, and the mean bandwidth allocation can be acceptable, for example, when calculated in a daily basis, but unacceptable if during peak use intervals the network produces unacceptable packet delay.

In this paper we present a simulation-based study that analyses the end-to-end delay observed by individual flows of delay sensitive applications. It shows that this delay can vary widely in relation to the one observed in aggregate traffic. This variation must be considered when one establishes network provisioning levels. Also, some empirical evidences are investigated in order to show the relation between individual flows and aggregate traffic in terms of end-to-end delay, considering network utilization rate observed during the determined period of analysis. The paper is organized as follows. Section 2 reviews some related work. Section 3 presents our end-to-end delay analysis methodology for the study of individual flows performance. Section 4 presents the simulation results and their analysis. Finally, Section 5 summarizes the main aspects in this study and points to future work.

2   Related Work

In their seminal work, Fraleigh, Tobagi, and Diot have analyzed several backbone traffic measurements and have shown that the average traffic rate is much lower than link capacities (around 50%) suggesting that low utilization could be a strategy for network resources provisioning [11]. They have concluded that delay is not a relevant issue when dealing with aggregate traffic within high capacity backbones (above 1 Gbits/s), considering 50% of utilization level. Moreover, they showed that network utilization could reach 80% to 90% and delay values would remain acceptable for almost all applications. Their conclusions have influenced the overprovisioning approach to deal with delay requirements on IP networks. However, as said before, overprovisionig may be costly and sometimes impossible to be implemented. For example, leased-lines, wireless links and other access networks have typically low capacity, what renders the approach unfeasible.

Another issue usually not covered by overprovisioning is to take into account individual flow delay. Indeed, many propositions for QoS management are based on the definition of special DiffServ classes for aggregate traffic, and they assume that end-to-end delay in aggregate class would be the same as those observed in each embedded individual flow. However, some studies show that end-to-end delay can vary sufficiently to produce service degradation. Jiang and Yao have investigated the impact of flow aggregation in end-to-end delay observed by individual flows in a DiffServ network [12]. This study considers a single aggregation traffic class and has evaluated multiple scenarios with the variation of network load and burstiness level. Results suggest that individual flow delay varies with respect to aggregate flow delay, according to bandwidth utilization level and the variation of the traffic burstiness level. A similar study realized by Siripongwutikorn and Banerjee has investigated individual flows delay embedded in a single traffic class, by considering the provisioning strategy based on aggregate traffic [13]. They considered several scheduling disciplines, such as FIFO and WFQ in their analysis, and the results indicate that traffic heterogeneity, network load and scheduling disciplines affect individual flows performance. Xu and Guérin have studied the performance of individual flows, in terms of packet loss rate, in a scenario where service level guarantees are offered to traffic classes [14]. They proposed an analytical model that measures the performance level of aggregate traffic, in order to foresee individual flows performance. Presented results show that when there are a great number of users it is desirable to avoid the aggregation of traffic flow with different profiles. They also evaluated what additional resources are necessary in order to reach the established loss rate assigned to individual flows.

Our work differs from above studies in several points. First, in the same way as previous studies, we relate delay analysis to network utilization rate, but differently we consider the variation of network utilization rate during simulation time. We show that it is important to consider variation of network utilization rate when evaluating individual flows delay. The second difference is the evaluation metrics. Xu and Guérin study does not consider delay but packet loss rate. Siripongwutikorn and Banerjee analyses the delay of the 99th percentile of packets of individual flows, while our work considers the 97th percentile, the one usually adopted as a reference for good quality voice flows[1]. Moreover, we propose the use of a new metric to evaluate the effects of the network load variation in the delay of individual flows. Beside of these differences, our work also brings a contribution by explicitly handling VoIP flows. We analyze two scenarios, the first handling just concurrent VoIP flows and the second handling concurrent VoIP flows mixed to data traffic. In summary, our work proposes new metrics to investigate the relation between end-to-end delays observed in individual flows with respect to that observed in the aggregate flow, by taking into account the probability distribution of network utilization rate computed for specific time intervals.

3   End-to-end Delay Analysis Methodology

3.1   Delay Requirements and Simulation Hypothesis

Real time applications have typically their SLAs specified in terms of end-to-end delay bounds with deterministic or probabilistic guarantees [11]. In the former case, one hard delay limit is defined, while, in the latter case, delay limits are associated to percentiles

---

[1] Typically, the 97th percentile is used in SLAs to establish performance metrics. For example, in VoIP systems a general loss of 3% or less is acceptable which indicates that the 97th percentile is the minumum required quantity for delivered packets on a flow basis. This work used this approach considering the highest delay observed by the 97th percentile of delivered packets of individual VoIP flows.

of delivered packets, as can be seen in Table 1. When using deterministic guarantee, every delivered packet should experience at most 50ms end-to-end delay, whereas in the probabilistic guarantee case, 97% of delivered packets should experience at most 50ms end-to-end delay and 99% should experience not more than 60ms.

Table 1. End-to-end delay guarantees example

Deterministic Guarantee	Probabilistic Guarantee
50ms	97,0% - 50ms 99,0% - 60ms

Network delay is a function of several sources: (i) Transmission delay: time to transmit a packet on a link; (ii) Queueing delay: time spent in node buffers waiting for service; (iii) Propagation delay: time related to physical media and link extension; (iv) Processing delay: time related to the switching process. The end-to-end delay observed by a packet is affected differently by each delay source. For example, for low capacity links and depending on packet lengths transmission delay could be relevant but it is negligible for high capacity ones. Propagation delay should be considered only in long distance links (e.g., continental links). Processing delay is negligible for the majority of recent network devices. Finally, queuing is the most challenging delay source for researchers and network engineers because of its dependence to traffic behavior, due to the difficulty of developing analytical models that renders the arrival processes non predictable.

Delay requirements for voice applications are well known. For example, ITU-T states that real time applications will not be affected by end-to-end delay lower than 150ms [15]. This value can be used as a deterministic limit for high quality flows. Actually, a sufficient condition for considering a VoIP flow as a high quality one is 97% of delivered packets to observe an end-to-end delay lower than 150ms [15]. However, the choice of appropriate provisioning levels to assure fine grain SLAs involving end-to-end delay in IP networks remains as a major challenge. A simple and usual solution is overprovisioning, but as mentioned before, it may be costly and sometimes impossible to be implemented.

From previous analysis of provisioning strategies two questions remain unanswered: (i) Is it possible to guarantee service level agreements based on probabilistic guarantees for individual flows of delay sensitive applications by considering provisioning levels assigned to aggregate traffic classes? (ii) How is individual flows end-to-end delay affected by variation of network utilization rate, especially during periods of higher network utilization rates? To answer these questions we performed simulations using the Network Simulator version 2 (NS-2) to observe end-to-end delay behavior of individual flows considering several network load conditions in order to obtain the relation between individual flow end-to-end delay with respect to aggregate traffic end-to-end delay.

3.2   Topology and Stages of Simulation

Fig. 1 shows the network topology adopted in simulation. Several traffic pairs (S_i, D_i) were instantiated, where each pair generates only one VoIP flow during simulation period. Every generated flow is analyzed in order to evaluate the end-to-end delay of its packets. In fact, the highest end-to-end delay observed within the 97th percentile is recorded to compute the performance metrics (see section 3.4). Bandwidth of link L is set to 2 Mbps, because high network utilization rates should be reached. This would be difficult to achieve with higher capacity links, due to low throughput required by each individual VoIP flow (around 30kbps). Propagation delay was not considered as well as processing time at codecs. Although both delay sources must be considered in the overall performance evaluation of a VoIP flow, in the context of this work, which focus is on the analysis of the individual flows performance in terms of delay taking into account variation of network utilization rate, the conclusions would be not modified by those fixed values (i.e., propagation and codec delays). Buffers of routers R_1 and R_2 were adjusted in order to avoid packet loss because its occurrence would affect the determination of target packets for delay analysis and we are just interested in delay analisys of delivered packets.

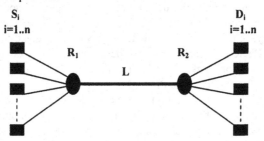

Fig. 1. Network Topology for Simulation

In order to get a more precise analysis the simulation was organized in two stages: stage 1, involving just VoIP traffic and stage 2, involving mixed VoIP and data traffic. They were defined because the distribution of the network utilization rate observed during simulation period has shown distinct behavior when mixed traffic was introduced, as shall see in Section 4. Stage 1 can be seen as a scenario where one queue is used to serve all aggregate traffic formed by VoIP flows. Here we intend to analyze the influence of DiffServ aggregation strategy in the performance of individual VoIP flow, with respect to end-to-end delay. On the other hand, Stage 2 can be seen as a scenario where voice traffic is mixed with data traffic with no service differentiation. Here we want to see how data traffic would interfere with VoIP flows.

3.3   Traffic Source Parameters

VoIP applications usually are simulated as a constant bit rate flow. Depending on the codec, traffic may vary widely. For example, G.711 codec requires higher bandwidth than other codecs, however, it provides the best mean opinion score (MOS) [15], a numerical metric that indicates the quality of human speech in a voice circuit. Silence suppression is an important feature to reduce the required bandwidth for VoIP applications. In this case, we have used the same traffic model adopted in [16], where talk-spurts and silence gaps are both exponentially distributed with the mean equals to 1.5 seconds. Also, the VoIP packet size (payload and headers) is 74 bytes and during transmission periods the packet interarrival time is 20 milliseconds. A major issue in our simulation is the traffic intensity generated by concurrent VoIP flows. In this case, based on the study presented in [17] we use two traffic parameters: the average flow duration (AFD) that establishes an average value in seconds for the duration of a VoIP flow; and the time between flows (TBF) that establishes an average value in seconds for the flow arrival process. AFD and TBF are both exponentially distributed according to the specified mean.

Fig. 2 illustrates the VoIP flows generation process. It shows four VoIP flows starting at instants t_1, t_2, t_3 and t_6, respectively, representing the exponential distribution of the TBF parameter. VoIP flows have different duration times, due to exponential distribution of the AFD parameter. The duration time of flows f_1 and f_4 have are respectively given by t_4-t_1 and t_8-t_6. For data traffic, we have adopted a combined traffic model based on the Internet distribution packet size presented in [18]. It is composed by 58% of 40-byte packets, 33% of 552-byte packets and 9% of 1500-byte packets. In terms of simulation, the Pareto distribution was used to implement this traffic source considering the ON and OFF parameters, respectively, 500ms and 125ms. The shape parameter adopted was 1.5 as suggested in [19].

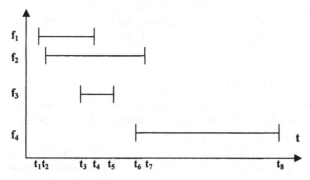

Fig. 2. VoIP flows: Generation process example

3.4 Simulation Scenarios

Simulation time was set to 400s because of the average duration of each VoIP flow and its arrival process, as can be seen in the AFD and TBF parameters in Tables 2 and 3. In this case, this simulation time permits an adequate period for the proposed analysis methodology since a value of 210s for the AFD parameter and a value of 3.5s for the TBF parameter allow the observation of several concurrent VoIP flows during this simulation time. This approach allows clearly the simulation of the arrival and termination processes of VoIP flows usually observed in real scenarios. As presented in section 3.2, simulation scenarios are divided into two stages. Tables 2 and 3 show, respectively, the configuration of each scenario in each stage.

Table 2. Simulation Stage 1

Sc.	VoIP flows	AFD (s)	TBF (s)
1	80	210	3.5
2	90	210	3.5
3	100	210	3.0
4	120	210	2.5

Table 3. Simulation Stage 2

Sc.	VoIP Flows	AFD (s)	TBF (s)	% Data Traffic
1	50	210	3.5	20.0
2	50	210	3.5	25.0
3	50	210	3.5	30.0
4	50	210	3.5	40.0

The TBF parameter in stage 1 (see Table 2) was decreased in order to generate higher load conditions; a lower TBF represents a lower average time between flows, thus, increasing the number of VoIP flows during a specific time. Four scenarios have been simulated in each stage. In Stage 1, the number of concurrent VoIP flow increases at each new scenario, in order to increase network load. In Stage 2, the number of concurrent VoIP flows is kept constant, but the data traffic rate increases at each new scenario.

3.5 Performance metrics

In order to investigate the relation between end-to-end delays observed in individual flows with respect to that observed in aggregate traffic we define some performance metrics, as shown in Table 4, which were analyzed under several simulation scenarios. These metrics will be used to investigate empirical relations between network load and delay of individual flows. Delay performance for individual flows and aggregate traffic can be verified by inspecting $d97_i$ and $d97_a$. The $d97_i$ and $\sigma97$ metrics are analyzed with respect to the variation of the ρ_Δ metric, i.e., its probability density function (pdf), in order to seek a possible empirical relation between aggregate traffic, individual flows and the distribution of the network utilization rate. In this context, a cumulative distribution function (cdf) of ρ_Δ is calculated by the integral of pdf(ρ_Δ) and can be denoted as follows:

$$F_{\rho\Delta}(x) = P[\rho_\Delta \le x] \quad (1)$$

Defining a complementary function of (1), we obtain:

$$\overline{F}_{\rho\Delta}(x) = 1 - F_{\rho\Delta}(x) = P[\rho_\Delta > x] \quad (2)$$

Table 4. Performance Metrics

Metric	Description
$d97_i$	Maximum end-to-end delay in milliseconds observed in the 97th percentile for the i-th individual VoIP flow.
$d97_a$	Maximum end-to-end delay in milliseconds observed in the 97th percentile for the aggregate VoIP traffic.
ρ_Δ	Mean of network utilization ratio during interval Δ, where Δ is measured in seconds.
$d97_m$	$d97_i$ mean.
$P[\rho_\Delta > x]$	Probability of ρ_Δ to be greater than x. (see equation (2)).

4   Simulation Results and Analysis

4.1   Stage 1: VoIP Traffic

Mean of network utilization ratio during interval Δ (ρ_Δ) is a major parameter in simulation and it is obtained as follows: simulation is repeated 20 times for each scenario and we compute the network load given by the input traffic due to the aggregation of independent VoIP sources in intervals defined by Δ. Figs. 3 and 4 show, respectively, the probability density function and the cumulative distribution function with normalized values for the ρ_1 metric observed during stage 1. These graphs represent the results given by all simulations. End-to-end delay values shown later in this section will be presented along with their 95% confidence intervals.

One of the main issues to be investigated in this work is the delay experienced by packets under different load conditions and, mainly, how their variation affect this delay. Observing the average network load during the simulation period, i.e., ρ_{400}, in scenarios 1, 2, 3 and 4, respectively, 40.74%, 50.21%, 55.58% and 64.86%, and considering the overprovisioning rule, these values were supposed to be adequate for supporting delay sensitive applications. However, in all scenarios, we can observe the network utilization rate given by ρ_1 above 90%, which could affect considerably the end-to-end delay of individual VoIP flows[2]. In fact, when computed for smaller intervals (Δ), ρ_Δ reaches unacceptable values which sometimes could represent a SLA violation. From Fig. 4, for example, one can observe that the probability of ρ_1 to be higher than 90% is, respectively, 0.41%, 2.28%, 7.02% and 20.00% for scenarios 1, 2, 3 and 4. We can conclude that it is meaningless to discuss the mean of network utilization rate without taking into account the interval in which it is computed (Δ). Figs. 5, 6, 7 and 8 show the frequency distribution (normalized values) of $d97_i$ for scenarios 1, 2, 3 and 4, where end-to-end delay axis has been plotted on a logarithmic scale. $d97_i$ is computed by considering all values registered in all simulation repetitions, that is, 1600, 1800, 2000 and 2400 VoIP flows for scenarios 1, 2, 3 and 4. The vertical line in each graphic depicts the maximum end-to-end delay observed in the 97th percentile for the aggregate VoIP traffic ($d97_a$). In all scenarios we can see several VoIP flows where $d97_i$ is greater than the $d97_a$. This result can be justified by the strategy of grouping all packets of every individual flow in order to compute the 97th percentile of the aggregate traffic. In this context, it is important to mention that either $d97_a$ or $d97_i$ are computed using the same data set. Using this grouping scheme, it is clear that the 97th percentile of the aggregate traffic is below the 97th percentile of some individual flows (i.e., flows that ocurred during higher load conditions) and, therefore, their $d97_i$ are expected to be higher than the associated $d97_a$.

---

[2] Values of network utilization rate above 100% means that the arrival process is higher than the service process given by the output link. Thus, for such periods packets are buffered waiting for service.

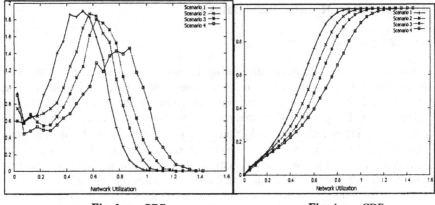

Fig. 3. ρ_1 - PDF   **Fig. 4.** ρ_1 - CDF

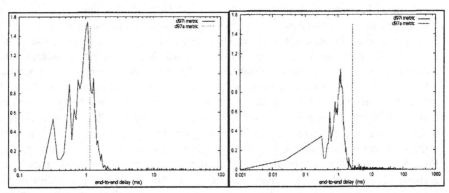

Fig. 5. $d97_i$-Frequency Distribution – Sc.1   **Fig. 6.** $d97_i$-Frequency Distribution – Sc.2

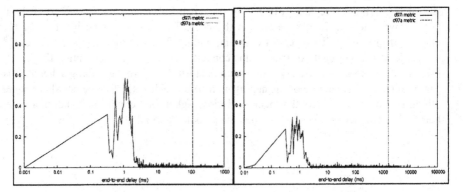

Fig. 7. $d97_i$-Frequency Distribution – Sc.3   **Fig. 8.** $d97_i$-Frequency Distribution – Sc.4

4.2   Stage 2: Mixed VoIP and Data Traffic

The difference between stage 1 and stage 2 is that we have mixed data traffic with VoIP flows to generate background traffic. We calculated the same performance metrics, only for packets of VoIP flows. Figs. 9 and 10 show the normalized values for ρ_1 frequency distribution observed during stage 2. Here we can observe higher average network utilization rates than those observed in stage 1. The calculated values for ρ_{400} (Δ= simulation time) in scenarios 1, 2, 3 and 4 are 55.65%, 61.12%, 64.87% and 75.29%, respectively. However, when comparing Figs. 4 and 10, we observe more instances of higher values of ρ_1 in stage 1 than in stage 2. This explains the better results even under higher average network utilization rates observed in stage 2.

Figs. 9, 10, 11 and 12 show the frequency distribution of the $d97_i$ for scenarios 1, 2, 3 and 4 as explained before. As in stage 1, in all scenarios we can see several VoIP flows where $d97_i$ is greater than the $d97_a$.

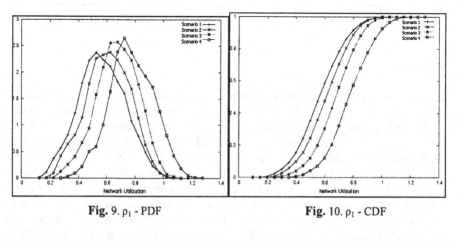

Fig. 9. ρ_1 - PDF   **Fig. 10.** ρ_1 - CDF

Fig. 11. $d97_i$ -Frequency Distribution – Sc.1   **Fig. 12.** $d97_i$ -Frequency Distribution – Sc.2

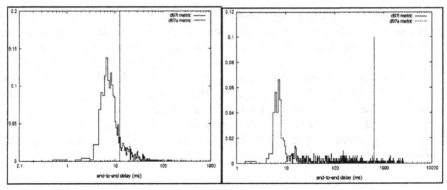

Fig. 13. d97$_i$ -Frequency Distribution – Sc.3   **Fig. 14.** d97$_i$ -Frequency Distribution – Sc.4

4.3 Remarks

Tables 5 and 6 present the computed values for d97$_m$ and σ97 metrics in each scenario, along with their 95% confidence intervals. Also, the corresponding values of P[ρ$_1$ > 100%] and ρ$_{400}$ are presented. For scenarios 1 and 2 of both stages the P[ρ$_1$ > 100%] is almost negligible. As can be seen, the end-to-end delay remains very steady under these load conditions. In addition, due to the similar value of P[ρ$_1$ > 100%], the scenario 3 in Table 6 also showed an acceptable performance in terms of the d97$_m$ metric and its variability (i.e., the σ97 metric). This behavior cannot be seen in scenario 3 in Table 5, where a slightly increase of P[ρ$_1$ > 100%] (i.e., to 2.39%) caused a sensible variation of the d97$_m$ and σ97 metrics. Finally, the scenario 4 of both stages experienced a significant increase of the network utilization rate, easily noted in the values of P[ρ$_1$ > 100%] in Tables 5 and 6, causing exponential augment of the d97$_i$ and σ97 metrics to prohibitive levels.

Table 5. Stage 1: d97$_m$; σ97 ; P[ρ$_1$ > 100%] metrics

Sc.	d97$_m$	Confidence Interval (95%)	σ97	P[ρ$_1$ > 100%]	ρ$_{400}$
1	1.46	[1.27 ; 1.64]	3.48	0.31%	40.74%
2	3.90	[3.40 ; 4.39]	9.78	0.97%	50.21%
3	81.50	[73.00 ; 89.99]	176.46	2.39%	55.58%
4	1000.84	[903.57 ; 1098.10]	2202.51	9.82%	64.86%

Table 6. Stage 2: d97$_m$; σ97 ; P[ρ$_1$ > 100%] metrics

Sc.	d97$_m$	Confidence Interval (95%)	σ97	P[ρ$_1$ > 100%]	ρ$_{400}$
1	7.11	[6.43 ; 7.80]	10.05	0.56%	55.65%
2	8.64	[7.82 ; 9.46]	12.06	1.06%	61.12%
3	16.63	[14.93 ; 18.33]	24.86	1.23%	64.87%
4	504.06	[457.44; 550.68]	684.52	7.34%	75.29%

It is important to examine the values in Tables 5 and 6 in light of the frequency distribution of the ρ_Δ. For example, ρ_{400} is 64.86% in scenario 4 of stage 1 and 75.29% in scenario 4 of stage 2, but $d97_m$ was twice higher in the former case which can be explained by the PDF of ρ_Δ. It is clear from the analysis of Figures 3 and 9 that in stage 1 (see Figure 3) the system remains under higher load conditions which affects directly the overall delay performance given by $d97_m$ and $\sigma97$ metrics, regardless of the fact that the value of ρ_{400} could indicate the contrary. On the other side, in the scenarios under lower network utilization, this anomaly does not verify, what clearly indicates the importance of considering the network utilization distribution in the context of individual flows performance.

5   Conclusion

This paper presented a study in order to investigate the end-to-end delay behavior observed by individual flows. It is important to understand this behavior and its relation with aggregate traffic and network utilization, mainly when one considers the SLA management for delay sensitive applications. In order to perform this analysis, this study has considered delay requirements for VoIP applications, which defines a maximum end-to-end delay to be experienced by the 97th percentile of packets from each individual VoIP flow. New metrics were defined to evaluate empirical relations between network load and delay of individual flows. Empirical relations were established by an extensive two stage simulation experiment, with multiple scenarios simulating several traffic configurations and a multiplicity of load conditions.

Results confirmed that network utilization ratio is one the parameters that affect the most the delay in IP networks. Moreover, the study presented a new approach to relate network load with delay. It is shown that it is meaningless to consider the mean of network utilization rate without taking into account the interval in which it is computed. Analyzed scenarios indicate that even when the average network utilization rate observed is acceptable, for example under overprovisioning empirical rules, the delay performance observed by several individual flows is impracticable. This new approach suggests that any statement about network utilization rate should also state the time interval in which it is computed, mainly when one considers the SLA specification based on individual flows performance metrics.

References

1.   S. Blake, D. Black, M. Carlson, E. Davies, Z. Wang, and W. Weiss, RFC 2475: An architecture for differentiated service. IETF (1998).

2.   A. Westerinen, J. Schnizlein, J. Strassner, M. Scherling, B. Quinn, S. Herzog, A. Huynh, M. Carlson, J. Perry, and S. Waldbusser, RFC 3198: Terminology for policy-based management. IETF (2001).

3.   W. Rhee, J. Lee, J. Yu, and S. Kim, Scalable quasi-dynamic-provisioning based admission control mechanism in differentiated service networks. ETRI Journal, 26(1):22–37 (2004).

4. R. Liao and A. Campbell, Dynamic core provisioning for quantitative differentiated service. IEEE IWQoS (2001).

5. Z. Zhang, D. Zhenhai, and Y. Hou, On scalable design of bandwidth brokers. EICE Transactions on Communications, e84-b(8) (2001).

6. C. Bouras and K. Stamos, An adaptive admission control algorithm for bandwidth brokers. Third IEEE International Symposium on Network Computing and Applications(NCA) (2004).

7. V. Elek, G. Karlsson and R. Ronngren, Admission control based on end-to-end measurements. IEEE INFOCOM (2000).

8. L. Breslau, S. Jamin and S. Shenker, Measurement-based admission control: What is the research agenda? IEEE IWQoS (1999).

9. F. Kelly, P. Key and S. Zachary, Distributed admission control. IEEE Journal on Selected Areas in Communications, 18:2617–2628(2000).

10. C. Filsfils and J. Evans, Deploying diffserv in backbone networks for tight sla control. IEEE Internet Computing Magazine(2005).

11. C. Fraleigh, F. Tobagi, and C. Diot, Provisioning ip backbone networks to support latency sensitive traffic. The 22nd Annual Joint Conference of the IEEE Computer and Communications Societies, Infocom(2003).

12. Y. Jiang and Q. Yao, Impact of fifo aggregation on delay performance of a differentiated services network. The International Conference on Information Networking, ICOIN (2003).

13. P. Siripongwutikorn and S. Banerjee, Per-flow delay performance in traffic aggregates, Proceedings of IEEE Globecom(2002).

14. Y. Xu and R. Guérin, Individual Qos versus Aggregate Qos: A loss performance study. IEEE/ACM Transactions on Networking, 13:370–383(2005).

15. ITU-T (2003). Recommendation g.114: One-way transmission time. ITU-T.

16. C. Boutremans, G. Iannaccone and C. Diot, Impact of link failures on voip performance. Proceedings of NOSSDAV Workshop (ACM Press) (2002).

17. Cisco. Traffic analysis for Voice over Ip. Cisco Document Server (2001).

18. K. Claffy, G. Miller and K. Thompson, The nature of the beast: Recent traffic measurements from an internet backbone. Proceedings of INET'98 (1998).

19. C. Dovrolis, D. Stiliadis and P. Ramanathan, Proportional Differentiated Services: Delay Differentiation and Packet Scheduling. IEEE/ACM Transactions on Networking (2002).

Proportional Service Differentiation with MPLS

João Neves, Paulo Rogério Pereira, Augusto Casaca
INESC ID, Rua Alves Redol, 9. 1000-029 Lisboa, Portugal.
Phone: +351-213100345. Fax: +351-213145843.
Email: {Joao.Neves, Paulo.Pereira, Augusto.Casaca}@inesc-id.pt

Abstract. This paper describes two traffic engineering techniques for implementing proportional differentiated services based on Multiprotocol Label Switching constraint based routing. Both use a dynamic bandwidth allocation scheme to modify the bandwidth reserved by each traffic class according to the current network load. The first scheme uses an adaptive algorithm that qualitatively determines the required average throughput per source for each class and moves bandwidth between classes for each path as necessary. The second scheme mathematically divides the existing bandwidth through the traffic classes for each path. The quality of service that users get with both techniques is assessed by simulation and compared with a fixed bandwidth allocation scheme.

1 Introduction

Quality of service (QoS) has been a major research topic in the networking community for the last 20 years [1]. Different user applications have different QoS requirements. Depending on the user application, parameters such as end-to-end delay, jitter, packet loss and throughput may be critical. The simplest answer to provide the QoS that the user applications need is to increase the capacity of the links. This is known as overprovisioning and results in a waste of resources, especially for end-to-end QoS.

The Differentiated Services architecture [2] offers a scalable solution for providing end-to-end QoS. Packets from different user applications with different QoS requirements are classified into different traffic classes and marked accordingly. Only ingress edge routers perform classification, marking and policing functions. The network core only deals with the aggregate of flows in each traffic class, giving them a common queue or scheduling behavior. This allows a scalable service differentiation according to the traffic class.

Please use the following format when citing this chapter:

Neves, J., Pereira, P.R., Casaca, A. 2006, in IFIP International Federation for Information Processing, Volume 213, Network Control and Engineering for QoS, Security, and Mobility, V, ed. Gaïti, D., (Boston: Springer), pp. 157–169.

However, if a fixed bandwidth allocation is used for each traffic class, a priority inversion may occur when a high priority class has higher load than a low priority class. A possible solution is to use flow admission control to avoid this situation. It has the disadvantage of refusing the requested traffic class to flows that would degrade the QoS of existing flows. Although the admission control is necessary to limit the maximum total network load and avoid QoS degradation, if the network resources in the core devoted to each traffic class are made to depend on the actual load of the traffic classes, fewer flows will see their traffic class changed by the admission control.

Towards this objective, the paper proposes two kinds of dynamic bandwidth allocation schemes based on traffic engineering (TE) techniques for implementing differentiated services supported by Multiprotocol Label Switching (MPLS) constraint based routing (CR) [3].

MPLS uses a label switching technique that consists in the addition of a label to each packet. This label indexes a forwarding table in each router, determining the outgoing link and the new label to use. The processing involved can be made much faster than looking at the destination address in the packet as in a routing process. Constraint-based routing (CR) is a mechanism used to meet Traffic Engineering requirements. It allows for a path to be setup based on explicit route constraints, QoS constraints and other constraints. The use of MPLS-CR was selected because it allows reserving and dynamically modifying the bandwidth in a path between a network core ingress and egress node. It can be used to configure the bandwidth, as necessary, for every traffic class in each path of the core network.

The first scheme proposed in this paper uses an adaptive algorithm that determines the required average throughput per source for each traffic class, according to the current network load, and moves bandwidth between classes for each path in the network core as necessary.

The second scheme proposed in this paper mathematically divides the existing bandwidth through the traffic classes for each possible path in the network core according to the current network load.

We propose to use an Olympic service model with three traffic classes: Gold, Silver and Bronze. We propose also to use a proportional differentiation mechanism between the Gold and Silver classes to give the Gold class the best QoS. The Bronze class is a best effort class that gets a very small fraction of the existing bandwidth along with the unused bandwidth of the other classes. This nomenclature is slightly different from the Olympic service nomenclature proposed in [4]. A proportional differentiation mechanism [5] is a refinement of a differentiated services mechanism, where an adjustable and consistent differentiation between classes is provided. The proportional differentiation has the advantages of being controllable, consistent and scalable. The proportional differentiation mechanism should try to give to each Gold flow the double of the bandwidth as to each Silver flow. This factor of two was chosen arbitrarily, as an example. In practice, it should depend on the relation of the prices charged to clients in the different classes.

The Gold and Silver classes could be further divided according to the specific QoS needs of the applications. For simplicity, we assumed that all applications have similar QoS requirements, except for the transport protocol used. TCP applications tend to increase their transmission rate until there is a packet loss, which should not affect the transmission rate of UDP applications. Accordingly, we propose to have different classes for TCP and UDP traffic, resulting in four MPLS-CR reservations: Gold TCP, Silver TCP, Gold UDP and Silver UDP.

Both proposed dynamic bandwidth allocation schemes were analyzed by simulation and compared with a fixed bandwidth allocation scheme for the QoS that users get. Section 2 describes the dynamic bandwidth allocation schemes. Section 3 describes the simulation scenario and the simulation results. Finally, section 4 draws conclusions and raises further work topics.

2   Dynamic Bandwidth Allocation Schemes

2.1   *Adaptive Dynamic Bandwidth*

In the first dynamic bandwidth allocation technique proposed, an adaptive algorithm divides the bandwidth between the traffic classes according to a few rules that determine when the reserved bandwidth should be moved from a traffic class to another.

First, a value for the required throughput per source (TpS) is determined. This is done independently for the Gold and Silver classes and for the UDP and TCP protocols. The TpS values are tabled, as shown in table 1, using steps that become smaller as the number of sources in a node increases, so as to accommodate the throughput of all the sources in a given path. The required TpS for the Gold class is about twice the TpS for the Silver class, favoring the Gold class for higher loads, so that the QoS is higher for the Gold class. The values chosen depend on the characteristics of the sources that were used.

Table 1. Throughput per Source (TpS) values according to the number of sources

Number of Sources	Gold Class	Silver Class
up to 4	100 Kbps	50 Kbps
5 to 8	50 Kbps	25 Kbps
9 to 10	40 Kbps	20 Kbps
11 to 12	30 Kbps	15 Kbps
13 or more	25 Kbps	10 Kbps

If the total bandwidth required for a class, determined as (TpS × number of sources), is higher than what is currently reserved with MPLS-CR, the dynamic algorithm searches in all the links of the path if it is possible to increase the reserve, considering the sources of the different paths sharing the same links. If possible, the reserve for the path is increased. If not possible, the algorithm will try to decrease the reserves of other paths. The Silver class is always the first one to be decreased, even if the predefined TpS steps for the Silver class are not respected. The Gold class is only decreased if the TpS allows it. If no decrease is possible, the bandwidth remains unchanged, which usually happens with high congestion. For all classes, there is always a minimum bandwidth guaranteed, considering the number of existing sources.

2.2 Mathematical Dynamic Bandwidth

In the second dynamic technique, a mathematical approach to divide the bandwidth among the classes is used. The idea is that the bandwidth available per source, for the Gold class should be twice the bandwidth available per source for the Silver class. The bandwidth available per source is related to the QoS users get.

The corresponding expressions are:

$$\begin{cases} bwGoldTCP + bwSilverTCP + bwGoldUDP + bwSilverUDP = TOTALbw \\[6pt] \dfrac{bwGoldTCP}{NrSourcesGoldTCP} = 2 \times \dfrac{bwSilverTCP}{NrSourcesSilverTCP} \\[6pt] \dfrac{bwGoldUDP}{NrSourcesGoldUDP} = 2 \times \dfrac{bwSilverUDP}{NrSourcesSilverUDP} \\[6pt] \dfrac{bwGoldTCP}{NrSourcesGoldTCP} = \dfrac{bwGoldUDP}{NrSourcesGoldUDP} \end{cases}$$

The first expression says that the total available bandwidth in a link has to be divided through the 4 existing aggregated flows, one for each combination of the existing classes with the different application protocols. The 4 aggregated flows follow the same source-destination path, whose bottleneck bandwidth is given by the value TOTALbw. This restriction does not exist in the adaptive algorithm. There are also fixed fractions of the link bandwidth that are reserved for signaling and best effort traffic, both excluded from the above expressions.

The second expression says that the bandwidth per Gold TCP source should be twice the bandwidth per Silver TCP source. The factor of two was chosen as an example of QoS proportionality between the Gold and Silver classes. The bandwidth per source is determined by dividing the total bandwidth of the aggregated flow by the number of flows existing in the aggregated flow. If the TCP applications continuously generate traffic, this expression results in the throughput QoS parameter for each Gold TCP flow to be twice as in the Silver TCP class.

The third expression is similar for the UDP protocol: the bandwidth per Gold UDP source should be twice the bandwidth per Silver UDP source. This usually results in a better QoS (lower delays, jitter and loss) for the Gold class.

The fourth expression says that each flow should get the same bandwidth, whether it is using TCP or UDP. Only the class should influence the QoS, not the protocol chosen.

Solving these equations, we get the bandwidth allocation for each class, corresponding to the reservations to be made in the network, as:

$$
\begin{cases}
bwSilverUDP = \dfrac{TOTALbw \times NrSourcesSilverUDP}{2.NrSrGoldTCP + NrSrSilverTCP + 2.NrSrGoldUDP + NrSrSilverUDP} \\[2ex]
bwSilverTCP = bwSilverUDP \times \dfrac{NrSourcesSilverTCP}{NrSourcesSilverUDP} \\[2ex]
bwGoldUDP = 2 \times bwSilverUDP \times \dfrac{NrSourcesGoldUDP}{NrSourcesSilverUDP} \\[2ex]
bwGoldTCP = 2 \times bwSilverTCP \times \dfrac{NrourcesGoldTCP}{NrSourcesSilverUDP}
\end{cases}
$$

The mathematical algorithm periodically modifies the bandwidth reserved for each source-destination path, according to these expressions.

3   Simulations and Results

3.1   *Network Configuration*

The network topology used for the simulations is shown in figure 1. The network has a core containing 12 nodes with at least 5 link-disjoint paths between each pair of nodes. This allows for some redundancy, so that there are several alternative paths between each source-destination pair that can be used by traffic engineering. Additionally, there are 3 ingress routers and 3 egress routers where traffic sources and traffic sinks are placed. The core links were configured with 1 Mbit/s capacity and 2 ms delay. Since we only wish to study the behavior of the core, the access links were configured with a sufficient large capacity. The network topology is described and discussed in [6]. It was simulated in the NS2 network simulator [7].

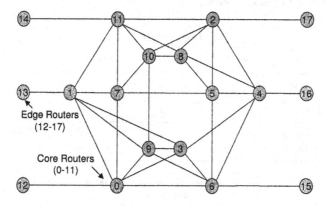

Fig. 1. Network topology

Three types of traffic sources were used simultaneously: long lived FTP/TCP sources, constant bit rate (CBR) sources over UDP and Pareto On/Off sources over UDP. Sources are randomly generated with equal proportions of the three traffic types. Therefore, there might be paths more congested than others in some simulations.

Paths are reserved in the core through MPLS-CR for each pair of source-destination nodes. The Bronze class has no paths reserved through MPLS. For Gold and Silver classes, there are 2 classes × 2 protocols × 3 source nodes × 3 destination nodes = 36 aggregated flows mapped onto MPLS reservations. All these aggregated flows are created initially. The dynamic bandwidth allocation schemes only modify the MPLS-CR bandwidth reservations for each path as necessary.

3.2   Fixed Bandwidth

The fixed bandwidth scenario is used only as a term of comparison in this paper. It divides the bandwidth along the classes as follows: 30% for Gold UDP, 30% for Gold TCP, 15% for Silver UDP, 15% for Silver TCP, 1% for signaling and 9% for Bronze. These values were chosen so that at least 10% of the bandwidth is available for the best effort traffic, the Gold class has the double of the bandwidth of the Silver class and the UDP and TCP classes have the same bandwidth available. Naturally, these values should depend on the services sold by the Internet Service Provider and the expected traffic pattern. But, in this scenario, they are fixed, whatever the actual traffic pattern is, while in the following two scenarios, they change according to the two algorithms proposed.

From the different simulations performed, the most interesting case is the one where the number of Gold class sources increases with a fixed number of 6 Silver sources and 60 Bronze sources. The results for the three different types of traffic sources (FTP/TCP, Pareto/UDP, CBR/UDP) are shown in figures 2, 3 and 4, respectively. Several simulations runs were made with different random number seeds and the same number of traffic sources. The results presented correspond to the average of the different simulations.

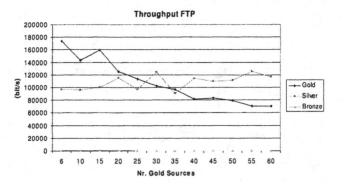

Fig. 2. FTP throughput per source for fixed bandwidth scenario

The results show a priority inversion between the throughput for the Gold and Silver classes for high loads: the fixed bandwidth available for the Gold class is divided by a large number of sources, resulting in less throughput per source and worse QoS than for the Silver class.

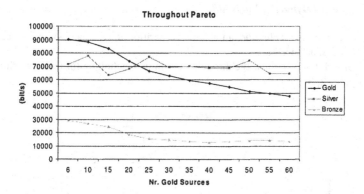

Fig. 3. Pareto throughput per source for fixed bandwidth scenario

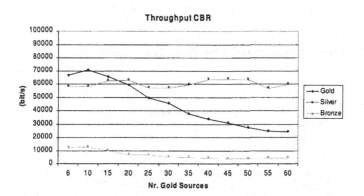

Fig. 4. CBR throughput per source for fixed bandwidth scenario

As the order in which the MPLS-CR paths between sources and destinations are created influences the paths chosen, two orders are used.

The first possibility is to create first the UDP paths for Gold and Silver classes and then the TCP paths for Gold and Silver classes. This will enable that several paths with different source-destination pairs share links in the core. This possibility was used in the adaptive algorithm.

The second possibility is for all source-destination pairs, no matter what their class or protocol, to use the same path. This will enable a better division of the bandwidth between the different classes. This possibility was used in the mathematical algorithm.

The first possibility results into a slightly worse delay and jitter for TCP flows, as they use the longest paths. Otherwise, there are no significant differences in the QoS.

3.3 *Adaptive Dynamic Bandwidth*

In the first dynamic technique, an adaptive algorithm moves bandwidth between the traffic classes, as necessary.

Figures 5, 6 and 7 show the throughput with this technique for the same situation as in figures 2, 3 and 4.

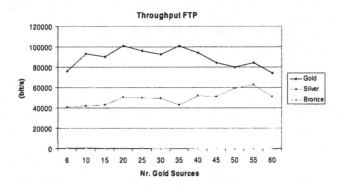

Fig. 5. FTP throughput per source for the adaptive dynamic technique

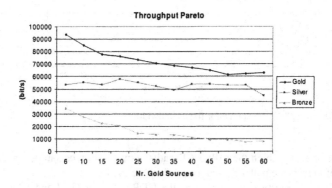

Fig. 6. Pareto throughput per source for the adaptive dynamic technique

Now there is no priority inversion for the throughput of FTP and Pareto applications, as the load increases. However, as a certain minimum bandwidth is assured to each class, the throughput variation is small as the load increases. This minimum bandwidth assured for the Silver class still causes a QoS priority inversion for high loads on the Gold class for CBR traffic. Although this priority inversion is a disadvantage from the proportional differentiation point of view, it might make sense, depending on the service being sold to users, since a minimum assured bandwidth is also of some value to users. The mathematical algorithm removes this minimum, as it does not use any steps.

For the FTP sources, the relation between the Gold throughput and the Silver throughput is 1.8 on the average, not far from the configured value of 2. But for the other types of sources, the relation is far from 2 on the average.

The other QoS parameters (end-to-end delay, jitter and packet loss) will be analyzed in section 3.5, so that all proposed techniques are evaluated together for these parameters and compared to the fixed bandwidth scenario.

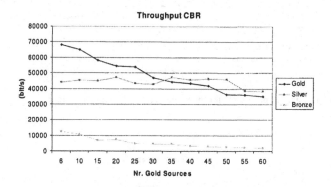

Fig. 7. CBR throughput per source for the adaptive dynamic technique

3.4   *Mathematical Dynamic Bandwidth*

In this second dynamic technique, the existing bandwidth is divided between the traffic classes according to the proposed mathematical expressions.

Figures 8, 9 and 10 show the throughput with this technique for the same situation as in figures 2, 3 and 4.

Now there is a better proportionality between the QoS in the Gold and Silver classes, with an increased throughput for low loads as compared with the adaptive algorithm.

For the FTP sources, the relation between the Gold throughput and the Silver throughput is 2.4 on the average, not far from the configured value of 2. For low loads, the Silver class is not much loaded and gets more than half the throughput of the Gold class. For high loads, there are many packet retransmissions, lowering the Silver class throughput.

For Pareto and CBR sources, the proportionality is not so easily obtained, but the Gold class always gets better QoS. For low loads, all Gold and Silver source applications can transmit all their packets, so the throughput is similar for both classes. When the load increases, the Silver class is much more affected than the

Gold class. The relation between the Gold throughput and the Silver throughput is 2.2 on the average for the Pareto sources and 1.9 for the CBR sources.

The other QoS parameters (end-to-end delay, jitter and packet loss) are analyzed in the next section.

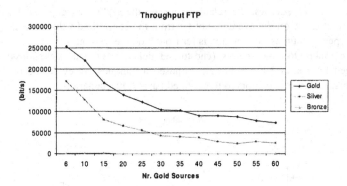

Fig. 8. FTP throughput per source for the mathematical dynamic technique

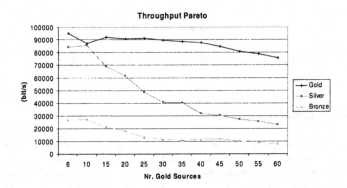

Fig. 9. Pareto throughput per source for the mathematical dynamic technique

3.5   QoS Comparison

Figure 11 shows the end-to-end delay averaged over the different types of user applications, for the different algorithms, for the Gold class on the left and for the Silver class on the right. The evolution of the remaining QoS parameters (jitter and packet loss) is very similar to the evolution of the delay, so they are not shown. The conclusions are the same as for the delay.

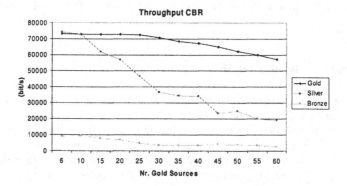

Fig. 10. CBR throughput per source for the mathematical dynamic technique

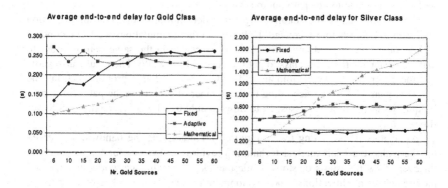

Fig. 11. Average end-to-end delay for the Gold and Silver classes

From figure 11, it can be observed that the end-to-end delay for the Gold class with the mathematical algorithm has a similar evolution as in the fixed bandwidth scenario, but with smaller values, resulting in better QoS. On the other hand, the end-to-end delay for the Silver class with the mathematical algorithm increases much faster as the load increases, when compared with the fixed bandwidth scenario. This means that the mathematical algorithm moves bandwidth from the Silver to the Gold class, increasing the Gold QoS and degrading the Silver QoS, when the load on the Gold class increases.

As regards the adaptive algorithm, the end-to-end delay for the Gold class is about constant when the load increases, while the end-to-end delay for the Silver class degrades much more slowly than for the mathematical algorithm.

The mathematical algorithm offers better QoS to the Gold class, but for high loads, the QoS of the Silver class is better for the adaptive algorithm, as it assures a minimum bandwidth to the Silver sources, independently of the load in the Gold class.

4   Conclusions and Further Work

This paper proposes and evaluates two techniques for implementing proportional differentiated services based on MPLS-CR.

The results show that with both techniques proposed it is possible to improve the QoS users get, as compared with the situation of fixed bandwidth division.

The results show that the mathematical technique makes a more uniform division of the bandwidth, according to the number of existing sources, resulting in a better overall QoS and better proportional differentiation of the throughput.

The main restriction to the mathematical approach is that the paths for the same source-destination pair need to be always the same for all the protocols and classes, otherwise the value for the TOTALbw in the equations will not make sense, since it will not correspond to one path but to several ones.

On the other hand, the adaptive algorithm does not have that kind of restriction and paths can be randomly created. However, in these simulations we had a concern which was to put a Gold and a Silver class aggregate in the same path in order to make it easier for the Gold class to get the needed bandwidth. The results also show that the difference between Gold and Silver QoS is not always proportional, but the aim is to guarantee a TpS according to the number of sources in the path. If the path is equally shared by both classes, Gold flows should usually get twice the QoS Silver flows get.

As regards the signaling traffic required for modifying the bandwidth reserved for the paths, the mathematical technique provides new values for the reservations for every flow that starts or stops, while the adaptive technique works in steps and requires fewer modifications. The development of a technique to keep the signaling traffic within a certain limit, say 1% of the network capacity, was left for further study. The removal of some simplifications was also left for further study. These include: the use of other network topologies; the simultaneous use of sources with different QoS requirements; the use of different proportionality factors between the Gold and Silver bandwidths; and the use of multiple paths for each source-destination pair.

References

[1] S. Giordano, S. Salsano, S. Van den Berghe, G. Ventre, D. Giannakopoulos, "Advanced QoS Provisioning in IP Networks: The European Premium IP Projects", *IEEE Communications Magazine*, 41(1):30-36, January 2003.
[2] S. Blake, D. Black, M. Carlson, E. Davies, Z. Wang, W. Weiss, "An Architecture for Differentiated Services", IETF RFC 2475, December 1998.

[3] B. Jamoussi, L. Andersson, R. Callon, R. Dantu, L. Wu, P. Doolan, T. Worster, N. Feldman, A. Fredette, M. Girish, E. Gray, J. Heinanen, T. Kilty, A. Malis, "Constraint-Based LSP Setup using LDP", IETF RFC 3212, January 2002.

[4] J. Heinamen, F. Baker, W. Weiss, J. Wroclawski, "Assured Forwarding PHB Group", IETF RFC 2597, June 1999.

[5] Y. Chen, C. Qiao, M. Hamdi, D. Tsang, "Proportional Differentiation: A Scalable QoS Approach", *IEEE Communications Magazine*, 41(6):52-58, June 2003.

[6] P. Pereira, P. Lepera, A. Casaca, "DiffServ Traffic Management with MPLS", 5th Conference on Telecommunications, ConfTele'2005, Tomar, Portugal, April 2005. ISBN: 972-98115-9-8.

[7] UCB/LBNL/VINT Network Simulator (version 2). http://www.isi.edu/nsnam/ns/

A Model of Signaling for Establishing of LSPs for Multicast Communication over GMPLS Networks

Rafael P. Esteves[1], Antônio J. G. Abelém[1], Ewerton Vaz[2] and Michael A. Stanton[3]

1 Federal University of Pará, Department of Informatics
Rua Augusto Corrêa, 01, 66075-110, Belém, Pará, Brazil
{esteves, abelem}@ufpa.br
WWW home page: http://www.cultura.ufpa.br/abelem

2 Federal University of Pará, Computer Science Graduate Program
Rua Augusto Corrêa, 01, 66075-110, Belém, Pará, Brazil
ewerton@ufpa.br
WWW home page: http://www.ufpa.br/ppgcc

3 Fluminense Federal University, Institute of Computing
Rua Passo da Pátria, 156, bloco E, sala 350, 24210-240, Niterói, RJ, Brazil
michael@ic.uff.br
WWW home page: http://www.ic.uff.br/~michael/

Abstract. Label switching, which in IP networks is exemplified by MPLS and its extensions MPLambdaS and GMPLS, appears as one of the best alternatives to offer a reliable and flexible control plane for WDM networks, since it allows the integration of the IP Protocol with WDM technology, when lambdas are associated with labels, implements powerful traffic-engineering mechanisms, and provides several alternative schemes for fault-tolerance, as well as support for quality of service (QoS). However, almost all the definitions and standardizations for MPLS are restricted to unicast communication, leaving support for multicast communication for future work. In the specific case of the triggering problem for LSPs (Label Switched Paths), there is still no consensus about the best strategy for multicast communication. This paper proposes an algorithm for traffic-driven triggering of LSPs, based on MFCs (Multicast Forwarding Caches), and has the advantage of being a schema which is compatible with several multicast routing protocols. To validate the proposed algorithm we carry out simulation studies using the NS-2 (Network Simulator) simulation platform.

Please use the following format when citing this chapter:

Esteves, R.P., Abelém, A.J.G., Vaz, E., Stanton, M.A., 2006, in IFIP International Federation for Information Processing, Volume 213, Network Control and Engineering for QoS, Security, and Mobility, V, ed. Gaïti, D., (Boston: Springer), pp. 171–186.

1 Introduction

The increasing demand for sophisticated network applications, allied to the growth of the Internet traffic, has lead to great efforts in the search of improvements in data transmission technologies with the intention of satisfying the increasing demand for bandwidth.

So far as optical networking is concerned, WDM (Wavelength Division Multiplexing) appears as the main advance in the transmission area, because it allows transmission rates near to the theoretical limit of optical fibers, of the order of dozens of terabits a second [1]. An essential issue in optical network design is defining how the network will be controlled, that is, what type of signalling will be responsible for resource reservation, route determination and fault handling, among other functions that constitute the control plane.

Label switching, which in IP networks is exemplified by MPLS (Multiprotocol Label Switching) [2], was extended through GMPLS (Generalized Multiprotocol Label Switching) [3] to operate with several different network technologies, where the label can be represented in other ways, for example, as time-slots in TDM networks, as physical switch ports and as wavelengths (lambdas) in WDM networks.

GMPLS appears as one of the best alternatives to offer a reliable and flexible control plane for WDM networks, since it allows the integration of the IP Protocol with WDM technology, when lambdas are associated with labels, implements powerful traffic-engineering mechanisms, and provides several alternative schemes for fault-tolerance, as well as support for quality of service (QoS). However, almost all the definitions and standardizations for MPLS are restricted to unicast communication, leaving support for multicast communication for future work.

In multicast based on label switching, the establishment of a label-switched path (LSP) can be made in three ways [4]: request-driven, topology-driven or traffic-driven. However, there is no consensus on which is the best alternative, since all three present pros and cons. In a similar way, controversies exist about the type of control to be adopted in multicast communication (independent or ordered) and about the method for distributing labels for a certain equivalence class, which can either be initiated by the egress LSR of the link, using the on-demand or unsolicited approaches, or by the ingress LSR of the link, using the on-demand, unsolicited or implicit approaches [4]. Thus we may conclude that a great opportunity is presented to analyze and reformulate some aspects of multicast communication and its use in a label switching context.

The objective of this paper is to propose an algorithm for the traffic-driven triggering of LSPs based on MFCs (Multicast Forwarding Caches), which are structures derived from the multicast routing tables found in the implementations of IP multicast (DVMRP, PIM), with the purpose of obtaining a scheme which is compatible with several implementations of multicast routing protocols. Basically, in this approach, when a node needs to create an entry in an MFC to store information about multicast groups, an LSP request is sent and processed by all the nodes in the direction of the source node. To validate the proposal, simulations were carried out using the NS-2 (*Network Simulator*) simulation platform.

As our proposal is related to label-switching in a general way, it can be associated, in addition to MPLS, to the improvements developed to bring label switching to the next-generation networks, such as GMPLS.

In addition to this introductory section, the paper is organized in more 4 sections. Section 2 discusses the characteristics of existing LSP triggers, presented in the literature. The algorithm for establishing LSPs is described in Section 3. Section 4 presents the simulation experiments used to validate the proposed algorithm. Section 5 presents conclusions and proposals for future work.

2   Triggering Multicast LSPs

One of the main discussion points concerning the use of label switching for multicast communication is the choice of method to be used to establish the label-switched paths.

Ooms et al. [4] define three approaches to this task: request-driven, topology-driven and traffic-driven. In the request-driven approach the label advertisement messages are encapsulated in control messages of the multicast routing protocol, such as *Join* messages, or in RSVP messages. This approach takes advantage of the characteristics of existing routing protocols, but can require that such protocols include explicit control messages, such as in PIM-SM, restricting its applicability to this class of protocol.

The encapsulation of label advertisements in native control messages of the multicast routing protocol is usually referred as "*piggy-backing*". This method has some problems, such as the fact that it excludes dense-mode protocols, since these do not use explicit control messages, and the modifications needed to add these messages to the protocol would be very expensive. Piggy-backing also makes impractible the use of other approaches to LSP triggering, as well as requiring extensions to the routing protocol to handle other LDP (*Label Distributon Protocol*) functions, such as peer discovery, and contributing to an increase in control traffic.

The topology-driven approach maps a level 3 multicast tree to a level 2 tree. The disadvantage of this is that labels are consumed even if there is no traffic for a certain multicast tree.

Traffic-driven LSP triggering has the advantage of consuming less labels than the other methods, because LSPs will only be established if there is demand for traffic. To achieve this, the technique monitors data structures known as MFCs (Multicast Forwarding Caches). MFCs are subsets of multicast routing tables that store information relating only to multicast groups that handle traffic [5]. If no entry exists in the MFC for a given multicast packet, one will be created. If the routes change afterwards, the MFC will be updated.

MFCs are used in most IP multicast implementations in UNIX systems and, as they are kept in the kernel of the operating system, traffic-driven triggering can be used with several different multicast routing protocols, making this approach more attractive than the alternatives.

Although these different approaches have all been proposed, a detailed definition of their mechanisms is needed, and some of them are not compatible with all existing multicast routing protocols. In this paper we describe an algorithm to establish LSPs based on traffic-driven triggering, since this approach has the advantage of being compatible with several multicast routing protocols and also consumes fewer labels than other multicast LSP triggers.

3   An Algorithm for LSP Establishment for Multicast Communication Based on MFCs

3.1   Reference Model

The reference model used in this article consists of IP/MPLS (we will use the MPLS term to refer to MPLS and its extensions MPλS and GMPLS) routers connected by means of an optical internetwork, using dynamically switched lightpaths (Fig. 1). The optical networks composing this internetwork are based on OCS (*Optical Circuit Switching*) [6] and MPLS paradigms. The choice of OCS is due to its low complexity, and, consequently, low implementation cost compared with other optical switching paradigms. On the other hand, the choice of MPLS, as pointed out in Section II, is justified by its flexibility and support for traffic engineering, as well as its being extensible to work with WDM technology, with the use of wavelengths as labels.

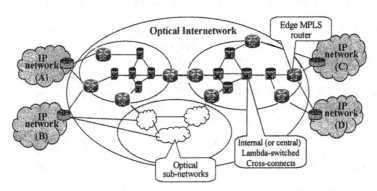

Fig. 1. Model network used in this proposal, composed of multiple optical switching devices (LSC) interconnected by an optical mesh.

We assume that the optical internetwork consists of a number of optical networks, each of which might be operated by a separate administrative entity. Each optical network can be made up of subnetworks comprised of a number of optical switching devices capable of label switching (Lambda Switching Crossconnects - LSCs) and interconnected by some non-specific topology of optical links. For simplicity, we assume there exists a one-to-one mapping between WDM switches and their IP-addressable controllers.

Signaling in an optical internetwork is performed out of band, and uses just one (high capacity) signaling channel (or lambda) per fiber. Signaling messages are electronically processed by all nodes, including internal ones. Data packets are not processed at internal nodes, and we make no assumptions about the data transmission rate. Network intelligence is concentrated essentially at the network edge, and no global synchronization is required.

We further assume the use of the integrated control model, as presented in [7], where both the IP and optical domains are managed in a unified way, with a single routing protocol and a single control plane based on MPLS. In the case of the internetwork consisting of a single Autonomous System (AS), a single intradomain routing protocol will be considered. When several ASs are involved, an interdomain routing protocol will also have to be used. Both intra- and interdomain routing protocols need to include the necessary extensions for optical technologies.

We also consider that all devices run IP Multicast and that optical devices have full light-splitting capability. The equipment must support both level 2 (MPLS) and level 3 routing.

3.2   Description of the proposed algorithm

In this section we describe an algorithm for traffic-driven LSP triggering. Our purpose is to detail the actions needed to establish LSPs, using as few resources as possible. The algorithm works as follows:

Every time a node receives a multicast packet, it verifies if there is information about the destination in the multicast forwarding cache (MFC). If this information is not found this node requests the creation of an entry in this structure.

When a leaf node (a node that is a destination of the multicast data) needs to request an entry in the MFC it acquires a label (Label can be represented by a wavelength in a MPλS/GMPLS context) for itself and propagates to the previous node on the route from the source the following information: the label to be used and the FEC (Forwarding Equivalence Class) of the LSP that is being built.

This same information will be used to create entries in the LIB (Label Information Base) of the node. The LIB in each LSR (Label Switched Router) stores data that will later be used in label-processing. A LIB entry usually contains the following fields: FEC, incoming label, incoming interface, outgoing label and outgoing interface [8].

The label sent will be used by the previous node (following the traffic direction) on the label swapping operation, that is to change the incoming label value with the outgoing label value (the incoming label of the next hop towards the leaf-nodes).

An intermediate node will also assign a label, create a LIB entry and forward this information along the path to the previous node in a similar way.

The multicast traffic source node does not request labels because it gets them from the downstream nodes belonging to the multicast tree.

When an intermediate node needs to replicate packets, it will receive several labels for the same equivalence class from the outgoing interfaces of the multicast distribution tree. If this happens, the node creates the additional entries in the LIB with the same FEC and the same incoming label. Fig 2. illustrates the algorithm.

This upstream signaling approach was designed to guarantee that all the nodes along the path have labels for a given FEC. The FECs are associated with the traffic source in this approach, in other words, the packets that originate at a given node and belong to the same multicast group also belong to a single FEC. It is worth pointing out that in this approach a single FEC is associated with several LSPs that have a common source.

To initiate this LSP triggering process, traffic has to arrive at a leaf node belonging to a multicast group. This data forwarding demands level 3 routing, since there is still no LSP to route these packets at level 2, therefore, the devices used in this approach must support this functionality.

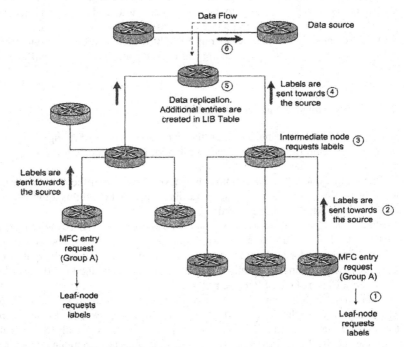

Fig. 2. Proposed algorithm for LSP triggering.

We now describe the format of the LIB entries created by the algorithm for each type of node (leaf, intermediate and source). On LSP triggering a LIB entry at the leaf node is created using the following format:

Table 1. LIB entry for a Leaf Node

FEC	Incoming Interface	Incoming Label	Outgoing Interface	Outgoing Label
Source node identifier	Next upstream node	Requested at this moment	-1	-1

FEC: The forwarding equivalence class that is associated with the source node in this case.

Incoming Interface: Defines where the traffic that arrives to that node comes from, that is, the next upstream node in this case.

Incoming Label: The incoming label consists of the label that is assigned by this node. It is requested at this moment, because this parameter will be forwarded to the upstream node to guarantee the creation of a consistent LSP between the leaf node and the data source.

Outgoing Interface: Represents the next hop of the packets. Here the value -1 is used because this is a leaf node, and there is no downstream node.

Outgoing Label: It represents the new value of the label. Here the value -1 is defined because it is a leaf node.

As the signaling messages reach intermediate nodes, the one of more entries are created in each of their LIBs, using the following format:

Table 2. LIB entry for intermediate nodes

FEC	Incoming Interface	Incoming Label	Outgoing Interface	Outgoing Label
Source node identifier	Upstream node	Requested at this moment	Next downstream node	Incoming label of the next downstream node

FEC, Incoming Interface and Incoming Label are interpreted and defined in a similar way to the leaf node.

Outgoing Interface: It is defined with the identifier of the next node towards a certain downstream leaf node, where an LSP was already triggered.

Outgoing Label: Defined with the value of the incoming label corresponding to the next downstream node in Outgoing Interface.

If this node is a data replicator, additional similar entries are created in the LIB with the same incoming interface and label but different outgoing interfaces and labels.

When the signaling message reaches the source node, one or more entries will be created in its LIB with the following format:

Table 3. LIB entry for the source node

FEC	Incoming Interface	Incoming Label	Outgoing Interface	Outgoing Label
Source node identifier	-1	-1	Next downstream node	Incoming label of the next downstream node

FEC, Outgoing Interface and Outgoing Label are interpreted and defined as shown in Table 2.

Incoming Interface: Here the value -1 is defined since, because it is the source node, there is no further upstream node.

Incoming Label: Here the value -1 is defined because it is the source node.

4   Validation and Analysis of the Proposed Mechanism

4.1   Tools Used

In order to analyze the proposed signaling and to verify its applicability, simulations were carried out using the NS-2 (*Network Simulator*) platform. NS-2 [9] is a discrete event-oriented simulator for computer networks much used by the scientific community for analysis and validation of proposals, having as a main attraction an extensible architecture that can easily incorporate new functionality.

NS-2 has modules for label switching, MNS (*"MPLS Network Simulator"*) [10], and for WDM optical networks simulations based in lambda (circuit) switching, OWNS (*"Optical WDM Network Simulator"*) [11]. It also supports multicast communications through the implementation of dense-mode protocols (PIM-DM, DVMRP), sparse-mode protocols (PIM-SM) and shared trees.

OWNS is an extension module for NS-2 that allows simulation of WDM networks that use circuit switching, also known as lambda switching. It also has components as optical switching nodes, wavelength multiplexed links, and routing and wavelength assignment algorithms.

MNS adds MPLS simulation capabilities to NS-2, including some characteristics as label switching, support for LDP and CR-LDP protocols, flow aggregation and constraint-based routing, and it allows the use of some LSP protection and restoration techniques.

The version of NS-2 used in this study was 2.1b6, because it has better compatibility with the NS-2 extensions, OWNS and MNS, that are fundamental for the required simulation context.

However, these modules do not cooperate with each other, and they do not support multicast communication. Therefore, the simulation of the proposed LSP triggering mechanism demands the following preliminary conditions:

- The integration of OWNS and MNS modules, described in detail in [12] [13], which enables us to characterize the GMPLS architecture, where the labels are associated with wavelengths (lambdas). It is worth pointing out that GMPLS adds new functions to the existing ones in MPLS: however, in our case, the other characteristics of GMPLS were not implemented, as we just needed the mapping between labels and lambdas and the functionalities already defined in the MNS module.

- Modifications and adaptations to extend the previously developed combined WDM-MPLS structure, to add support for multicast communication, including the development of replicators that can handle labels and the implementation of the proposed algorithm. Boudani and Cousin [14] have proposed a simulation tool based on

NS-2 that implements multicast communication in MPLS networks. However, this latter proposal is limited to the PIM-SM multicast routing protocol, which distributes labels through explicit signaling, using *Join* messages, while our proposal works with several protocols since it implements the traffic-driven LSP triggering.

Fig. 3 shows the NS-2 node structure developed to support multicast transport in networks with label switching.

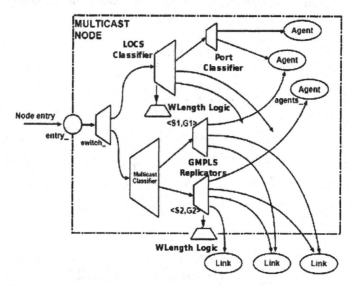

Fig. 3. NS-2 node structure developed for simulations

The LOCS classifier is the union of the MPLS node classifier and the WDM node classifier belonging to MNS and OWNS respectively. The classifier is responsible for forwarding the packets to the appropriate simulation object, such as an agent that simulates a transport protocol. In addition to this new classifier, we have built a structure (Wavelength Logic) that keeps the information on the wavelengths allocated in each link in accordance with the established LSPs, using for this purpose the MPLS Label Information Base (LIB).

In the part of the node that deals with multicast communication we have added a new replicator, the GMPLS replicator, that produces several copies of incoming information and sends the copies to its outgoing interfaces. The replicator object is essential to implement the multicast communication in NS-2.

The actions taken by this node when receiving a data packet are described below:

1. When a packet arrives at the node entry point, it is analyzed to check whether or not it is addressed to a multicast address.

2. If it is a multicast packet, then it is forwarded to the Multicast Classifier, that, in its turn, sends the packet to the appropriate GMPLS replicator. Otherwise, the information is sent to LOCS Classifier.
3. If the next hop IP address is of this node, then the packet is passed on to the Port Classifier, to determine which agent will be responsible for handling the arriving information.
4. Otherwise, the packet is sent to the next node through the optical links using label switching.

The label switching mechanisms in the new node works as illustrated in Fig. 4.

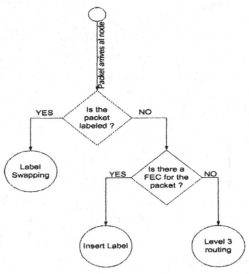

Fig 4. Label switching on the developed node

1. When a packet arrives at the LOCS classifier, it is analyzed to verify if it is labeled or not.
2. If the packet is labeled, the label swapping operation is processed (the value of the incoming label may be different from the value of outgoing label) and the information is sent for the correspondent outgoing interface. In the case that the value of the incoming label is different from the value of the outgoing label, wavelength conversion is characterized. When the packet arrives at its final destination no label swapping will be carried out.
3. If the packet is not already labeled, but there exists a FEC for it (that defines a group of packets routed in the same way), a label is inserted and Wavelength Logic is updated.
4. If no FEC is defined for the packet, it is routed at level 3 in the conventional way.

After integrating these components, we were then able to adapt the existing functionalities of MNS, such as label switching, traffic engineering, protection and restoration, and others, to the context of optical networks provided by OWNS.

Finally, the proposed LSP triggering algorithm was implemented and incorporated in the LDP protocol of MNS and associated with the event of creation of entries in the MFC.

4.2   A Case Study

In this section, we present a case study to illustrate the proposed LSP triggering scheme in a possible multicast backbone in Brazil interconnecting the metropolitan networks of the state capitals of the Amazon Region with the national capital of Brasília, using optical fibers. This network could be implemented through OCTL (Optical Cables in Transmission Lines) cables that use the OPGW technology [6].

This proposed backbone is represented in Fig. 5 and will be used in the simulations.

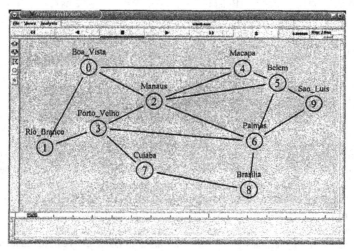

Fig. 5. Topology used in simulations

The network has 10 nodes, each one representing a capital city. In the simulations, 10Gbps optical links were assumed. Their propagation delays in milliseconds are listed. These delays are based in real distances.

Boa Vista	Rio Branco	11ms
Boa Vista	Manaus	4ms
Boa Vista	Macapá	30ms
Rio Branco	Porto Velho	3ms
Manaus	Porto Velho	5ms
Manaus	Macapá	25ms
Manaus	Belém	26ms
Manaus	Palmas	20ms
Porto Velho	Cuiabá	7ms
Porto Velho	Palmas	16ms
Macapá	Belém	2ms
Belém	Palmas	6ms
Belém	São Luís	4ms
Palmas	São Luís	7ms
Palmas	Brasília	5ms
Cuiabá	Brasília	6ms

The traffic type used is CBR (Constant Bit Rate) with a 4Mb rate. This rate can be associated with multimedia transmission in the MPEG-2 format. It was defined that the node in Brasília (Node 8) sends data for a multicast group composed by Belém (Node 5), Boa Vista (Node 0) and São Luís (Node 9) nodes. The multicast routing protocol used is PIM-SM (in NS-2 this protocol is known as centralized multicast) with node 6 (Palmas) as the rendezvous point. The choice for PIM-SM is due to the low density of the multicast group defined. This does not interfere in our analysis.

4.3   Results

We present below some of the LIBs generated by the use of the proposed LSP triggering algorithm based on the scenario described in the previous section. The purpose is to illustrate the functioning of the proposed algorithm for LSP setup.

```
··) __PFT dump__ [LSR 8] (··
```
....

FEC	Fid	PRio	LIBptr	SLIBptr	AlternativePath
8	-1	0	0	-1	-1

```
__LIB dump__ [LSR 8]
```
....

#	iIface	iLabel	oIface	oLabel	LIBptr	Linkerror?
0:	-1	-1	6	1	-1	-1

Fig 6. PFT and LIB for Node 8 (source node)

Our simulation platform inherits from the MNS module a structure known as PFT (Partial Forwarding Table), that is used to map FECs to LIB entries. The FEC value 8 refers to all multicast packets that have this node as source. If there are others traffic sources, additional LIB entries must be created at the nodes that receive or forward packets from these sources.

```
··) __PFT dump__ [LSR 6] (··
```
....

FEC	Fid	PRio	LIBptr	SLIBptr	AlternativePath
8	-1	0	0	-1	-1
8	-1	0	1	-1	-1
8	-1	0	2	-1	-1

```
__LIB dump__ [LSR 6]
```
....

#	iIface	iLabel	oIface	oLabel	LIBptr	Linkerror?
0:	8	1	2	1	-1	-1
1:	8	1	5	1	-1	-1
2:	8	1	9	1	-1	-1

Fig. 7. PFT and LIB for Node 6 (intermediate node)

Node 6 replicates packets, hence, we observe the creation of three LIB entries for the same FEC. Entry 0 is related to the traffic destinated to Node 0 through outgoing interface number 2. Entry 1 was created to send packets to Node 5 and Entry 2 to the traffic destinated to Node 9. All these entries have the same incoming label. The outgoing labels may or not be the same.

```
··) __PFT dump__ [LSR 5] (··
..........................................................
  FEC      Fid      PRio     LIBptr   SLIBptr  AlternativePath
   8       -1        0         0        -1        -1


__LIB dump__ [LSR 5]
..........................................................
    #     iIface   iLabel   oIface   oLabel   LIBptr   Linkerror?
   0:       6        1        -1       -1       -1        -1
```

Fig. 8. PFT and LIB for Node 5 (leaf-node)

Node 5 is a destination of this multicast group. It is from this node and the other leaf nodes of this multicast group that the proposed LSP triggering scheme begins. From the LIBs generated it can be concluded that this part of LSP referring to FEC 8 (group that receives packets originated from Node 8) corresponds to the path composed by Nodes 8, 6 and 5, successively. The remaining parts of the LSP are built starting at Nodes 0 and 9, the other destinations of the group.

4.4   Considerations about the proposed algorithm

To initiate this LSP triggering process, traffic has to arrive at a leaf node belonging to a multicast group. This data forwarding demands level 3 routing, since there is still no LSP to route these packets at level 2, therefore, the devices used in this approach must support this functionality.

Some problems can occur in the process of creating an LSP, for instance, a label request cannot be satisfied. In this case, we need to send a signaling message from the node where the problem occurred to the leaf-nodes that triggered the LSP. This message must contain the information about the FEC related to the LSP that could not be established in order to remove the LIB entries created for this FEC. Fig. 9 illustrates this feature.

The scheme proposed here is similar to unsolicited downstream label distribution [2], with the added advantage of eliminating the signaling delay imposed when the LSP triggering is initiated at the source node, without threatening the integrity of already established LSPs, or unnecessary resource allocation, since the LSP is triggered only if there is traffic in the multicast tree.

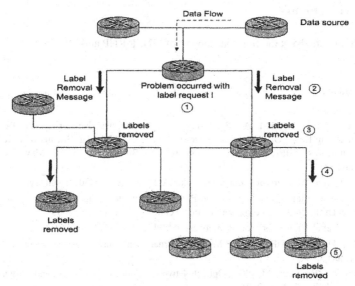

Fig. 9. Procedure in case of problems with label request.

5   Conclusion and Future Work

Several issues regarding to the adaptation of label switching to multicast communication in optical networks are currently being discussed and defined. This paper presents a concrete proposal for the establishment of label-switched paths using traffic-driven triggering, that is more attractive than the request-driven and topology-driven approaches, for reasons of independence of the multicast routing protocol used and lower label consumption.

The scheme proposed here is similar to unsolicited downstream label distribution [2], with the added advantage of eliminating the signaling delay imposed when the LSP triggering is initiated at the source node, without threatening the integrity of already established LSPs, or unnecessary resource allocation, since the LSP is triggered only if there is traffic in the multicast tree.

Simulations presented here show that the proposed algorithm can be implemented and satisfactorily perform the task of LSP creation. We can also see that the algorithm can minimize the blocking probability of connections, since wavelength assignment occurs in a controlled manner from the leaf nodes towards the source, and because the number of wavelength requests is small in a traffic-driven approach. Thus the probability of a wavelength being already allocated decreases.

Future studies will deal with the detailed evaluation of the impact caused by the proposed LSP triggering algorithm on the connection blocking probability, compared with other approaches, and with the analysis of traffic-engineering mechanisms in multicast communication in optical networks.

Ackowledgments

The authors thank the finnacial support of FINEP/RNP and Eletronorte.

References

1. Abelém, A.; Stanton, M. A. IP Internets Based on Optical Networks (Inter-Redes IP Baseadas em Redes Ópticas). Minicourses text book, 20° Simpósio Brasileiro de Redes de Computadores (SBRC2002), Cap. 2, pp. 63-123, Búzios, RJ, Brazil. May, 2002. (in Portuguese)

2. Rosen, E. et al. Multiprotocol Label Switching Architecture. RFC3031. January, 2001.

3. Mannie E. (Editor). Generalized Multi-Protocol Label Switching (GMPLS) Architecture. Internet Draft, draft-ietf-ccamp-gmpls-architecture-04.txt. February, 2003.

4. Ooms, D. et al. Framework for IP Multicast in MPLS. RFC 3353. August, 2002.

5. Ooms, D. et al. MPLS for PIM-SM. Internet Draft, draft-ooms-mpls-pimsm-00.txt. November, 1998.

6. Murthy, C.; Gurusamy, M. WDM Optical Networks: Concepts, Design, and Algorithms, Prentice Hall PTR, Nov. 2001.

7. Rajagopalan, B. et al. IP over Optical Networks: A Framework. *RFC3717*. March, 2004.

8. Magalhães, M.; Cardozo, E. Introduction to IP Label-switching through MPLS (Introdução à comutação IP por rótulos através de MPLS). Minicourses text book, 19° Simpósio Brasileiro de Redes de Computadores (SBRC2002), Cap. 3, Florianópolis, SC, Brazil. May, 2001. (in Portuguese)

9. Fall, K.; Varadhan, V. The *ns* Manual. Url: http://www.isi.edu/nsnam/ns . Accessed in: July, 2005.

10. Ahn, G; Chun, W. Design and Implementation of MPLS Network Simulator. Url: http://flower.ce.cnu.ac.kr/~fog1/mns/. Accessed in: July, 2005.

11. Wen, B; Bhide, N. M.; Shenai, R. K.; Sivalingam, K. M.Optical Wavelength Division Multiplexing (WDM) Network Simulator (OWns): Architecture and Performance Studies. In: SPIE Optical Networks Magazine Special Issue on Simulation, CAD, and Measurement of Optical Networks, March, 2001.

12. Esteves, R.; Nagahama, F.; Abelém, A.; Stanton, M. A Proposal to Adjust the GMPLS Control and Signaling Mechanisms for Optical Burst Switched Networks. In: Annals of 3rd International Information and Telecommunication Technologies Symposium (I2TS2004). São Carlos, SP, Brazil. December, 2004.

13. Viana, J.; Esteves, R; Abelém, A; Costa, J. C.; Stanton, M. Analysis of Failure-Recovery Mechanisms in Next-Generation Optical Networks with Control Plane Based on GMPLS (Análise de Mecanismos de Recuperação de Falhas em Redes Ópticas de Nova Geração com Plano de Controle Baseado no GMPLS). In: IV Workshop em Desempenho de Sistemas Computacionais e de Comunicação-WPERFORMANCE (SBC2005), São Leopoldo, RS, Brazil. July, 2005. (in Portuguese)

14. Boudani, A.; Cousin, B. Multicast Routing Simulator over MPLS Networks. 36th Annual Simulation Symposium, Orlando, Florida, USA, March 2003.

Agent-Based Self-Management of MPLS DiffServ-TE domain

Rana Rahim-Amoud, Leila Merghem-Boulahia, and Dominique Gaiti
Institut Charles DELAUNAY, University of Technology of Troyes
12, rue Marie Curie, BP 2060, 10 010 TROYES CEDEX, FRANCE
{rana.amoud, leila.boulahia, dominique.gaiti}@utt.fr,
WWW home page: http://www.utt.fr/labos/LM2S/

Abstract. MPLS DiffServ-TE presents the solution awaited so much by the network service providers by allowing a differentiation of services and a traffic engineering based on a fast packet switching technology. However, the management of such a network is not a simple function and could not be done manually. In this paper, we propose a novel architecture based on the Multi-Agent Systems (MAS) capable of managing automatically MPLS DiffServ-TE domains. Based on the network states, our intelligent agents take the appropriate decisions. They, for example, reconfigure the network accordingly.

1 Introduction

The Multi-Protocol Label Switching (MPLS) [28] is an Internet Engineering Task Force (IETF) framework that performs label switching between layer 2 and layer 3 protocols. It is a versatile solution to address the problems faced by present-day networks like speed, scalability, quality of service (QoS) and traffic engineering [19].

In recent years, there has been active research in the field of MPLS and an increasing number of networks are supporting MPLS [3]. One of the most significant applications of MPLS is traffic engineering (TE) [4]. MPLS-TE enables resource reservation, fault-tolerance and optimization of transmission resources [23]. However, MPLS does not define a new QoS architecture [11] and cannot provide service differentiation by itself.

DiffServ (Differentiated Services) [5] defines an architecture for implementing scalable service differentiation in the Internet by defining multiple classes of service. The combination of DiffServ and MPLS [16] presents a very attractive strategy to backbone network service providers with scalable QoS and traffic engineering capabilities using fast packet switching technologies. The result is the MPLS

Please use the following format when citing this chapter:

Rahim-Amoud, R., Merghem-Boulahia, L., Gaiti, D., 2006, in IFIP International Federation for Information Processing, Volume 213, Network Control and Engineering for QoS, Security, and Mobility, V, ed. Gaïti, D., (Boston: Springer), pp. 187–199.

DiffServ-TE which will be able to satisfy users' requests like the QoS guarantees while optimizing the use of network resources.

As networks grow rapidly and traffic conditions change frequently, the management of the above MPLS network presents many complexities and could not be done manually. Therefore, automated management is required to minimize this complexity and to engineer traffic efficiently [8]. Moreover, recent researches showed the effectiveness of Multi-Agent Systems (MAS) for the dynamic management of distributed systems [13, 29].

In this paper, we propose a novel architecture based on MAS capable of managing automatically MPLS DiffServ-TE domains. Based on the network states, our intelligent agents take the appropriate decisions. They, for example, reconfigure the network accordingly.

This paper is organized as follows. In the second section we discuss MPLS-TE and DiffServ. A brief description of the multi-agent systems is done in section 3. Our proposition and our proposed architecture are presented in sections 4 and 5 respectively. The LSP creation strategy is presented in section 6. Conclusion and future work are given in section 7.

2   MPLS-TE and DiffServ

2.1   MPLS

MPLS [28] is a new technology that uses labels to forward packets by specifying the Forwarding Equivalence Class (FEC). A FEC is a representation of a group of packets that share the same requirements for their transport. All packets in such a group receive the same treatment in the domain.

MPLS domain contains two types of equipments: LER (Label Edge Router) and LSR (Label Switch Router). The LERs are also called I-LSR (Ingress LSR) for the LSR that puts the label to an incoming packet and E-LSR (Egress LSR) for the one which removes the label from the outgoing packet to return it to its initial nature. LSR is a high speed router device in the core of the MPLS network. The path between two LERs is called LSP (Label Switched Path).

2.2   MPLS-TE

Traffic engineering is used to achieve performance objectives such as optimization of network resources and placement of traffic on particular links [23]. In other terms, MPLS traffic engineering routes traffic flows across a network based on the resources the traffic flow requires and the resources available in the network [25].

Current Interior Gateway Protocols (IGPs) always use the shortest path to forward traffic in order to conserve network resources. However, using shortest path is not always the best choice and it may cause the following problems [30]:

1.   Different shortest paths from different sources overlap at some links causing congestion on those links.

2. The shortest path between a source and a destination is over-utilized while a longer path between these two routers is under-utilized.

TE is needed to avoid these problems by optimizing resource utilization and network performance. In order to control the path of LSPs effectively, one or more attributes can be assigned to each LSP. Such attributes are Bandwidth, Path attribute, Setup Priority, Holding Priority, Affinity, Adaptability, Resilience, etc. [30].

2.3   MPLS - DiffServ

There are many similarities between the functioning of MPLS and DiffServ. In MPLS domain, the classification of incoming packets is done just at the entry of the domain by the I-LSR router, by assigning a particular packet to a particular FEC. Within the domain, there is no reclassification and packets are just switched by LSRs according to labels.

In DiffServ domain, the traffic classification is also done by edge routers by setting the DSCP (Differentiated Service Code Point) field. In the core network, there is also no reclassification, routers use the DSCP value in the IP header to select a PHB (Per-Hop Behavior) for the packet and provide the appropriate QoS treatment [12].

It is clear that the functioning of MPLS and DiffServ is very similar and it consists of 3 main steps:
1. Traffic classification,
2. Labeling of packets after classifying them,
3. Traffic forwarding according to labels (DSCP in the DiffServ case).

In addition, both MPLS and DiffServ are based on the aggregation.

The mapping between DiffServ and MPLS is still an open research [3]. Currently, there are two solutions [16], the first one is applied to networks that support less than eight PHBs and it uses the 3 Exp (experimental) bits of the MPLS label to determine the PHB. In this case LSPs are called E-LSPs. The second solution is applied to networks that support more than eight PHBs. In this solution, the PHB is determined from both the label and the Exp bits and LSPs are called L-LSPs. Each solution has its advantages and its disadvantages and the use of one of them depends on the particular application scenarii [23]. In our proposition, we are going to consider the second solution by using different LSPs for different classes of traffic. The effect is that the physical network is divided into multiple virtual networks, one per class. These virtual networks may have different topologies and resources [30]. In this case, three virtual MPLS networks are defined for EF, AF and BE classes. An example is showed in Fig. 1.

The bandwidth set by administrators on each physical link is partitioned among these MPLS virtual networks. As a result, each network has a percentage of the maximum bandwidth. This will provide better resource utilization and each DiffServ level can be treated alone. The most important thing in the management of such network is the management of LSPs.

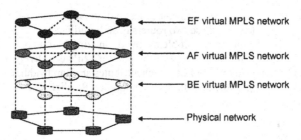

Fig. 1. Virtual MPLS networks

To summarize, we have seen that the TE is needed to avoid some serious problems. DiffServ is also needed to provide a differentiation of services into the MPLS network. However, the management of an MPLS DiffServ-TE network is not a simple function and an automated management is needed to reduce the complexity of the management tasks. Our proposed solution considers that the mapping between DiffServ and MPLS is done by the L-LSP method (multiple virtual networks). In addition, it is based on the use of multi-agent systems which are briefly described in the next section.

3 Multi-Agent Systems

Multi-Agent Systems are an innovative and interesting concept for a great number of researchers in different domains such as road traffic simulation [13, 18, 22], social phenomena simulation [6, 10], biological phenomena simulation [14, 15, 26], negotiation in electronic markets [1, 29], etc.

According to Ferber [17], an agent is a physical or virtual entity having trends and resources, able to perceive its environment, to act on it and to acquire a partial representation of it. It is also able to communicate with other peers and devices, and has a behavior that fits its objectives according to its knowledge and capabilities. Furthermore, agents can learn, plan future tasks and are able to react and to change their behavior according to the changes in their environment. A multi-agent system is a group of agents able to interact and to cooperate in order to reach a specific objective.

Agents are characterized by their properties that determine their capabilities. Different properties are defined like autonomy, proactive-ness, flexibility, adaptability, ability to collaborate and coordinate tasks and mobility. According to its role within its environment, the agent acquires some of these properties. Multi-agent approach is well suited to control distributed systems. Telecommunication networks are good examples of such distributed systems. This explains partly the considerable contribution of agent technology when introduced in this area which motivates us to use it.

4   Our proposition

Since the MPLS functioning is based on the use of LSP in order to forward packets, and the mapping between MPLS and DiffServ is also based on the LSP, it seems that the management of LSPs is the most important need. It includes LSP dimensioning, LSP setup procedure, LSP tear-down procedure, LSP routing, and LSP adaptation for incoming resource requests.

In order to effectively control and manage the path of LSPs, one or more attributes can be assigned to each LSP. Such attributes can be Bandwidth, Path attribute, Setup Priority, Holding Priority, Affinity, Adaptability, Resilience, etc. These attributes will be considered in computing the path for the LSP [30].

Agents that we will introduce into the MPLS domain have the role to introduce some decision-making abilities in the complex network management tasks. So the introduction of these agents will take place into the decision points of MPLS network. The first step of our research consisted in finding the decision points of the MPLS network which are especially identified on the entry of the domain on the LER routers [27].

An intelligent agent will be, as a result, introduced on the level of each LER router in the MPLS domain. In order to control and manage effectively the network and to benefit from the distribution feature of MAS, we decide to introduce also an agent on the level of each intermediate LSR. All these agents form a multi-agent system. These agents interact and communicate together and also interact with the routers and switches in the domain. Each agent has a local vision and takes local decisions in order to realize the main goal of the multi-agent system. The architecture of these agents is given in the next section.

5   The proposed architecture

Our principal idea is to control and manage the MPLS network by a simple automated way. This is the reason for which we decide to use Multi-Agent Systems. In fact, the most important feature of a multi-agent system, that we are interested in, is the distribution. An agent has a local view and takes local decisions in order to achieve the global goal of the system. In our case, an agent is introduced on the level of each router in the MPLS domain. Actually, each agent is responsible for the router on which it is introduced and for the corresponding interfaces.

The architecture of our intelligent agent is shown in Fig.2. It includes two entities: the collector entity (CE) and the management entity (ME) which includes, in its turn, two sub entities: the LSP resource management entity and the LSP route management entity. In addition, the architecture contains a Data Base (DB) which is shared between the CE and the ME.

The CE collects the information concerning the corresponding router and its interfaces. It collects various parameters like available bandwidth, delay, jitter, queue lengths, and the number of loosed packets. CE collects also the network topology information such as the new created LSPs, if an opened LSP is still useful or not, etc. Furthermore, the interaction between agents is done by their CEs by exchanging the collected information. This information is stored into the DB.

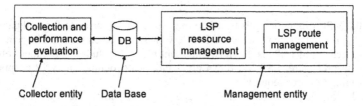

Fig. 2. Intelligent agent architecture

The ME is in charge of taking the corresponding decisions according to the collected information. Possible decisions are:

1. to create a new LSP,
2. to vary the resource allocated to a given LSP,
3. to tear down an LSP,
4. to establish a physical path for an LSP requiring a specified QoS.

After taking the appropriate decision, the next step done by the ME is to automatically implement this decision by configuring the corresponding router accordingly. The last step is done by the CE and consists in checking if the result obtained after the configuration corresponds to the intended one. The succession of these tasks is showed in Fig. 3.

The next section describes the function of the CE.

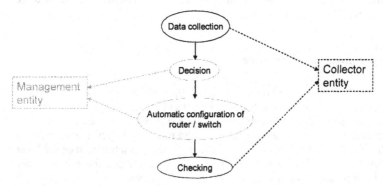

Fig. 3. The succession of tasks

5.1 Collector entity (CE)

The CEs collect the various parameters of the network and routers. Each CE collects only the information concerning the interfaces of its node. It uses SNMP (Simple Network Management Protocol) [9] to collect information from the MIB (Management Information Base) [21]. The objects collected from the MIB can have a read-only or a read-create access.

The collected information is stored into the DB. The ME which has access to the DB uses this information to take the suitable decisions and to configure the corresponding router accordingly.

We estimate that the available bandwidth is the most important parameter to be treated. It gives us a view of the current network state. At a first step, we will consider that the available bandwidth is the only parameter collected by the CEs and exchanged between agents (Fig. 4).

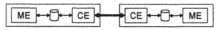

Fig. 4. The interaction between agents is done via the CEs

Each router is requested by the SNMP agent in order to collect the available bandwidth of its interfaces. One of the DB tables, called "LSP table", contains a list of the already created LSPs traversing the corresponding router, their current available bandwidths and the virtual topologies to which they belong. An example of this table can be showed in Fig .5.

Existant LSP	Available bandwith	Virtual topology
LSP1	150	EF
...	...	...

Fig. 5. An example of the LSP table. Each row contains the information concerning an LSP traversing the corresponding router.

5.2   Management entity (ME)

The ME is the most important part of our intelligent agent. In fact, it is responsible for the resource and route management. Precisely, it is responsible for determining when and where an LSP should be created. Based on the information collected by the CE, the ME takes the appropriate decision. The ME contains two sub entities: the LSP resource management entity and the LSP route management entity (Fig. 2).

5.2.1 LSP route management entity

The role of this entity is to route the new LSP on the physical network. More specifically, in case of creating a new LSP, the role of this entity is to decide, for a specific network state, how to select the most suitable route for the LSP avoiding placing many LSPs on a given link. Since the MPLS architecture does not specify any routing protocol, all standardized protocols can be used. The solution is then to choose the most appropriate protocol to be activated according to the network conditions. The decision rules of this entity will not be discussed in this paper.

5.2.2 LSP resource management entity

The role of this entity is to manage the LSP resources. In other terms, it is responsible for creating and re-dimensioning LSPs, etc. To take the suitable decision, the LSP resource management entity has to follow a strategy that we have proposed and called the "LSP creation strategy". This strategy is described in the next section.

6   The LSP creation strategy

The general goal of this strategy is to create LSP according to the network conditions. Currently, given the physical topology, the operator has to design a layout or virtual topology by finding an optimal set of paths and a flow distribution over it to accommodate a given demand, as well as to adapt the layout to varying traffic conditions [7].

To design the MPLS layout, there are on-line and off-line proposed approaches. Off-line approaches are based on the estimation of the traffic demand over time. According to Kodialam [20], off-line approaches are not appropriate to MPLS networks due to the high unpredictability of the Internet traffic. Another approach is based on the creation of a fully connected MPLS network. This approach consists of creating an LSP between each pair of nodes. This provides a large number of LSP introducing, as a result, high control traffic, high signaling cost, high management cost and high management complexity. Since these two methods present many disadvantages, they are to be avoided.

On-line methods calculate paths as demands arrive. Three different approaches can be distinguished:
1. Request-driven
2. Topology-driven
3. Traffic-driven

The request-driven approach is used when MPLS transmits multicast traffic [24]. We have avoided this approach because we are not interested in this paper by the multicast case.

In the topology-driven approach, a standard IP routing protocol runs and calculates the network's topology. In addition, a Label Distribution Protocol (LDP) constructs a mesh of labeled paths between ingress and egress LERs according to the routing entry generated by the routing protocol [2]. The constructed path is released only if the corresponding routing entry is deleted. In this approach, LSP already exists before traffic is transmitted. Thus, a constructed path may be not used because its creation was based only on the routing information. That is the big disadvantage of this approach.

In the Traffic-driven approach, the LSP is created according to the traffic information. When a new request arrives, the corresponding path is established and it is maintained until the request becomes inactive. In this approach, only the required LSPs are setup. This approach conserves labels, bandwidth, signaling and management.

It should be noted that the available bandwidth on a link is equal to the maximum bandwidth of the physical link minus the total bandwidth reserved by LSPs traversing the link. It does not depend on the actual amount of available bandwidth on that link [30]. The available bandwidth on a physical link is given by the following equation (1):

$$B_a = B_{rt} - \sum_{i=1}^{n} B_i \qquad (1)$$

Where B_a is the available bandwidth on the link, B_{rt} is the maximum reserved bandwidth of the physical link and B_i is the bandwidth reserved for the LSP_i.

We remark that the establishment of a non used LSP will have bad consequences on the total behavior of the MPLS network. A part of the bandwidth will be reserved without being used. Moreover, another LSP may be prevented from taking a path fault of the lack of the bandwidth. In this context, the traffic-driven technology is more advantageous than the topology-driven technology.

The solution, which seems the most logical and the most advantageous to design an MPLS network, is to determine an initial MPLS network topology and to adapt it to the traffic load. A topology change will take place, by consequence, when a new LSP is created or released after receiving a real request. Our goal is to decide when to create a new LSP and when to pass a new traffic in an already created LSP. To do that we define the most important factors which can have an influence on the possible decision, these factors are:

1. The requests
2. The network state
3. The cost

A request can be a new bandwidth request, a disabled bandwidth request or a request for disabling an existing LSP. The request is a very important factor because the type and the number of requests occurred at a precise instant have a big influence on the decision to be taken.

The network state includes the current MPLS topology (the virtual topology) such as the created LSP, the existence or not of an LSP between a pair of routers. The network state includes also the LSP attributes (i.e. the available bandwidth, the priority, etc.) and finally, it includes the physical link attributes (i.e. the available bandwidth, the delay, etc.). As we have mentioned above concerning the LSP attributes and the physical link attributes, our strategy takes into account only the available bandwidth. The other parameters will not be treated in this paper.

The cost includes three different components [3], (1) the signaling cost which is considered only when creating a new LSP or re-dimensioning an LSP. In the other cases, signaling is not needed. (2) The switching cost which depends on the switched bandwidth and the switching cost defined by the operator. (3) The bandwidth cost which depends on the carried bandwidth and the number of traversed nodes.

Taking into account these factors, we can distinguish many cases. The first and trivial case is when a request for disabling an already created LSP arrives. In this case, the LSP resource management entity takes the decision (1) to tear down the LSP, (2) to release the corresponding labels and (3) to liberate the bandwidth. As a result, the available bandwidth on the physical link is increased by the value of the liberated bandwidth.

A second trivial case is when a request for bandwidth is deactivated. In this case, the LSP resource management entity takes the decision (1) to liberate the corresponding bandwidth and (2) to increase the available bandwidth of the corresponding LSP by the value of the liberated bandwidth. Thus, the available bandwidth on the physical link remains the same.

Another case more complex than the previous ones is when a new bandwidth (BW) request arrives. The LSP creation strategy for this case is defined in the diagram showed in Fig.6.

Consider that a new BW request arrives between a pair of routers demanding a certain level of QoS. The first step consists of verifying the existence of an LSP between these two routers in the corresponding virtual topology (EF, AF or BE). This verification is done by consulting the "LSP table". If the LSP exists, the next step is to compare the available BW of that LSP with the requested BW. If the available BW is higher than the requested one, the requested BW is allocated on that LSP and its available BW is reduced accordingly.

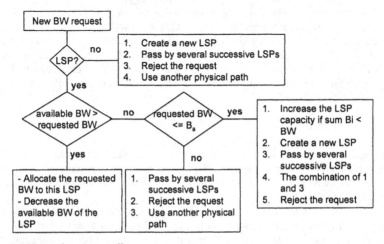

Fig. 6. LSP creation strategy diagram

If the available bandwidth is lower than the requested one, two cases can be distinguished:

a.   The requested BW is lower than or equal to the available BW on the physical link. In this case, several possibilities take place:

1.   According to Eq. 1 it is possible to increase the capacity of the LSP. In other words, the BW reserved for the LSP in question will be increased by a value equal to the requested BW to be able to forward the new traffic.

2.   Another possibility will be to create a new LSP and to reserve a BW to him equal to that requested.

In these two cases the available BW of the physical link is decreased by the value of the requested BW.

3.   A third possibility will be to pass by several successive LSPs by using the label stack, an example can be showed in Fig. 7.

In the case of Fig.6 there are two LSPs: LSP1 (Igress-LSRx-LSRy) and LSP2 (LSRy-LSRz-Egress). These two LSPs have one LSR in common and the idea is to use the LSP (Igress-LSRx-LSRy-LSRz-Egress).

The Ingress LSR pushes two labels onto the label stack of the incoming packet, label1 to be used to forward the traffic in LSP1 and label 2 to be used to forward the traffic in LSP2. When the packet arrives to the LSRy, LSRy pops off label1 and forwards the packet according to the label2.

4. The combination of the possibilities 1 and 3. An example can be to increase the capacity of LSP1 and use LSP1+LSP2 to forward the incoming traffic.

5. The last possibility will be to reject the request.

b. The requested BW is higher than the available capacity of the physical link. In this case, only the two possibilities (3 and 5) will be valid. Another solution is to pass by other physical links indicated by the routing protocol. In this case, a new LSP will be created between the pair of routers traversing another physical path.

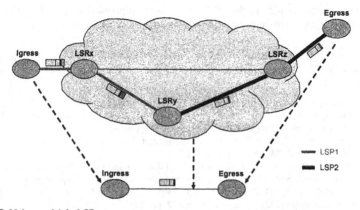

Fig. 7. Using multiple LSPs

If there is no LSP between the pair of routers, only the possibilities 2, 3 and 5 can be valid. Another solution is also to pass by other physical links as in b.

The previous cases correspond to the arrival of only one request. If several requests having the same type or different types arrive at the same moment, the decision will be much more complex. The decision will be a generalization of the previous cases. Considering the multitude of the possible cases, the most practical method which appears to us is the use of an optimization method which enables us to choose the best decision according to the various conditions and various factors. To do that, we have to choose the suitable optimization method and to formulate our problem as a mathematical model.

7   Conclusion and future work

In this paper, we propose a novel architecture based on the Multi-Agent Systems capable of managing automatically MPLS DiffServ-TE domains. Based on the network states, our intelligent agents take the appropriate decisions. In our approach, we determine an initial MPLS network topology and then we adapt it to the traffic load. The challenge is to determine when an LSP should be created and when to pass a new traffic in an already created LSP. In order to do that, we propose an LSP creation strategy based on the traffic-driven approach. Our decision rules consider many factors like the cost, the request, the available bandwidth and the network topology information. As future work, we are intended to complete our proposed LSP creation strategy by choosing an optimization method and formulating our problem as a mathematical model. Once done, we will test this proposition and compare the results. As long term future work, we will define the decision rules of the LSP route management entity and test it.

Acknowledgment

This work is one of the results of PhD research supported in part by "Conseil Régional Champage-Ardenne" (district grant) and the European Social Fund.

References

1. Aknine S, Pinson S, Shakun MF (2004) An Extended Multi-agent Negotiation Protocol. International Journal on Autonomous Agents and Multi-agent Systems, Sycara, K., Wooldridge, M. (eds.), Vol. 8, no. 1, pp.5-45
2. Armitage G (2000) MPLS: The magic behind the myths. IEEE Communications Magazine, Vol. 38, no. 1, pp. 124-131
3. Anjali T, Scoglio C, de Oliveira JC, Akyildiz IF, Uhl G (2002) Optimal Policy for LSP Setup in MPLS Networks. Comp. Networks, vol. 39, no. 2, pp. 165-183
4. Awduche D O (1999) MPLS and traffic engineering in IP networks, IEEE Communications Magazine, vol. 37, no.12, pp. 42-47
5. Blake S, Black D, Carlson M, Davies E, Wang Z, Weiss W (1998) Architecture for Differentiated Services. RFC2475
6. Ben Said L, Bouron T, Drogoul A (2002) Agent-based interaction analysis of consumer behavior. AAMAS' 2002, ACM, Bologna, Italy, pp. 184-190
7. Beker S, Kofman D, Puech N (2003) Off Line MPLS Layout Design and Reconfiguration: Reducing Complexity Under Dynamic Traffic Conditions. International Network Optimization Conference, INOC, Evry, France, N. ISSN: 1762 5734, pp. 61-66
8. Callon R (2000) Predictions for the Core of the Network. IEEE Internet Comp., vol. 4, no. 1, pp. 60-61
9. Case J, Fedor M, Schoffstall M, Davin J (1990) A Simple Network Management Protocol (SNMP). RFC 1157
10. Conte R, Gilbert N, Sichman JS (1998) MAS and Social Simulation: A Suitable Commitment. MABS'98. Lecture Notes in AI, Vol. 1534, Paris, France, pp. 1-9
11. Cisco Systems, Inc. (2001) Quality of Service for Multi-Protocol Label Switching Networks. Q & A
12. Cisco Systems (2005) Implementing Quality of Service Policies with DSCP.
13. de Oliveira D, Bazzan ALC, Lesser VR (2005) Using cooperative mediation to coordinate traffic lights: a case study. AAMAS, Utrecht, Netherlands, pp. 463-470
14. Doran J (2001) Agent-Based Modelling of EcoSystems for Sustainable Resource Management. 3rd EASSS'01. Lecture Notes in AI, Vol. 2086, Prague, Czech Republic, pp. 383-403

15. Drogoul A (1995) When ants play chess. In From reaction to cognition. Lecture Notes in AI, Vol. 957. C. Castelfranchi & J.P. Müller (Eds). Springer-Verlag, Berlin-Heidelberg, pp. 13-27
16. Le Faucheur F et al (2002) Multi-Protocol Label Switching (MPLS) Support of Differentiated Services. RFC3270
17. Ferber J (1999) Multi-Agent System: An Introduction to Distributed Artificial Intelligence. Harlow: Addison Wesley Longman
18. El Hadouaj S, Drogoul A, Espié S (2000) How to Combine Reactivity and Anticipation: the Case of Conflicts Resolution in Simulated Road Traffic. MABS'2000 workshop. Lecture Notes in AI, Vol. 1979, Boston, USA, pp. 82-96
19. The Internal Engineering Consortium (2005) Multi Protocol Label Switching. Web ProForums Tutorials, http://www.iec.org
20. Kodialam M, Lakshman TV (2000) Minimum interference routing with applications to MPLS traffic engineering. IEEE INFOCOM 2000, Tel Aviv, Israel
21. McCloghrie K, Rose M (1990) Management Information Base for Network Management of TCP/IP-based internets.
22. Moukas A, Chandrinos K, Maes P (1998) Trafficopter: A Distributed Collection System for Traffic Information. CIA'98. Lecture Notes in AI, Vol. 1435, Paris, France, pp 34-43
23. Minei I (2004) MPLS DiffServ-aware Traffic Engineering, Juniper Networks
24. Ooms D, Sales B, Livens W, Acharya A, Griffoul F, Ansari F (2002) Overview of IP Multicast in a Multi-Protocol Label Switching (MPLS) Environment. RFC 3353
25. Osborne E, Simha A (2003) Traffic Engineering with MPLS. Cisco Systems
26. Pave A, Bousquet F, Cambier C, Mullon C, Morand P, Quensiere J (1993) Simulating the Interaction between a Society and a Renewable Resource. Journal of Biological Systems, Vol. 1, pp 199-213
27. Rahim-Amoud R, Merghem-Boulahia L, Gaiti D (2005) Improvement of MPLS Performance by Implementation of a Multi-Agent System. Intelligence in Communication Systems - IntellComm 2005, pp. 23-32, Springer. Montreal, CANADA, Oct. 17-19
28. Rosen E, Viswanathan A, Callon R (2001) Multiprotocol Label Switching Architecture. RFC3031, IETF
29. Sandholm T eMediator (2002) A Next Generation Electronic Commerce Server". Computational Intelligence Vol. 18, no. 4, pp. 656-676, Special issue on Agent Technology for Electronic Commerce
30. Xiao X, Hannan A, Bailey B, Ni L (2000) Traffic engineering with MPLS in the Internet. IEEE Network Magazine, pp. 28-33

NSME: A Framework for Network Worm Modeling and Simulation

Siming Lin1, 2, Xueqi Cheng1

1 Software Lab, Institute of Computing Technology, Chinese Academy of
Sciences, Beijing
2 Graduate School of the Chinese Academy of Sciences, Beijing
linsiming@software.ict.ac.cn, cxq@ict.ac.cn

Abstract. Various worms have a devastating impact on Internet. Packet level
network modeling and simulation has become an approach to find effective
countermeasures against worm threat. However, current alternatives are not fit
enough for this purpose. For instance, they mostly focus on the details of lower
layers of the network so that the abstraction of application layer is very coarse.
In our work, we propose a formal description of network and worm models,
and define network virtualization levels to differentiate the expression
capability of current alternatives. We then implement a framework, called
NSME, based on NS2 for dedicated worm modeling and simulation with more
details of application layer. We also analyze and compare the consequential
overheads. The additional real-time characteristics and a worm simulation
model are further discussed.

1   Introduction

Internet worms have become a serious threat to the Internet infrastructure and
users. It is important to study worm behaviors in order to find the effective
countermeasures. An ideal approach is to create a realistic mathematical model that
allows behavior prediction in a closed form. But in fact it is impossible to create such
a model because there are a number of random factors difficult to be introduced in.
For example, the epidemic model [1] greatly simplifies the details of the networks
and worms.

Much literature, such as [2-4], has taken a bottom-up approach which utilizes
packet level network simulators to simulate worms in detail. They model every
individual entity of the network, including hosts, routers and links, as well as every
worm entity. Each entity has its own attributes and interactive behaviors which can
be implemented by simulators. This approach can match the realistic topologies and
protocols, so it can provide more accurate data. The worm related countermeasures
can even be developed and tested directly on this kind of simulation models.

Please use the following format when citing this chapter:

Lin, S., Cheng, X., 2006, in IFIP International Federation for Information Processing, Volume 213, Network Control and Engineering for QoS, Security, and Mobility, V, ed. Gaïti, D., (Boston: Springer), pp.
201–212.

The alternatives of network modeling and simulation have been studied for many years. Some famous simulators/emulators, such as NS2 [5] and ModelNet [6], have come forth. In our work, according to the theory of automata and discrete event system, we propose a formal description of network and worm models. By defining the virtualization levels, we then find different alternatives of network modeling and simulation have different expression capability. As mentioned above, current worm related research is mainly based on existing network simulators. However, these simulators mostly focus on the details of lower layers of the network so that the functions of application layer are greatly simplified. In addition, it is possible that packet level worm simulation will degrade the performance of these simulators.

We have developed a framework, called Network Security Modeling Environment (NSME), based on NS2 for dedicated worm modeling and simulation. We remove some inherent structures in NS2, such as Agent, and add some new features, such as host TCP/IP protocol stack, IP address supporting and external interfaces. These features make our framework support realistic application layer logic and make it achieve stronger expression capability, which means that it can be used in all worm related research, such as propagation simulation, honeypot and IDS test.

The remainder of this paper is organized as follows. Section 2 provides information on packet level worm simulation by others. Section 3 formalizes the problem. Section 4 describes our implementation in detail. Section 5 analyzes the performance of NSME and shows a worm simulation model based on it. Section 6 gives some conclusions and future directions.

2   Related Work

At present, there is much related work on packet level worm simulation. Riley et al [2] implement a worm model propagating with TCP and UDP protocols by using the GTNetS simulator [7]. In their work, the entire design of the worm model depends closely on many inherent and excellent features of GTNetS. However, a lot of attack packets with random destination IP Address generated by this model trend to degrade the performance of the NIx–Vector routing mechanism of GTNetS. To solve this problem, they take some enhancements, such as Routing Proxy, NIx–Vector Aggregation and so on. They have successfully simulated more than 50,000 nodes without exploiting the parallel and distributed simulation features of GTNetS.

Another significant work in this field is made by Liljenstam et al [3]. They point out that worm simulation is a challenge to the scale and performance of packet level simulators. They extend the SSFNet simulator [8] to implement a mixed abstraction worm simulation model. In this work, they use both epidemic model and packet level network model consisting of BGP routers. A pseudo-protocol is used to link the two parts. Although less accurate, this hybrid method can achieve a scale of $10^2 \sim 10^3$ autonomous systems (ASes) under the assumption that one BGP router represents one AS.

In [4], Sewani et al discuss the difference among analytical model, testbed emulation and packet level simulation. They use PDNS [9], a parallel version of NS2, to simulate 15,000 nodes on 8 machines. In this work, they extend a lightweight TCP protocol to simplify computing. In addition, they point out some advantages and disadvantages of PDNS for worm simulation.

We find that most simulators usually cannot support the expression of application logic. For instance, NS2 does not have the functions related with IP address. Its Agent structure makes it static and trivial to configure protocols and connections in Otcl [5], which means all behaviors in NS2 are semiautomatic. These even affect its emulation function. Our framework will solve these problems.

3   Problem Formalization

3.1   Network Model

Given that R is a set of routers in the network, H is a set of hosts, L is a set of point to point data links, and C is a set of shared data links, the network topology can be defined as $T = (R, L, \varphi)$, where $\varphi : L \to R \times R$ represents the adjacent relationship. If both set H and set C are not empty, their partitions $\{H_1, H_2, \cdots, H_n\}$ and $\{C_1, C_2, \cdots, C_n\}$ exist, which makes $\forall i \in [1,n]$, $\exists r \in R$, $LAN_i = (\{r\} \cup H_i, C_i, \varphi_i)$ form the completely connected graphs, where n is the number of LANs.

Furthermore, characteristics of discrete packets transmission in computer networks are conform to the discrete event system (DEVS) [10]. Therefore, according to the theory of automata and discrete event system, we can get the general representation of the network modeling alternatives. We define a structure:

$M = (Q, V, \Sigma, \Gamma, \Upsilon, q_0, F)$, where:

① Q is a set of states;

② V is a set of functional nodes;

③ Σ is a set of external events;

④ Γ is a set of internal events;

⑤ Υ is a set of transition functions, and

$$\Upsilon = \begin{cases} \{\delta_{ext}, \delta_{int1}\} & \Sigma \neq \varnothing \\ \{\delta_{int2}\} & \Sigma = \varnothing \end{cases}, \quad \begin{pmatrix} \delta_{ext} : Q \times \Sigma \times V \times \mathbb{N} \to Q \times \Gamma \\ \delta_{int1} : Q \times \Gamma \times \mathbb{N} \to Q \times P(\Gamma) \times P(\Sigma) \\ \delta_{int2} : Q \times \Gamma \to Q \times P(\Gamma) \times \mathbb{N} \end{pmatrix}$$

⑥ $q_0 \in Q$ is the initial state;

⑦ $F \subseteq Q$ is a set of termination states.

The elements in V denote the handlers. Therefore, $V \subseteq R \cup H \cup L \cup C$. Σ is the set of packets caused by the interaction between M and the external. A list is used to deal with the internal events. The elements in the list can be represented as $(\lambda, v, t) \in \Gamma$. It means the internal event with value λ will be received and processed by v at the time of t. The ability of M to generate a variety of simulated behaviors vastly depends on its abundant transition functions, e.g.:

$\delta_{ext}(q_1, p, v, t) = (q_2, e)$ denotes that receiving the external event p under the state q_1 from v at the time of t will lead to the state transition to q_2, and generate the internal event e.

$\delta_{int1}(q_1, e_1, t) = (q_2, E, P)$ denotes that receiving the internal event e_1 under state q_1 at the time of t will cause the state transition to q_2, and generate a set of internal events E and a set of external events P.

$\delta_{int2}(q_1, e_1) = (q_2, E, t_1)$ denotes that receiving the internal event e_1 will cause the state transition from q_1 to q_2, and generate a set of internal events E, with the time going to t_1.

In δ_{int1} and δ_{int2}, the received event e_1 should be the one in the event list with the minimum t and it will be removed from the list after the state transition is completed. In addition, whether Σ is empty determines the values and natures of the set of transition functions Υ. δ_{int2} depends on the value of t in the event e_1 to maintain a simulation clock, so it is not constrained by the real-time condition, while δ_{ext} and δ_{int1} meet the real-time constrains, which are:

$c_1 : rt(\delta) < t_\delta$, where $rt(\delta)$ is the time after δ is executed, $(\lambda_\delta, v_\delta, t_\delta)$ is the event with minimum t in the event list after δ is executed;

$c_2 : \delta_{int1}(q_1, (\lambda_1, v_1, t_1), t) = (q_2, E, P)$ holds if and only if $0 \le t - t_1 \le \varepsilon$, where t is the current time and ε is the adjustment factor.

3.2   Virtualization Levels

For $M = (Q, V, \Sigma, \Gamma, \Upsilon, q_0, F)$, we give the following 3 definitions:

Definition 1: When $V = R \cup L$ and $\Sigma \neq \varnothing$, M can create a network model in low virtualization level. The receivers of the internal events in the model are limited to the virtual routers and data links. That is, the model only simulates the communication network. The hosts are outside the model and interact with it.

Definition 2: When $V = R \cup H \cup L \cup C$ and $\Sigma \neq \varnothing$, M can create a network model in medium virtualization level. The receivers in the model are extended to all layers of the network. Furthermore, since Σ is not empty, the model must support the communication between the external hosts and the internal virtual hosts.

Definition 3: When $V \subseteq R \cup H \cup L \cup C$ and $\Sigma = \varnothing$, M will create a network model in high virtualization level. Since Σ is empty, the model implements full abstraction from physical data link, routing mechanism to data generation and response. Thus, it is a closure system.

The existing alternatives usually can only create models in one of the virtualization levels. The network emulators, such as ModelNet and Netbed [11], can reach low virtualization level. The network simulators, such as NS2 and SSFNet, can reach high virtualization level. The medium virtualization level is rigorous but less useful for traditional network research. Only few emulators, such as IP-TNE [12], can reach it.

It is significant for worm related research to get models in both high and medium virtualization levels. Using a high level model, the worm propagation can be simulated, and using a medium level model, living honeypot [13], another countermeasure against worms, can be constructed.

3.3   Behaviors of Worm-Daemon

Using the methods described in section 3.1, we can also formalize the worm behaviors. Since the real OS environment does not exist, the method to simulate the worm propagation is to run a virtual daemon, which can simulate how a host interacts with the worms. We define the daemon as $(Q_w, H, \Gamma_w, \delta_w, q_{w0})$, where:

① $Q_w = \{q_{w0}, q_s, q_v, q_h, q_i\}$ is a set of states;

② H is a set of hosts;

③ $\Gamma_w \subset \Gamma$ is a set of internal events;

④ δ_w is similar to δ_{int2}, but there is an probability parameter *prob* in it. $\delta_w(q_1, e_1, prob) = (q_2, E, t_1)$ means it will happen with the probability *prob* that receiving the internal event e_1 under the state q_1 will cause the state transition to q_2, and generate a set of internal events E, with the time going to t_1;

⑤ $q_{w0} \in Q_w$ is an initial state.

Let state q_r denotes a robust host that cannot be infected by any worms; q_v represents a host with vulnerabilities; q_l is the latent state after the host has been infected; and q_i is the propagating state. We can also define the following behaviors.

A host is vulnerable with the probability p_v and it can be upgraded by patches to become a robust host with the probability p_u. An infected host can become a robust host by upgrading with the probability p_s, or resume the vulnerable state with the probability p_r. Worms do not infect the same victims, and they alternate between the latent and propagating states. Based on these assumptions, Figure 1 shows the state transition graph of a worm-daemon.

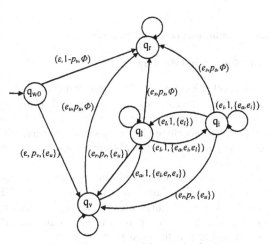

Fig. 1. The state transition graph of a daemon

4   Implementation

4.1   Topology and Event Scheduling

The topology basically consists of virtual hosts, virtual routers and related data links. In low or medium level models, the mapping hosts and interface routers can be additional used, acting as the interfaces between NSME model and the real network. Like a virtual host, an abstract subnet can handle all the data streams within a sub-network with a uniform protocol stack. By this way, it is flexible to control over the scale and the complexity.

When being transmitted in a network model, the packets are treated as the timestamp events, scheduled by kernel. The links will calculate a new timestamp for every packet handled by them, according to the packet size, their bandwidth and

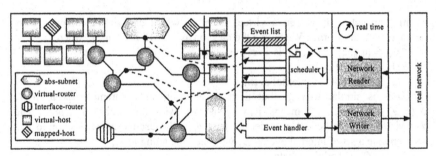

Fig. 2. The architecture of the topology and the event scheduling in NSME framework

delay. Figure 2 shows the architecture of the topology and the event scheduling in NSME framework.

4.2   Communication Architecture

4.2.1   Packet and Routing

The packet headers in NSME follow the structures in the real network protocols instead of the inherent structures in NS2, such as ns_addr_t. Furthermore, in order to generate low or medium level models, the real data field has been supported. However, for generating high level models, the abstract packets are also used, which means the size of a packet can be greater than the sum of the actual size of its header and data field.

We use the classical algorithm, Dijkstra, to compute routes and implement a RadixTreeClassifier class which inherits from the NSObject class to perform IP packet forwarding. In this class, the routing table is constructed with realistic Radix tree structure. Therefore, it is available to allocate IP addresses and partition the network segments in the simulation model.

4.2.2   Protocol Stack

The major difference from NS2 is that each NSME virtual host has a mini but fully functional TCP/IP protocol stack. Therefore, the application layer is no longer a dispensable structure. Virtual application programs can gain the ability to access the network model via Virtual Sockets which replace NS2 Agents to process the protocols in lower layers. These sockets are no longer pre-configured, but controlled jointly by the protocol stack and virtual programs. The main benefit from this change is that virtual programs can directly use the real data and protocols to communicate without caring about whether the other end is a virtual host or an external real host.

In order to support the programming logic in application layer, we imitate Visual C++ (MFC) socket classes to implement a set of Virtual Socket classes, including RawSocket, UDPSocket, TCPListenSocket, and TCPSocket. RawSocket provides the ability to access the network layer. It can not only send the packets with any protocols, but also intercept the packets arriving at the local host. UDPSocket is responsible for the UDP packet encapsulation on the transportation layer. The more complicated TCP connections are managed by both TCPListenSocket and TCPSocket. TCPSocket, derived from FullTCPAgent in NS2, provides the ability of flow control, packet assembly and retransmission. TCPListenSocket is used to manage passive connection requests. These socket classes are not associated with the Otcl classes. The developers do not need to care about the details of the connections and protocols. In a word, programming with Virtual Sockets in NSME is the same as writing a normal network program except that the Socket APIs are different.

Furthermore, ip_local_deliver is used to replace the old PortClassifier class to dispatch packets locally. Figure 3 shows the design of NSME protocol stack. It is easy to find our stack is quite similar to that in real systems (e.g. Linux). When a Virtual Socket is created, it will be registered on ip_local_deliver. When any packets arrive, ip_local_deliver will send them to rawip_filter for filtering. If an instance of RawSocket derived class is registered to intercept a certain protocol, rawip_filter will replicate the related packets and send them to it. Rawip_filter will also forward all packets to protocol handler entries according to their protocol types, and the packets that are not matched will be discarded. Icmp_handler will directly process ICMP packets without forwarding them to the upper layers. However, tcp_demuxer and udp_demuxer are more complicated. They need to create quick indices for all the registered sockets. In addition, tcp_demuxer needs to distinguish active and passive connections. Our protocol stack can response UDP or TCP requests that are not matched by sending special packets, such as ICMP destination-unreachable packets and TCP RST packets. It will be also possible to imitate the stack fingerprint of a certain OS.

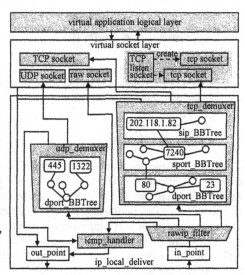

Fig. 3. NSME protocol stack

4.3   External Interfaces

Based on NS2, two types of external interfaces are implemented in NSME. One of them is the file interface which saves the packets in the network model to files in tcpdump format. The other is the interface for communication between the network model and the real network. For example, the interface routers can connect the model with the real network, and the mapping hosts can logically map the real hosts into the network model. Meanwhile, the proper routing configuration and IP address allocation strategy are needed. It should be compatible with the management of the real network. Below is an example of the possible configuration for communication between the real network and the model network.

We run NSME on host A with IP address 202.118.19.128, and there is another host B with IP address 202.118.19.132. First, we deploy two class C sub-networks (210.120.2.0, 202.118.19.0) connected by a virtual router into NSME model. Second, we allocate IP address 202.118.19.132 to a mapping host in this simulation model. Finally, we add a new routing entry to host B:

route add 210.120.2.0 mask 255.255.255.0 202.118.19.128

Now, host B has been partially mapped to the above mapping host so that it can communicate with the sub-network 210.120.2.0 in this model. However, it can still communicate with other real local hosts. We then add another routing entry to host B:

route add 202.118.19.0 mask 255.255.255.0 202.118.19.128

Now, host B is fully mapped into the simulated sub-networks (both 210.120.2.0 and 202.118.19.0), and can no longer communicate with other real local hosts, except host A.

5   Experiment and Analysis

In this section, we will analyze and compare the related overheads between our framework and NS2, then discuss real-time characteristics of our framework. Finally, we simulate a random scanning worm.

5.1   Routing Overheads

Figure 4 shows the comparison of the look-up time overhead (LTO) and basic memory overhead (BMO) between NSME routing and NS2 routing (The experimental hardware is a PC with a P4, 2.6GHz CPU and 4GB memory). On axel x, different scales of 1~10,000 are drawn in order to illuminate the issue of scale. It is easy to see that the LTO approximates a constant (0.96 us) in NS2. The BMO is about 2GB when it obtains the maximal scale of 5,000 nodes. The LTO and BMO in NSME are both close to those in NS2 when the number of nodes is less than or equal to 1,000. But the up-limit in NSME is 4,000 nodes with the LTO of 1.2 us and the BMO of about 2GB.

When greater than 1,000 nodes, BMO is very high either in NS2 or in NSME. The reason is that a routing table must be maintained for each router, whose space complexity is $O(n^2)$. In NSME, the routing table is implemented by Radix tree but not linear array, which makes the LTO and BMO are higher than those in NS2.   Note that in this experiment, we only use virtual routers in NSME (for the ease of comparison). In fact virtual hosts do not need routing tables in NSME, which makes it

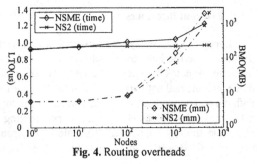

Fig. 4. Routing overheads

different from NS2.

5.2   Structure Overheads

With the same experimental hardware, we measure the overheads brought by the Virtual Socket structure in NSME and the Agent structure in NS2 respectively. Figure 5 shows both time and memory overheads when the TCP connections are assigned in the phase of initialization. In NSME, two virtual hosts, H_{v1} and H_{v2}, are configured, and N ($1 \le N \le 10,000$) virtual clients with TCP sockets on H_{v1} are assigned to prepare for connections to the virtual server on H_{v2}. Corresponsively, the similar configuration is given in NS2, in which FullTcpAgents are used and the number of them is equal to that of virtual clients.

As we can see in Figure 5, the time and memory overheads are both linear to the number of the connections in the phase of initialization. In NSME, however, the average time (about 1.7ms) is apparently less than that in NS2 (about 13.9ms). And its average memory consumption (about 2.93KB) is also less than that in NS2 (about 3.74KB). These differences are due to the fact that in NS2 each Agent must be created in Otcl space, and then Otcl translator creates a core instance of it in C++ space by invoking the splitting object model, which brings huge time and memory consumption. This proves that some structures in NS2, such Agent, Otcl, are not appropriate enough for achieving better performance.

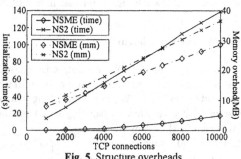

Fig. 5. Structure overheads

5.3   Real-time Characteristics

We designed five scenarios in order to observe the real-time characteristics in NSME. Scenario 1 includes a 1,000Mbps (0.1ms delay) LAN L_1, where mapping hosts H_{s1}, H_{s2} and virtual host H_{v1} are deployed. An additional LAN L_2 exists in other 4 scenarios, where L_1 and L_2 are connected through one-hop or ten-hop link(s) respectively, and the delay of each hop is 0.1ms or 1ms respectively (1,000Mbps bandwidth). In the 4 scenarios, the difference from scenario 1 is that we deploy H_{s1}, H_{s2} in L_1 and H_{v1} in L_2 (for medium virtualization), or H_{s1} in L_1 and H_{s2} in L_2 (for low virtualization).

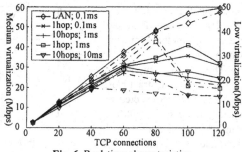

Fig. 6. Real-time characteristics

The experimental environment consists of 3 PCs (P4 2.8GHz, 256M memory) in a 100Mbps LAN. Host A runs NSME and hosts B, C are mapped to H_{s1}, H_{s2} respectively.

For medium virtualization, clients on hosts B and C request TCP connections to server on H_{v1}. Each connection utilizes a timer to try to send data at 0.78Mbps. For low virtualization, clients on hosts B and C communicate with each other. The solid line in Figure 6 illustrates the transmission rate of all the connections in medium virtualization level and the dashed line shows the situation in low virtualization level. We can see the rate increases linearly when the number of connections is less than 60, which means the good real-time performance. When the number of connections is more than 60, the performance drops if the number of hops increases. Meanwhile, the link delay affects the real-time performance. When the number of connections is greater than 80, the utility rate of CPU of host A generally drops to 90% and below, which means the performance of the network interfaces should be improved. In addition, since NSME model actually acts as a relay between host B and host C in low virtualization level, it is more sensitive to the bandwidth of the physical links and the performance of the network interfaces. Consequently, application layer can only achieve a lower transmission rate in this situation.

5.4   Worm Experiment

In order to observe the runtime characteristics of worm simulation, we used NSME to simulate a random scanning worm like Slammer which duplicates itself by transmitting in UDP. Without concerning whether the target hosts exist or not, Slammer has a very fast propagating speed and has been the top threat for the recent two years [14]. We write a daemon and simplify its actions (no update and no recovery). This worm model exploits random scanning strategy to select target, and then sends it a single attack packet. If the target is vulnerable and has not been infected, it will be infected a short time later after receiving the attack packet. We list in table 1 several major parameters for this worm model.

This worm model is deployed to 10 abstract class B subnets interconnected by virtual routers (1,000Mbps bandwidth, 1ms delay). Each available IP address is

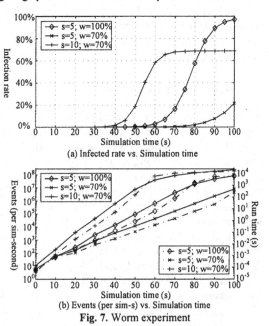

(a) Infected rate vs. Simulation time

(b) Events (per sim-s) vs. Simulation time

Fig. 7. Worm experiment

occupied by a virtual host. The scanning strategy is random scanning in 2^{26} addresses space. We find that the parameter t has no obvious effects on the propagation of the worm. The parameter i does affect the propagation, but it is not essential. Figure 7(a), where $t=0.1$s and $i=1$, illustrates the variation of the infection rate vs. simulation time brought by different s and w. Increasing either one will obviously aggravate the infection rate. In contrast to (a), figure 7(b) shows the relationship between NSME events (run time) and simulation time. It illustrates that the scan rate and weak degree will also affect the number of events which eventually determines the run time of the worm model. It is obvious that the large scale worm simulation will be a challenge to the discrete event simulators.

Table 1. Parameters for the worm experiment

Parameter	Description
s	the scan rate of the worm
w	the weak degree which is a percentage of vulnerable hosts in a subnet
t	the time delay when a host is infected
i	the number of the initial infected hosts

6   Conclusion and Future Work

In this paper, we propose a formal description of network and worm models. We then implement the NSME framework based on NS2 for dedicated worm modeling and simulation. Our framework extends the details of the network modeling and simulation, so it is unavoidable to consume more memory and CPU time. Therefore, we must trade off between the accuracy and scale. In our worm model, we use abstract subnets to achieve large scale simulation, but it is not accurate. Furthermore, the flat routing mechanism is a bottleneck of the memory utility.

Our future work is to improve the scale and performance of the NSME framework. The approach mentioned in literature [15] is valuable for us. However, the technology of parallel and distributed simulation is essential to enhance the scale and performance, so we will focus on it. In this aspect, PDNS will be naturally compatible with our framework.

References

1. H. Andersson, T. Britton, and K. Krickeberg et al, *Stochastic Epidemic Models and Their Statistical Analysis*, Springer-Verlag, New York, 2000
2. G. F. Riley, M. I. Sharif, and W Lee, "Simulating Internet Worms", In *Proceedings of the 12th Annual International Symposium on Modeling, Analysis, and Simulation of Computer and Telecommunications Systems (MASCOTS'04)*, IEEE Computer Society, Washington DC, 2004, pp. 268-274
3. M. Liljenstam, Yougu Yuan, and BJ Premore, et al, "A Mixed Abstraction Level Simulation Model of Large-Scale Internet Worm Infestations", In *Proceedings of*

the *10th IEEE Int'l Symp. on Modeling, Analysis and Simulation of Computer and Telecommunications Systems (MASCOTS'02)*, IEEE Computer Society, Washington DC, 2002, pp. 109-116

4. Anil Sewani, Bowei Du, "Packet Level Worm Simulation and Analysis", http://www.eecs.berkeley.edu/~anil/, 2004
5. L. Breslau, D. Estrin, and K. Fall, et al, "Advances in Network Simulation", *IEEE Computer*, 2000, pp. 59-67
6. A. Vahdat, K. Yocum, and K Walsh, et al, "Scalability and Accuracy in a Large-Scale Network Emulator", In *Proceedings of the 5th Symposium on Operating Systems Design and Implementation*, ACM Press, New York, 2002, pp. 271-284
7. G. F. Riley, "The Georgia Tech Network Simulator", In *Proceedings of the ACM SIGCOMM workshop on Models, methods and tools for reproducible network research*, 2003, pp. 5-12
8. SSFNet, "Scalable Simulation Framework Network Models", http://www.ssfnet.org/homePage.html, 1999
9. G. F. Riley, M. H. Ammar, and R. Fujimoto, "A Federated Approach to Distributed Network Simulation", *ACM Transactions on Modeling and Computer Simulation*, 2004, pp. 116-148
10. B P Zeigler, *Theory of Modeling and Simulation*, Wiley, New York, 1976
11. B. White, J. Lepreau, and L. Stoller, et al, "An Integrated Exerimental Environment for Distributed Systems and Networks", In *Proceedings of the 5th Symposium on Operating Systems Design and Implementation*, ACM Press, New York, 2002, pp. 255-270
12. R. Simmonds, R. Bradford, and B Unger, "Applying Parallel Discrete Event Simulation to Network Emulation", In *Proceedings of the Fourteenth Workshop on Parallel and Distributed Simulation*, IEEE Computer Society, Washington DC, 2000, pp. 15-22
13. I. Kuwatly, M. Sraj, and Z. A. Masri, et al, "A Dynamic Honeypot Design for Intrusion Detection", In *Proceedings of the IEEE/ACS International Conference on Pervasive Services (ICPS'04)*. IEEE, 2004, pp. 95-104
14. Symantec Corporation, "Symantec Internet Security Threat Report", http://enter-prisesecurity.symantec.com, 2004
15. K. Walsh, E. G. Sirer, "Staged simulation: A General Technique for Improving Simulation Scale and Performance", *ACM Transactions on Modeling and Computer Simulation (TOMACS)*, 2004, pp. 170-195

Algorithms for network service guarantee under minimal link usage information

Sugwon Hong[1], Hwang-Kyu Lee[2], Seonuck Paek[3]

[1]Department of Computer Software, Myongji University
San 38-2 Namdong, Yongin, Gyeonggi-do, 449-728 Korea, swhong@mju.ac.kr
[2] Tecoware, 823-21 Yeoksam-dong, Kangnam-gu, Seoul, Korea, exarch@korea.com
[3] Division of Information Technology & Communication
Sangmyung University, paeksu@smu.ac.kr

Abstract. One way to guaranteeing service for an application flow even if a network happens to fail is to establish a restoration path with the bandwidth that amounts to the same of the flow. If the flows can share the bandwidth for their restoration paths with others, we can reduce bandwidth consumption required for restoration. It is also required that deciding sharable bandwidth among flows should be done using controllable link information at each node. This paper proposes an algorithm to determine the sharable bandwidth among application flows given local link usage information at each node, validates the results of the algorithm and analyze the conditions required to achieve the goal by simulation.

1 Introduction

Fast restoration time and service guarantee are the important goals to achieve the network reliability and survivability. One way to continuing traffic delivery when a network happens to fail is to establish an alternative path to detour to destination avoiding the point of failure. The network protection or recovery schemes using alternative paths and the classification are explained in [1]. Various rerouting methods using alternative paths have been extensively studied for network survivability [2].

For service guarantee of application flows, it is also required to guarantee traffic delivery without any service degradation. For this purpose not only do networks have to provide a restoration path, but also provide enough bandwidth to secure detoured traffic of an application flow. One simple way to guaranteeing service for an application flow when network failure happens is to establish a restoration path with the same bandwidth of a working path at the same time. However, it requires exact twice as much as the bandwidth for an application flow whenever a working path is established.

In order to reduce bandwidth consumption for restoration paths, those paths should share their bandwidths each other as long as the sharing does not degrade original service. One problem of sharing bandwidth between restoration paths is the complexity of keeping the necessary information at each node to determine which flows can share bandwidth at each link for this purpose. The information that each node should

Please use the following format when citing this chapter:

Hong, S., Lee, H.-K., Paek, S., 2006, in IFIP International Federation for Information Processing, Volume 213, Network Control and Engineering for QoS, Security, and Mobility, V, ed. Gaïti, D., (Boston: Springer), pp. 213–222.

maintain is enormous, and up-to-date information should be propagated to every node whenever new paths are established. Therefore, when we try to find a solution to determine sharable bandwidth, it is required that the method should be done using controllable information at each node.

In this paper we first define the problem in section 2. In section 3 we propose two algorithms to set up a bandwidth-guaranteed path for restoration with local link usage information. In section 4 and 5 we do simulation and analyze the results. In section 6 we conclude the paper.

2   Problem Definition

In this paper we assume that when a working path is established, its corresponding restoration path is set up simultaneously. The ingress node of the restoration path becomes the point, where traffic is transferred from the working path to the restoration path when links fail. In general this node is not a point of failure.

An example of establishing working and restoration paths is shown in figure 1. As shown in this figure, the traffic for session k1, k2, k3 flowing through the working paths will be transferred to the corresponding restoration paths respectively when any link or links on working paths happen to fail.

In order to guarantee traffic delivery without any service degradation when links fail on the working paths, we have to provide the equivalent bandwidth for their restoration paths. However, bandwidth consumption will become twofold.. Thus the problem to be raised is how much bandwidth should be assigned for a restoration path for guaranteeing service of an application flow, and at the same time minimizing bandwidth consumption as a whole.

To approach this problem we postulate the following two conditions.

Condition 1: The service must be guaranteed regardless of any link failure on a working path.

Condition 2: More than two working paths never fail simultaneously.

In order to satisfy the condition 1, a restoration path should take a disjoint path of the corresponding working path. The condition 2 is realistic assumption because more than two working path are unlikely to fail at the same time. If working paths do not have any shared link each other, they can use the same restoration path, consequently reducing the bandwidth consumption incurred due to the restoration path.

In figure 1, the bandwidth of the link (u, v) for the restoration path of the session k1 can be shared with the restoration paths of the other sessions if the sessions take disjoint links of working paths each other. However, suppose that session k1 and k2 take routes with at least one same link on their paths, say link (i, j). In this case if they have a shared link on their restoration paths, say link (u, v), the service will not be guaranteed when the link (i j) is broken. Thus the bandwidth for the session k1 and k2 at link (u, v) should be assigned as much as the sum of the bandwidths required for each working path.

In order to decide whether or not the bandwidths for restoration paths at each link can be shared with others, each node needs to have the following information:

$$\{\{k_1, k_2, ..., k_n\}, (L^{k1}, L^{k2}, ..., L^{kn}), (a^{k1}, a^{k2}, ..., a^{kn})\} \tag{1}$$

where $K = \{k_1, k_2, ..., k_n\}$ is the set of sessions for the restoration paths established at this moment passing through link (i, j). L^k is the set of links on the working path for the session k, and a^k is the bandwidth requested for the session k. To keep such information imposes enormous burden on each node. Thus not only do we need to find an algorithm to determine sharable bandwidths among restoration paths, the algorithm should be based on minimal link information as well.

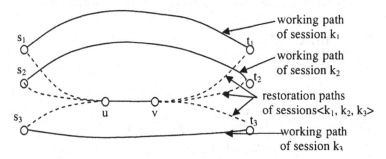

Fig. 1. The working paths and restoration paths of sessions $<k_1, k_2, k_3>$

3. Algorithms

3.1 Algorithm 1

One way to avoid keeping all information shown in equation (1) is to use the maximum bandwidth assigned to the links on a working path as the bandwidth required for its restoration path. This method was proposed and the effect of bandwidth reduction was shown in [3] and [4]. When a session establishes a working path and its restoration path, the source examines the bandwidths of all links assigned on the working path. Then it chooses the maximum bandwidth among them, and uses it as the bandwidth for its restoration path to be established. In this case the only information needed at each node is the total bandwidth assigned at this moment for working paths passing through the link.

This method satisfies the condition 1 if a restoration path takes disjoints routes of the corresponding working path. Since the bandwidth for a restoration path is the maximum bandwidth among those assigned to all links on the working path, any link failure on the working path will not degrade the service of a session whose traffic flows on the restoration path, which leads to satisfy the condition 2.

The following describes how we determine the bandwidth for a working path at link (i, j) and the bandwidth of its restoration path at link (u, v) when a new path request occurs.

a_{ij}^k : bandwidth for the working path of session k passing through link (i, j)

b_{uv}^k : bandwidth for the restoration path of session k passing through link (u, v)

m_{ij}^k : bandwidth requested by session k passing through link (i, j)

R_{uv} : bandwidth left at link (u, v)

G_{uv} : total bandwidth of all restoration paths to be established at link (u, v)

M : the maximum bandwidth among the links on a working path

F_{ij} : the total bandwidth assigned to all working paths passing link (i, j)

L(s,t) : a set of links consisting of a path from source s to destination t

$$M = \max_{all \ (i,j) \ \in \ L(s,t)} F_{ij} \tag{2}$$

$$a_{ij}^k = \begin{cases} m_{ij}^k & if \ R_{ij} > m_{ij}^k \\ \infty & if \ R_{ij} < m_{ij}^k \end{cases}$$

$$b_{uv}^k = \begin{cases} 0 & if \ M < G_{uv} \\ M - G_{uv} & if \ M > G_{uv} \quad and \quad R_{uv} \geq M - G_{uv} \\ \infty & if \ R_{uv} \leq M - G_{uv} \end{cases}$$

3.2 Algorithm 2

The goal of the algorithm is to find the bandwidth that can not be sharable among restoration paths since their working paths pass through the same link or links. The algorithm is also required to solve the problem using minimal link usage information. The algorithm 1 of section 3.1 uses the maximum bandwidth among the links which a working path passes through in order to determine the bandwidth for its restoration path.

We modify the algorithm 1 by allowing each node to have some information about links, which we call a link usage database, B(u, v) where (u, v) belongs to all links of a network. Every node keeps B(u, v) where the link (u, v) has the accumulated bandwidth of only the working paths whose restoration paths are passing through the link (u, v). So, when new restoration path is set up, we can look up B(u, v) to determine its bandwidth instead of finding M in equation (2) of the algorithm 1. This algorithm is described as follows:

a^k : bandwidth requested by session k

b_{ij}^k : bandwidth required for the restoration path of session k at link (i, j)

$B(u,v)$: the sum of bandwidths assigned for working paths which are assigned at link (u,v)

$G(u,v)$: the sum of bandwidths assigned for the restoration paths which are established at link(u,v)

L : the set of links in a network
L^k : the set of links which consists of the working path of session k

1. initialize: $B(u,v) = 0$ *for* *all* $(u,v) \in L$
2. If a working path of session k is passing through link (i,j),
   $B(u,v) = B(u,v) + a^k$ *for* *all* $(u,v) \in L^k$
3: $b_{ij}^k = \max_{(u,v) \in L^k} B(u,v) - G(i,j)$

4 Experiment

In the experiment we simulate two kinds of network models. The model 1 consists of 5 nodes and 8 bi-directional links shown in figure 2. The model 2 is composed of 28 nodes and 45 bi-directional links shown in figure 3. The model 2 is a real transport network which has some backbone links to connect between local groups of nodes [5]. The model 1 is an artificial network where traffic is evenly distributed over all links. The reason we choose the model 1 is that this model highlights the sharing effect and might mislead results comparing to the model 2 which reflects real traffic distribution.

In this simulation, each node has the information about the bandwidths assigned to the links which are connected to the node. At each request, the simulation takes the following steps. First, two nodes are randomly selected as source and destination nodes, and random amount of bandwidth between 1 and 10 required for the path is determined.

Second, a working path and its restoration path are calculated based on the shortest pairs of disjoint path algorithm [6],[7]. The path is also chosen to satisfy the sharable bandwidth described by the algorithms. The simulation runs on requests varying from 20 to 700 at one batch run, and does 10 batch runs in total.

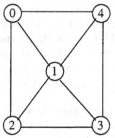

Fig. 2. The network model 1

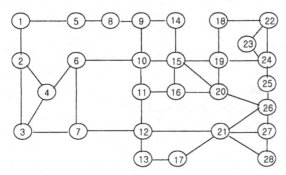

Fig. 3. The network model 2

5   Results and Analysis

The results of the algorithm 1 for the model 1 are shown in figure 4 and 5. In these figures, the bandwidth consumption means the sum of all bandwidths assigned to all links. This amounts to the total bandwidth requested for the paths multiplied by the average hops of links which each path consists of. NS denotes the case that no sharing is applied, while SS means that the sharing is applied. And AP and BP denote a working path and a restoration path respectively. In this figure, since the results of the algorithm 2 are very close to those of the algorithm 1, we show only the results of the algorithm 1. As shown in these figures we can save considerable bandwidth as we expected when the algorithm is applied.

The algorithm 1, however, does not always guarantee the reduction of bandwidth which is required for restoration. The figures 6 and 7 show such contradictory results. In this experiment of 200 requests, the total bandwidth for working paths is 3318.9 and the total bandwidth for restoration paths is 4955.9 when no sharing is applied. But when the algorithm 1 is applied for sharing, the restoration paths consume the total bandwidth of 6748.9. So sharing incurs more consumption.

In order to analyze this anomaly of sharing effect, let us assume the following case. Let us suppose that a session that has a working path from s to t passing the link (i j) and requires bandwidth n. Let us also suppose that bandwidth m is already assigned at link (i, j) and $m > n$. Then by the algorithm 1 the session requires the bandwidth at least m for its restoration path. If m is shared with very few other sessions which have the working paths passing through link (i, j), it incurs unnecessary bandwidth allocation on their restoration paths.

This kind of undesired effect happens when a network has several groups of nodes which have proximity each other within a group, and has hot spot links to connect between those groups. When the bandwidth is distributed over the links fairly evenly, the sharing algorithm gets a benefit. This happens in the case of the model 1. However, when the hot spot links to which more bandwidth are assigned than other links, the algorithm 1 might consume more bandwidth for restoration paths than when no sharing is applied.

To see this effect more clearly, we do another experiment which shows the bandwidth assigned to each link. Figure 8 shows the total bandwidth assigned at each link for the working paths and restoration paths respectively for the model 1 when the algorithm 1 is applied. The bandwidth distribution is fairly even among the links in this result. The result in figure 9, however, shows that the distribution is lopsided on a couple of links for the model 2. Therefore the working paths passing through these hot spot links require much more bandwidth for their restoration paths unnecessarily.

The algorithm 2 modifies the algorithm 1 by allowing each node to have a link data base which stores the accumulated bandwidth of only the working path whose restoration paths are passing through the link. In this way the algorithm 2 can calculate more accurate sharable bandwidth, consequently reducing the bandwidth consumption even to the cases when traffic distribution is heavily lopsided on some links.

We simulate the algorithm 2 for the network model 2 and obtain the results in figure 10. All assumptions and procedures are the same as done in the case of algorithm 1. The results show that the algorithm 2 saves the bandwidth for restoration paths comparing the result of figure 7.

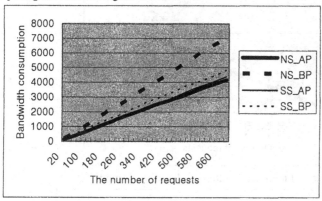

Fig. 4. Comparison of bandwidths for working and restoration path (model 1)

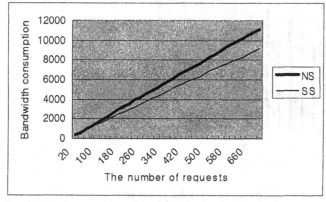

Fig. 5. Comparison of total bandwidths (model 1)

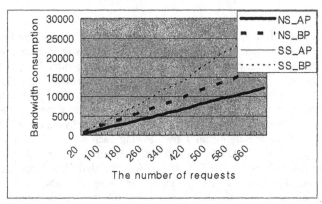

Fig.6. Comparison of bandwidths for working and restoration path by algorithm 1 (model 2)

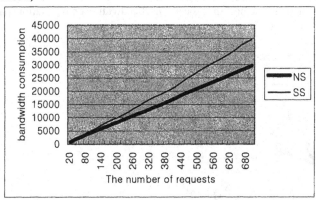

Fig. 7. Comparison of total bandwidths by algorithm 1 (model 2)

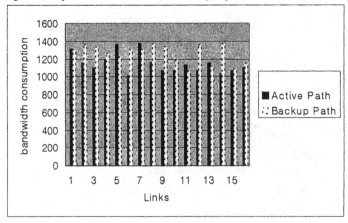

Fig. 8. The bandwidth assigned to each link by algorithm 1 (model 1)

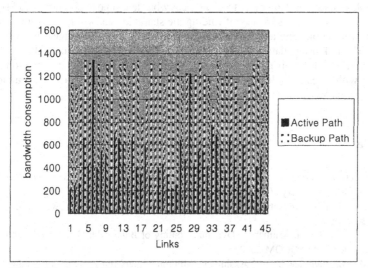

Fig. 9. The bandwidth assigned to each link by algorithm 1 (model 2)

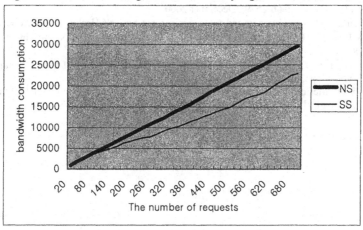

Fig. 10. Comparison of total bandwidths by algorithm 2 (model 2)

6. Conclusion

In this paper, we propose an algorithm to determine the bandwidth for restoration paths to guarantee service. For this purpose we approach the problem to meet two requirements. First, we should find the bandwidth required for restoration paths for assuring quality of service and at the same time use the least information of links at each node.

If we can use as much information as we need, it is not difficult to find the complete sharable bandwidth. However, to avoid heavy burden imposed on nodes to keep such information, we propose a way of finding the sharable bandwidth using minimal link usage information. The algorithm proposed here uses the link usage database at each node. The link usage database has the accumulated bandwidth of only the working paths whose restoration paths are passing through the link. The information is easily dealt with at each node. And we show that this algorithm works well under circumstances where traffic is unevenly distributed over links.

References

1. V. Sharma et al, " Framework for Multi-protocol Label Switching(MPLS)-based Recovery," RFC 3469, February 2003
2. R. Bhandari, " Survivable Networks: Algorithms for Diverse Routing," Kluwer Academic Publishers, 1999
3. M. Kodialam and T.V. Lakshman, " Dynamic Routing of Bandwidth Guaranteed Tunnels with Restoration," INFOCOM 2000
4. K. Kar, M. Kodialam, and T. V. Laskshman, "Minimum interference routing of bandwidth guaranteed tunnels with MPLS traffic engineering applications," IEEE, J. of Selected Area of Com. Vol. 16(12), pp2566-2579, December 2000
5. K. Murakami, " Optical Capacity and Flow Assignment for Self-Healing ATM Networks Based on Line and End-to-End Restoration," IEEE/ACM Trans. On Networking 6(2), April 1998
6. J.W. Suurballe R.E. Tarjan "A Quick Method for Finding Shortest Pairs of Disjoint Paths," Networks, vol. 14, pp325-226, 1984
7. C.-L. Li, S. T. McCormick, and D. Simchi-Levi, "Finding Disjoint Paths with Different Path-Costs: Complexity and Algorithms," NETWORKS, vol. 22, pp653-667, 1992

Dynamic Complexity of Autonomic Communication and Software Systems

Andrei Kirilyuk[1] and Mikaël Salaün[2]

[1] National Academy of Sciences of Ukraine, Institute of Metal Physics
36 Vernadsky Ave, 03142 Kiev-142, Ukraine
kiril@metfiz.freenet.kiev.ua
[2] France Télécom, Division R&D/MAPS/MMC/LAN
38-40 rue du Général Leclerc, 92794 Issy-les-Moulineaux Cedex 9, France
mikael.salaun@francetelecom.com

Dynamics of arbitrary communication and software system is analysed as unreduced interaction process. The applied generalised, universally nonperturbative method of effective potential reveals the phenomenon of dynamic multivaluedness of competing system configurations forced to permanently replace each other in a dynamically random order, which leads to universally defined dynamical chaos, complexity, fractality, self-organisation, and adaptability. We demonstrate the origin of the huge, exponentially high efficiency of the unreduced, complex network and software dynamics and specify the universal symmetry of complexity as the fundamental guiding principle for creation and control of such qualitatively new kind of network and software systems. Practical aspects of ICT complexity transition are outlined.

1 Introduction

Any communication and software system can be considered as a dynamical system formed by many interacting units. If system components can interact without *strict* external control (which is a rapidly growing tendency of modern ICT tools), then such *unreduced* interaction process leads to *complex-dynamical*, essentially *nonlinear* and *chaotic* structure emergence, or (*dynamically multivalued*) self-organisation [1–3], extending usual, regular self-organisation concept. Traditional information technologies and paradigm rely, however, on very strong human control and totally regular, predictable dynamics of controlled systems and environment, where unpredictable elements can only take the form of undesirable system failure or noise.

Growing sophistication of communication and software systems leads to dangerously rising probability of undesirable deviations from pre-programmed regular behaviour, thus largely compromising its expected advantages. On the other hand, such increasingly attractive system properties as intrinsic creativity and autonomous adaptability to changing environment and individual user demands should certainly involve another, much less regular and more diverse kind of

Please use the following format when citing this chapter:

Kirilyuk, A., Salaün, M., 2006, in IFIP International Federation for Information Processing, Volume 213, Network Control and Engineering for QoS, Security, and Mobility, V, ed. Gaïti, D., (Boston: Springer), pp. 223–236.

behaviour. In this paper we analyse these issues in a rigorous way by presenting the unreduced, nonperturbative analysis of arbitrary system of interacting communication and software units and show that such *unreduced interaction process* has the natural, dynamically derived properties of chaoticity, creativity (autonomous structure formation ability), adaptability, and exponentially high efficiency, which are consistently unified in the *universal* concept of *dynamic complexity* [1]. This concept and particular notions it unifies represent essential extension with respect to usual theory results always using one or another version of perturbation theory that strongly reduces real interaction processes and leads inevitably to regular kind of dynamics (even in its versions of "chaoticity"). We shall specify those differences in our analysis and demonstrate the key role of unreduced, interaction-driven complexity, chaoticity and self-organisation in the superior operation properties, as it has already been demonstrated for a large scope of applications [1–10].

The proposed universal theory of autonomic information system correlates positively with other emerging, usually empirically based approaches to growing sophistication of communication networks and software systems. One may evoke various recent research initiatives on "pervasive computing", "ambient intelligence", "autonomic communication networks", "knowledge-based networks", "context awareness", "semantic grid/web", "complex software", etc. (see e.g. [11–16] for representative overview sources and multiple further references). By providing the unambiguous, rigorously derived, reality-based and universally applicable definition of dynamic complexity and classification of possible dynamic regimes in *any* communication and software system, our theory can play the role of indispensable *unifying basis* for further research and applications, revealing existing possibilities for each particular case. Approximation of a real system dynamics by a simulative or metaphorical (mechanistic) "complexity" remains feasible, but now one can consistently estimate its validity, pertinence, losses and advantages.

We start, in Section 2, with a mathematical demonstration of the fact that the unreduced interaction process within *any* real system leads to *intrinsic*, genuine and omnipresent *randomness* in system behaviour realised in a few regimes and summarised by the *universally* defined *dynamic complexity*. We outline the change in strategy and practice of communication and software system construction and use, which follows from such unreduced analysis of system interactions. *Universality* of our analysis is of special importance here, since the results can be applied at various *naturally entangled* levels of ICT system operation, including e.g. autonomic communication network, related software clients, and human/environment components. We demonstrate the origin of huge, *exponentially high efficiency growth* of unreduced, causally random system dynamics with respect to usual, regular system operation (Section 3). Finally, the dynamically derived, *universal symmetry, or conservation, of complexity* is introduced as the new *guiding principle* and tool of complex system design extending usual, regular programming. The *paradigm of intelligent (complex-dynamic) communication and software systems* is thus specified, since we show also [1,5,6] that the property of *intelligence* can be consistently described as high enough levels of unreduced dynamic complexity. That *intelligent ICT* framework based on unreduced interaction complexity is the most complete realisation, and in fact unifying synonym, of *truly autonomous*, user-oriented and knowledge-based communication dynamics (Section 4).

2 Complex dynamics of unreduced interaction process

We begin with a general expression of multi-component system dynamics (or many-body problem) called here *existence equation*, fixing the fact of interaction between the system components, and generalising various model equations:

$$\left\{ \sum_{k=0}^{N} \left[h_k(q_k) + \sum_{l>k}^{N} V_{kl}(q_k, q_l) \right] \right\} \Psi(Q) = E\Psi(Q) , \tag{1}$$

where $h_k(q_k)$ is the "generalised Hamiltonian" for the k-th system component in the absence of interaction, q_k is the degree(s) of freedom of the k-th component (expressing its "physical nature"), $V_{kl}(q_k, q_l)$ is the (generally arbitrary) interaction potential between the k-th and l-th components, $\Psi(Q)$ is the system state-function, $Q \equiv \{q_0, q_1, ..., q_N\}$, E is the eigenvalue of the generalised Hamiltonian, and summations are performed over all (N) system components. The generalised Hamiltonian, eigenvalues, and interaction potential represent a suitable measure of dynamic complexity defined below and encompassing practically all "measurable" quantities (action, energy, momentum, current, etc.) at any level of dynamics. Therefore (1) can express unreduced interaction configuration at any level of arbitrary communication network. It can also be presented in a particular form of time-dependent equation by replacing the generalised Hamiltonian eigenvalue E with the partial time derivative operator (for the case of explicit interaction potential dependence on time).

One can separate one of the degrees of freedom, e.g. $q_0 \equiv \xi$, corresponding to a naturally selected, usually "system-wide" entity, such as "embedding" configuration (system of coordinates) or common "transmitting agent":

$$\left\{ h_0(\xi) + \sum_{k=1}^{N} \left[h_k(q_k) + V_{0k}(\xi, q_k) + \sum_{l>k}^{N} V_{kl}(q_k, q_l) \right] \right\} \Psi(\xi, Q) = E\Psi(\xi, Q),$$
$$\tag{2}$$

where now $Q \equiv \{q_1, ..., q_N\}$ and $k, l \geq 1$.

We then express the problem in terms of known free-component solutions for the "functional", internal degrees of freedom of system elements ($k \geq 1$):

$$h_k(q_k) \varphi_{kn_k}(q_k) = \varepsilon_{n_k} \varphi_{kn_k}(q_k) , \tag{3}$$

$$\Psi(\xi, Q) = \sum_{n} \psi_n(\xi) \varphi_{1n_1}(q_1) \varphi_{2n_2}(q_2) ... \varphi_{Nn_N}(q_N) \equiv \sum_{n} \psi_n(\xi) \Phi_n(Q), \tag{4}$$

where $\{\varepsilon_{n_k}\}$ are the eigenvalues and $\{\varphi_{kn_k}(q_k)\}$ eigenfunctions of the k-th component Hamiltonian $h_k(q_k)$, forming the complete set of orthonormal functions, $n \equiv \{n_1, ..., n_N\}$ runs through all possible eigenstate combinations, and $\Phi_n(Q) \equiv \varphi_{1n_1}(q_1) \varphi_{2n_2}(q_2) ... \varphi_{Nn_N}(q_N)$ by definition. The system of equations for $\{\psi_n(\xi)\}$ is obtained then in a standard way, using the eigen-solution orthonormality (e.g. by multiplication by $\Phi_n^*(Q)$ and integration over Q):

$$[h_0(\xi) + V_{00}(\xi)]\psi_0(\xi) + \sum_n V_{0n}(\xi)\psi_n(\xi) = \eta\psi_0(\xi)$$

$$[h_0(\xi) + V_{nn}(\xi)]\psi_n(\xi) + \sum_{n' \neq n} V_{nn'}(\xi)\psi_{n'}(\xi) = \eta_n\psi_n(\xi) - V_{n0}(\xi)\psi_0(\xi),$$

$$(5)$$

where $n, n' \neq 0$ (also below), $\eta \equiv \eta_0 = E - \varepsilon_0$, $\eta_n = E - \varepsilon_n$, $\varepsilon_n = \sum_k \varepsilon_{n_k}$,

$$V_{nn'}(\xi) = \sum_k \left[V_{k0}^{nn'}(\xi) + \sum_{l>k} V_{kl}^{nn'} \right], \qquad (6)$$

$$V_{k0}^{nn'}(\xi) = \int_{\Omega_Q} dQ\Phi_n^*(Q)V_{k0}(q_k, \xi)\Phi_{n'}(Q), \qquad (7)$$

$$V_{kl}^{nn'}(\xi) = \int_{\Omega_Q} dQ\Phi_n^*(Q)V_{kl}(q_k, q_l)\Phi_{n'}(Q), \qquad (8)$$

and we have separated the equation for $\psi_0(\xi)$ describing the generalised "ground state", i. e. the state with minimum complexity. The obtained system of equations expresses the same problem as the starting equation (2), but now in terms of "natural", dynamic variables, and therefore it can be obtained for various starting models, including time-dependent and formally "nonlinear" ones (see below for a rigorous definition of *essential* nonlinearity).

We try now to approach a "nonintegrable" system of equations (5) with the help of generalised effective, or optical, potential method [17], where one expresses $\psi_n(\xi)$ through $\psi_0(\xi)$ from the equations for $\psi_n(\xi)$ using the standard Green function technique and then substitutes the result into the equation for $\psi_0(\xi)$, obtaining thus the *effective existence equation* that contains *explicitly* only "integrable" degrees of freedom (ξ) [1–5, 8–10]:

$$h_0(\xi)\psi_0(\xi) + V_{\text{eff}}(\xi; \eta)\psi_0(\xi) = \eta\psi_0(\xi), \qquad (9)$$

where the operator of *effective potential (EP)*, $V_{\text{eff}}(\xi; \eta)$, is given by

$$V_{\text{eff}}(\xi; \eta) = V_{00}(\xi) + \hat{V}(\xi; \eta), \quad \hat{V}(\xi; \eta)\psi_0(\xi) = \int_{\Omega_\xi} d\xi' V(\xi, \xi'; \eta)\psi_0(\xi'), \quad (10)$$

$$V(\xi, \xi'; \eta) = \sum_{n,i} \frac{V_{0n}(\xi)\psi_{ni}^0(\xi)V_{n0}(\xi')\psi_{ni}^{0*}(\xi')}{\eta - \eta_{ni}^0 - \varepsilon_{n0}}, \quad \varepsilon_{n0} \equiv \varepsilon_n - \varepsilon_0, \qquad (11)$$

and $\left\{\psi_{ni}^{0}\left(\xi\right)\right\}$, $\left\{\eta_{ni}^{0}\right\}$ are complete sets of eigenfunctions and eigenvalues of a *truncated* system of equations:

$$\left[h_{0}\left(\xi\right) + V_{nn}\left(\xi\right)\right]\psi_{n}\left(\xi\right) + \sum_{n'\neq n} V_{nn'}\left(\xi\right)\psi_{n'}\left(\xi\right) = \eta_{n}\psi_{n}\left(\xi\right) . \qquad (12)$$

One can use now the eigenfunctions, $\left\{\psi_{0i}\left(\xi\right)\right\}$, and eigenvalues, $\left\{\eta_{i}\right\}$, of a formally "integrable" equation (9) to obtain other state-function components:

$$\psi_{ni}\left(\xi\right) = \hat{g}_{ni}\left(\xi\right)\psi_{0i}\left(\xi\right) \equiv \int_{\Omega_{\xi}} d\xi' g_{ni}\left(\xi,\xi'\right)\psi_{0i}\left(\xi'\right) , \qquad (13)$$

$$g_{ni}\left(\xi,\xi'\right) = V_{n0}\left(\xi'\right)\sum_{i'} \frac{\psi_{ni'}^{0}\left(\xi\right)\psi_{ni'}^{0*}\left(\xi'\right)}{\eta_{i} - \eta_{ni'}^{0} - \varepsilon_{n0}} , \qquad (14)$$

and the total system state-function, $\Psi\left(q_{0}, q_{1}, ..., q_{N}\right) = \Psi\left(\xi, Q\right)$ (see (4)):

$$\Psi\left(\xi, Q\right) = \sum_{i} c_{i}\left[\Phi_{0}\left(Q\right) + \sum_{n}\Phi_{n}\left(Q\right)\hat{g}_{ni}\left(\xi\right)\right]\psi_{0i}\left(\xi\right) , \qquad (15)$$

where coefficients c_{i} should be found from the state-function matching conditions at the boundary where interaction effectively vanishes. The measured quantity, generalised system density $\rho\left(\xi, Q\right)$, is obtained as state-function squared modulus, $\rho\left(\xi, Q\right) = \left|\Psi\left(\xi, Q\right)\right|^{2}$ (for "wave-like" complexity levels), or as state-function itself, $\rho\left(\xi, Q\right) = \Psi\left(\xi, Q\right)$ (for "particle-like" structures) [1].

Since EP expression in the effective problem formulation (9)–(11) depends essentially on the eigen-solutions to be found, the problem remains "nonintegrable" and equivalent to its initial formulation (1), (2), (5). However, it is the effective version of a problem that leads to its unreduced solution and reveals the nontrivial properties of the latter [1–10]. The key property of unreduced interaction result (9)–(15) is its *dynamic multivaluedness* meaning that one has a *redundant* number of individually complete and therefore *mutually incompatible* solutions describing *equally real* system configurations. We call each such locally complete solution (and real system configuration) *realisation* of the system and problem. Realisation plurality follows from unreduced EP expressions due to nonlinear and self-consistent dependence on the solutions to be found, reflecting physically real and evident plurality of interacting eigen-mode combinations [1–10]. It is important that dynamic multivaluedness emerges only in the unreduced problem formulation, whereas a standard theory, including EP application (see e.g. [17]) and scholar "science of complexity" (theory of chaos, self-organisation, etc.), resorts invariably to one or another version of perturbation theory, whose approximation, used to obtain an "exact", closed-form solution, just "kills" *redundant* solutions by eliminating *dynamically* emerging nonlinear links and retains *only one*, "averaged" solution, usually expressing but *small* deviations from initial system configuration. That *dynamically single-valued*, or *unitary*, problem reduction forms the basis of the whole canonical science paradigm.

Since we have many *incompatible* system realisations explicitly appearing from the same, driving interaction, we obtain a major property of *causal, or dynamic, randomness* in the form of permanently *changing* realisations that replace each other in a *truly random* (unpredictable, undecidable, noncomputable) order. Therefore dynamic multivaluedness, rigorously derived simply by unreduced, correct solution of a real many-body (interaction) problem, provides the *universal dynamic origin* and *meaning* of *omnipresent, unceasing* randomness in system behaviour, also called *(dynamical) chaos* (it is essentially different from any its unitary version, reduced to "involved regularity" or *incorrectly postulated* "noise amplification"). It means that the truly complete *general solution* of arbitrary problem (describing a *real* system behaviour) has the form of *dynamically probabilistic* sum of measured quantities for different realisations:

$$\rho(\xi, Q) = \sum_{r=1}^{N_{\Re}} {}^{\oplus} \rho_r(\xi, Q) , \tag{16}$$

where summation is performed over all system realisations, $N_{\Re}$ is their number (its maximum value is equal to the number of system components, $N_{\Re} = N$), and the sign $\oplus$ designates the special, dynamically probabilistic meaning of the sum described above. It implies that any measured quantity (16) is *intrinsically unstable* and its current value *will* unpredictably change to another one, corresponding to another, *randomly* chosen realisation. Such kind of behaviour is readily observed in nature and actually explains the living organism behaviour [1, 4, 5], but is avoided in unitary theory and usual technological (including ICT) systems, where it is correctly associated with linear "noncomputability" and technical failure (we shall consider below that *limiting* regime of real system dynamics). Therefore, universal dynamic multivaluedness thus revealed by rigorous problem solution forms a fundamental basis for transition to "bio-inspired" and "intelligent" kind of operation in artificial, especially ICT systems, where causal randomness can be transformed from an obstacle to qualitative advantage (Section 3).

The obtained causal randomness of generalised EP formalism (9)–(16) is accompanied by the *dynamic probability definition*. Since elementary realisations are equal in their "rights to appear", the dynamically derived, *a priori probability*, α_r, of elementary realisation emergence is given by

$$\alpha_r = \frac{1}{N_{\Re}} , \quad \sum_r \alpha_r = 1 . \tag{17}$$

However, actual observations may deal with dense groups of elementary realisations because of their multivalued self-organisation (see below). Therefore the dynamic probability of observation of such general, compound realisation is determined by the number, N_r, of elementary realisations it contains:

$$\alpha_r(N_r) = \frac{N_r}{N_{\Re}} \quad \left(N_r = 1, ..., N_{\Re}; \ \sum_r N_r = N_{\Re} \right), \quad \sum_r \alpha_r = 1 . \tag{18}$$

An expression for *expectation value*, $\rho_{\text{exp}}(\xi, Q)$, can easily be constructed from (16)–(18) for statistically large event numbers:

$$\rho_{\text{exp}}(\xi, Q) = \sum_r \alpha_r \rho_r(\xi, Q) . \tag{19}$$

It is important, however, that our dynamically derived randomness and probability need not rely on such "statistical", empirically based definition and basic expressions (16)–(18) remain valid even for any *single* event of realisation emergence and *before* any event happens at all.

Realisation probability distribution can be obtained in another way, involving the *generalised wavefunction (or distribution function)* and *Born's probability rule* [1, 3, 5, 10, 18]. The wavefunction describes the system state during its transition between "regular", "concentrated" realisations and constitutes a particular, "intermediate", or "main" realisation with spatially extended and "loose" (chaotically changing) structure, where system components transiently disentangle before forming the next "regular" realisation. The generalised wavefunction is obtained in the unreduced EP formalism by *causal (dynamic) quantization* [1, 3, 5, 6, 10, 18] and provides, in particular, a totally realistic version of quantum-mechanical wavefunction at the lowest, "quantum" levels of complexity. The "Born probability rule", now also causally derived and extended to any level of world dynamics, states that realisation probability distribution is determined by wavefunction values (their squared modulus for "wave-like" complexity levels) for respective system configurations. The generalised wavefunction satisfies the universal Schrödinger equation (Section 3) rigorously derived by causal quantization, while Born's probability rule follows from the *dynamic* "matching conditions" mentioned in connection with the state-function expression (15) and actually satisfied during each system transition between a "regular" realisation and the extended wavefunction state. Note also that it is *only* that "averaged", weak-interaction state of the wavefunction, or "main" realisation, that remains in the dynamically single-valued, one-realisation "model" and "exact-solution" paradigm of unitary theory, which explains both its partial success and fundamental limitations.

Closely related to dynamic multivaluedness is the property of *dynamic entanglement* between interacting components, described in (15) by the dynamically weighted products of state-function components depending on different degrees of freedom (ξ, Q). It provides a *rigorous* expression of the tangible *quality* of emerging system structure and is absent in unitary models. The obtained *dynamically multivalued entanglement* describes a "living" structure permanently changing and probabilistically *adapting* its configuration, which provides a well-specified basis for "bio-inspired" technological solutions. The properties of dynamically multivalued entanglement and adaptability are further amplified due to complex-dynamic, *probabilistic fractality* of unreduced general solution [1, 4–6] obtained by application of the same EP method to solution of truncated system of equations (12) involved in the first-level EP expression (11).

We can now consistently and *universally* define the unreduced *dynamic complexity*, C, of *any* real system or interaction process as a growing function of the number of *explicitly obtained* system realisations, $C = C(N_{\Re})$, $dC/dN_{\Re} > 0$, or rate of their change, equal to zero for the unrealistic case of only one system realisation, $C(1) = 0$. Suitable examples are provided by $C(N_{\Re}) = C_0 \ln N_{\Re}$, generalised energy/mass (proportional to the temporal rate of realisation change), and momentum (proportional to the spatial rate of realisation emergence) [1, 5, 10, 18]. It becomes clear that the whole *dynamically single-valued* paradigm and results of canonical theory (including its versions of "complexity" and *imitations* of "multi-stability" in *abstract*, mathematical "spaces") correspond to exactly *zero* value of unreduced complexity equivalent to effectively zero-dimensional, point-like projection of reality.

Correspondingly, *any* dynamically single-valued "model" is strictly regular and *cannot* possess any true, intrinsic randomness (chaoticity), which should instead be introduced artificially (and inconsistently), e.g. as a *regular* "amplification" of "random" (by convention) *external* "noise" or "measurement error". By contrast, our unreduced dynamic complexity is practically synonymous to equally universally defined and genuine *chaoticity* (see above), since *multiple* system realisations, appearing and disappearing only in *real* space (and *forming* thus its tangible, changing structure [1, 3, 5, 10]), are *redundant (mutually incompatible)*, which is the origin of *both* complexity and chaoticity. Genuine dynamical chaos thus obtained has a complicated internal structure (contrary to ill-defined unitary "stochasticity") and contains *partial regularity* dynamically mixed with irregularity in *inhomogeneous* realisation *probability* distribution.

Universal dynamic complexity and related properties involve the *essential, or dynamic, nonlinearity* of unreduced problem solution. It is provided by feedback links of developing interaction as they are expressed by EP dependence on the problem solutions (see (9)–(11)). It is the *dynamically emerging* nonlinearity, since it appears even for a formally "linear" initial problem expression (1)–(2), (5), whereas usual, mechanistic "nonlinearity" is but a perturbative reduction of essential nonlinearity of unreduced EP expressions. Essential nonlinearity leads to irreducible *dynamic instability* of any system state (realisation): both are determined by the same mechanism of dynamic feedback development.

Universality of our description leads, in particular, to the unified understanding of the whole diversity of existing dynamical regimes and types of system behaviour [1, 2, 5]. One standard, limiting case of complex (multivalued) dynamics, called *uniform, or global, chaos*, is characterised by sufficiently different realisations with a homogeneous distribution of probabilities (i.e. $N_r \approx 1$ and $\alpha_r \approx 1/N_{\Re}$ for all r in (18)) and emerges when major parameters of interacting entities (suitably represented by frequencies) are similar to each other (which leads to a strong "conflict of interests" and resulting "big disorder"). The complementary limiting regime of *multivalued self-organisation, or self-organised criticality (SOC)* emerges for sufficiently different parameters of interacting components, so that a small number of relatively rigid, low-frequency components "enslave" a hierarchy of high-frequency and rapidly changing, but configurationally similar realisations (i.e. $N_r \sim N_\Re$ and realisation probability distribution is highly inhomogeneous). The difference of that extended, multi-valued SOC from usual, unitary self-organisation is essential: despite the rigid *external* shape of system configuration in this regime, it contains an intense "internal life" and *chaos* of changing "enslaved" realisations (which are *not* super-posable unitary "modes"). Another important advance with respect to unitary "science of complexity" is that the unreduced, multivalued self-organisation uni-fies extended versions of a whole series of separated unitary "models", including SOC, "synchronisation", "control of chaos", "attractors", and "mode locking". All intermediate dynamic regimes between the limiting cases of uniform chaos and multivalued SOC (as well as their multi-level, fractal combinations) are obtained for intermediate parameter values. The point of transition to strong chaos is expressed by the *universal criterion of global chaos onset*:

$$\kappa \equiv \frac{\Delta\eta_i}{\Delta\eta_n} = \frac{\omega_\xi}{\omega_q} \cong 1 \,, \tag{20}$$

where κ is the introduced *chaoticity* parameter, $\Delta\eta_i$, ω_ξ and $\Delta\eta_n \sim \Delta\varepsilon$, ω_q are energy-level separations and frequencies for the inter-component and intra-component motions, respectively. At $\kappa \ll 1$ one has the externally regular multivalued SOC regime, which degenerates into global chaos as κ grows from 0 to 1, and the maximum irregularity at $\kappa \approx 1$ is again transformed into a SOC kind of structure at $\kappa \gg 1$ (but with the "inverse" system configuration).

One can compare this transparent and universal picture with separated and incomplete unitary criteria of chaos and regularity. Only the former provides a real possibility of understanding and control of ICT systems of arbitrary com-plexity, where more regular regimes form a general direction of system dynamics, while less regular ones play the role of efficient search and adaptation means. That combination constitutes the basis of any "biological" and "intelligent" kind of behaviour [1, 4–7] and therefore determines the *intelligent ICT para-digm* supposed to extend the current practice of communication and software of (quasi-) regular limiting regime, $\kappa \to 0$. While the latter *inevitably* becomes inefficient with growing system sophistication (where chaos-bringing resonances of (20) *cannot* be avoided any more), it definitely lacks the "intelligent power" of unreduced complex dynamics to generate meaning and adaptable structure development.

3 Huge efficiency of unreduced interaction dynamics and the guiding role of the symmetry of complexity

Dynamically probabilistic fractality of system structure emerges naturally by the unreduced interaction development [1, 4–6]. It is obtained mathematically by application of the same EP method (9)–(14) to solution of truncated system of equations (12), then to solution of the next truncated system, etc., which gives the irregular and *probabilistically moving* hierarchy of realisations, containing an intermittent mixture of global chaos and multivalued SOC, which constitute together a sort of *confined chaos*. The total realisation number $N_{\Re}$, and thus the power, of that autonomously branching interaction process with a *dynamically parallel* structure grows *exponentially* with its volume [5].

Indeed, if our system of inter-connected elements contains N_{unit} "processing units", or "junctions", and if each of them has n_{conn} real or "virtual" (possible) links, then the total number of interaction links is $N = n_{\text{conn}} N_{\text{unit}}$. In most important cases N is a huge number: for both human brain and genome inter-actions N is greater than 10^{12}, and being much more variable for ICT systems, it will tend to similar "astronomical" ranges. The key property of *unreduced, complex* interaction dynamics, distinguishing it from any unitary "model", is that the maximum number $N_{\Re}$ of realisations taken by the system (also per time unit) and determining its real "power" P_{real} (of search, memory, cognition, etc.) is given by the number of *all possible combinations of links*, i.e.

$$P_{\text{real}} \propto N_{\Re} = N! \rightarrow \sqrt{2\pi N} \left(\frac{N}{e} \right)^N \sim N^N \ggg N \ . \tag{21}$$

Any unitary, sequential model of the same system (including its *mechanistically* "parallel" and "complex" modes) would give $P_{\text{reg}} \sim N^{\beta}$, with $\beta \sim 1$, so that

$$P_{\text{real}} \sim (P_{\text{reg}})^N \ggg P_{\text{reg}} \sim N^{\beta} \ . \tag{22}$$

Thus, for $N \sim 10^{12}$ we have $P_{\text{real}} \gg 10^{10^{13}} \gg 10^{10^{12}} = 10^N \rightarrow \infty$, which is a "practical infinity", also with respect to the unitary power of $N^{\beta} \sim 10^{12}$.

These estimates demonstrate the true power of complex (multivalued) com-munication and software dynamics remaining suppressed in its unitary, quasi-regular operation mode dominating in modern technologies. Huge power val-ues for complex-dynamical interaction correlate with emergence of new *quali-ties*, such as *autonomy (adaptability), intelligence* and *consciousness* (at higher complexity levels) [5,6], in direct relation to our *intelligent* communication and software paradigm meaning that such properties as *sensible*, context-related information processing, personalised *understanding* and autonomous *creativity* (useful self-development), desired for next-generation ICT tools, are natural *qualitative* manifestations of the above "infinite" power.

Everything has a price, however, and a price to pay for the above huge power and qualitative advantages of complex-dynamic information-processing systems is rigorously specified now as irreducible *dynamic randomness* and thus unpre-dictability of their operation details. We only confirm here an evident conclusion that *autonomous* adaptability and genuine *creativity* exclude any regular, pre-dictable pre-programming. But then what can serve as a guiding principle and practical strategy of design and control of complex communication networks and software tools? We show in our further analysis of unreduced interaction process that those guiding rules and strategy can be unified into a general law of complex (multivalued) dynamics, the *universal symmetry, or conservation, of complexity* [1,3,5,6]. That universal "order of nature" and evolution law unifies extended versions of all (correct) conservation laws, symmetries, and postulated "principles" (which are dynamically derived and realistically interpreted now). Contrary to any unitary symmetry, the universal symmetry of complexity is *irregular* in its structure, but always *exact* (never "broken"). Its "horizontal" manifestation (at a given level of complexity) implies actual, dynamic symmetry between realisations, which are really taken by the system and constitute thus its dynamics (and evolution) by contrast to usual abstract "symmetry operators". Therefore conservation, or symmetry, of system complexity totally determines its dynamics and explains the deep "equivalence" (link) between chaotically changing and often quite dissimilar realisation configurations.

Another, "vertical" manifestation of the universal symmetry of complexity is somewhat more involved and determines progressive emergence and development of different levels of complexity within a real interaction process. The system "potentiality", or (real) power to create new structure at the very beginning of interaction process (i.e. before any actual structure emergence) can be universally characterised by a form of complexity called *dynamic information* and generalising usual "potential energy" [1, 3, 5]. During interaction process development, or structure creation, that potential, latent form of complexity is progressively transformed into its explicit, "unfolded" form called *dynamic entropy* (it generalises kinetic, or thermal, energy). Universal *conservation of complexity* means that this important transformation, determining every system dynamics and evolution, happens so that the sum of dynamic information and dynamic entropy, or *total complexity*, remains unchanged (for a given system or process). It is the absolutely universal formulation of the symmetry of complexity that includes the above "horizontal" manifestation and, for example, extended and unified versions of the first and second laws of thermodynamics (i.e. conservation and degradation of energy). It also helps to eliminate a persisting (and inevitable) series of confusion around the notions of information, entropy, complexity, and their relation to real system dynamics in unitary theory (thus, really expressed and processed "information" corresponds rather to a particular case of our generalised dynamic entropy, see [1,5] for further details).

It is not difficult to show [1, 3, 5, 6, 10] that a natural, universal measure of dynamic information is provided by *generalised action* $\mathcal{A}$ known from classical mechanics, but now acquiring a much wider, essentially nonlinear and causally complete meaning applicable at any level of complexity. One obtains then a universal differential expression of complexity conservation law in the form of *generalised Hamilton-Jacobi equation* for action $\mathcal{A} = \mathcal{A}(x, t)$:

$$\frac{\Delta \mathcal{A}}{\Delta t}\Big|_{x=\text{const}} + H\left(x, \frac{\Delta \mathcal{A}}{\Delta x}\Big|_{t=\text{const}}, t\right) = 0 \,, \tag{23}$$

where the *Hamiltonian*, $H = H(x, p, t)$, considered as a function of emerging space coordinate x, momentum $p = (\Delta \mathcal{A}/\Delta x)|_{t=\text{const}}$, and time t, expresses an explicit, entropy-like form of differential complexity, $H = (\Delta S/\Delta t)|_{x=\text{const}}$ (note that discrete, rather than usual continuous, versions of derivatives and increments here reflect the naturally quantized character of unreduced complex dynamics [1, 3, 5, 10]).

Taking into account the dual character of multivalued dynamics, where every structure contains transformation from a localised, "regular" realisation to extended configuration of generalised wavefunction and back (Section 2), we obtain the *universal Schrödinger equation* for the wavefunction (or distribution function) $\Psi(x, t)$ by applying the causal, dynamically derived quantization procedure [1, 3, 5, 10, 18] to the generalised Hamilton-Jacobi equation (23):

$$A_0 \frac{\partial \Psi}{\partial t} = \hat{H} \left(x, \frac{\partial}{\partial x}, t \right) \Psi , \qquad (24)$$

where A_0 is a characteristic action value by modulus (determined by Planck's constant at quantum complexity levels) and the Hamiltonian operator, $\hat{H}$, is obtained from the Hamiltonian function $H = H(x, p, t)$ with the help of causal quantization (we put here continuous derivatives for simplicity).

Equations (23)–(24) provide a universal differential expression of the symmetry of complexity showing how it directly determines dynamics and evolution of any system or interaction process (they justify also our use of Hamiltonian form in the starting existence equation, Section 2). This universally applicable Hamilton-Schrödinger formalism can be useful for rigorous description of any complex network and its separate elements, provided we look for the *truly complete* (dynamically multivalued) general solution to particular versions of equations (23)–(24) with the help of unreduced EP method (Section 2).

4 ICT complexity transition

We have demonstrated in Sections 2 and 3 the fundamental, analytical basis of complex (multivalued) dynamics of real communication networks and related software systems, which can be further developed in particular applications in combination with other approaches. The main *practical proposition* of emerging intelligent (complex-dynamic) ICT paradigm is to open the way for *free, self-developing structure creation* in communication and software systems with strong interaction (including self-developing internet structure, intelligent search engines, and distributed, user-oriented knowledge bases). Liberated, autonomic system dynamics and structure creation, "loosely" governed by the hierarchy of system interactions as described in this report, will essentially exceed the possibilities of usual, deterministic programming and control.

Practical framework of intelligent ICT paradigm will be based upon permission for various *local* deviations and "mistakes" in system operation in exchange to its *unceasing* search for a *general purpose* realisation, in agreement with the above law of complexity conservation by its transformation (Section 3). The "purpose" represented by software structures of increasing sophistication expresses the "potential" form of complexity, dynamic information, which is transformed into the "accomplished" form of dynamic entropy in the course of chaotic search of ways towards the purpose realisation. One can start therefore with creation of suitable *motivation structures* and system *spaces* (containing a hierarchy of *multiple* possibilities) for their unreduced, *chaotic* interaction with other participating structures.

Complex-dynamical criteria and control parameters of detailed system development are provided by the universal criterion (20) of transition between chaos and regularity and expression (21)–(22) of huge efficiency growth upon transition to the unreduced complex dynamics (they can be specified for each particular case). They imply that emergence of a new, truly complex-dynamic kind of system behaviour will have the form of qualitative, clearly perceived transition in the system operation mode that can be designated as *complexity transition*. As there are many levels of a real interaction process with multiple participants (many frequencies in (20)), one will obtain eventually a whole hierarchy of such transitions, which can be unified into uneven groups of more or less pronounced changes.

Note that the basic criterion (20) can also be applied to the general transition from quasi-unitary (regular) to complex-dynamic (multivalued) kind of ICT structures, where it means that the rigid, low-frequency dynamics of an artificial structure (computer, network) enters in interaction with an effectively high-frequency dynamics of natural intelligence (cf. (21)–(22)) and actually *imposes* its low-efficiency, regular dynamics to the complex-dynamical human component, thus strongly limiting the huge efficiency of the latter. The resulting effective *enslavement* of natural intelligence complexity by a "machine" it has created provides a convincing demonstration of the necessity to realise the ICT complexity transition and profit from the advantages of unreduced intelligence of the *whole* system as they are outlined in the present report.

References

1. A.P. Kirilyuk, *Universal Concept of Complexity by the Dynamic Redundance Paradigm: Causal Randomness, Complete Wave Mechanics, and the Ultimate Unification of Knowledge* (Naukova Dumka, Kyiv, 1997). For a non-technical overview see also Physics/9806002 at http://arXiv.org.
2. A.P. Kirilyuk, Dynamically Multivalued Self-Organisation and Probabilistic Structure Formation Processes, *Solid State Phenomena* **97–98** (2004) 21–26. Physics/0405063 at http://arXiv.org.
3. A.P. Kirilyuk, Universal Symmetry of Complexity and Its Manifestations at Different Levels of World Dynamics, *Proceedings of Institute of Mathematics of NAS of Ukraine* **50** (2004) 821–828. Physics/0404006 at http://arXiv.org.
4. A.P. Kirilyuk, Complex-Dynamical Extension of the Fractal Paradigm and Its Applications in Life Sciences, in: *Fractals in Biology and Medicine. Vol. IV*, edited by G.A. Losa, D. Merlini, T.F. Nonnenmacher, and E.R. Weibel (Birkhäuser, Basel, 2005), pp. 233–244. Physics/0502133 at http://arXiv.org.
5. A.P. Kirilyuk, Dynamically Multivalued, Not Unitary or Stochastic, Operation of Real Quantum, Classical and Hybrid Micro-Machines, Physics/0211071 at http://arXiv.org.

6. A.P. Kirilyuk, Emerging Consciousness as a Result of Complex-Dynamical Interaction Process, Report at the EXYSTENCE workshop Machine Consciousness: Complexity Aspects (Turin, 29 Sep – 1 Oct 2003). Physics/0409140 at http://arXiv.org.

7. A.P. Kirilyuk, Complex Dynamics of Real Nanosystems: Fundamental Paradigm for Nanoscience and Nanotechnology, *Nanosystems, Nanomaterials, Nanotechnologies* **2** (2004) 1085–1090. Physics/0412097 at http://arXiv.org.

8. A.P. Kirilyuk, Theory of Charged Particle Scattering in Crystals by the Generalized Optical Potential Method, *Nucl. Instr. and Meth. B* **69** (1992) 200–231.

9. A.P. Kirilyuk, Quantum Chaos and Fundamental Multivaluedness of Dynamical Functions, *Annales de la Fondation Louis de Broglie* **21** (1996) 455–480. Quant-ph/9511034–36 at http://arXiv.org.

10. A.P. Kirilyuk, Quantum Field Mechanics: Complex-Dynamical Completion of Fundamental Physics and Its Experimental Implications, Physics/0401164 at http://arXiv.org.

11. M. Smirnov (Ed.), *Autonomic Communication: First International IFIP Workshop, WAC 2004, Berlin, Germany, October 18-19, 2004, Revised Selected Papers*, LNCS No. 3457 (Springer Verlag, Berlin, 2005). See also http://www.autonomic-communication.org/wac/wac2004/program.html.

12. European Commission FP6, FET Situated and Autonomic Communications, http://www.cordis.lu/ist/fet/comms.htm. Links to other related FET initiatives can be found at http://www.cordis.lu/ist/fet/areas.htm.

13. S. Bullock and D. Cliff, Complexity and Emergent Behaviour in ICT Systems, Foresight Intelligent Infrastructure Systems Project, UK Office of Science and Technology (2004), http://www.foresight.gov.uk/
Intelligent_Infrastructure_Systems/Complexity_and_Emergent_Behaviour.html.

14. G. Di Marzo Serugendo, A. Karageorgos, O.F. Rana, and F. Zambonelli (Eds.), *Engineering Self-Organising Systems: Nature Inspired Approaches to Software Engineering*, LNCS No. 2977 (Springer Verlag, Berlin, 2004).

15. T. Berners-Lee, K. Hendler, and O. Lassila, The Semantic Web, *Scientific American*, May (2001) 35–43.

16. ManyOne Networks, http://www.manyone.net/; Digital Universe Foundation, http://www.digitaluniverse.net/.

17. P.H. Dederichs, Dynamical Diffraction Theory by Optical Potential Methods, in: *Solid State Physics: Advances in Research and Applications*, Vol. 27, edited by H. Ehrenreich, F. Seitz, and D. Turnbull (Academic Press, New York, 1972), pp. 136–237.

18. A.P. Kirilyuk, 75 Years of the Wavefunction: Complex-Dynamical Extension of the Original Wave Realism and the Universal Schrödinger Equation, Quant-ph/0101129 at http://arXiv.org.